# ENGAGEMENTS
## AND
# MARRIAGES

FROM THE
PRINCE WILLIAM COUNTY
VIRGINIA

*Manassas Gazette*
&
*Manassas Journal*

1885–1910

*Carol Thompson Phillips*

HERITAGE BOOKS
2011

# HERITAGE BOOKS
*AN IMPRINT OF HERITAGE BOOKS, INC.*

### Books, CDs, and more—Worldwide

For our listing of thousands of titles see our website
at
www.HeritageBooks.com

Published 2011 by
HERITAGE BOOKS, INC.
Publishing Division
100 Railroad Ave. #104
Westminster, Maryland 21157

Copyright © 1998 Carol Thompson Phillips

Other Heritage Books by the author:

*Death Notices, Obituaries and Memoriams: From the
Prince William County, Virginia* Manassas Gazette
*and* Manassas Journal, *1885–1910*

All rights reserved. No part of this book may be reproduced or transmitted in any form or by any means, electronic or mechanical, including photocopying, recording or by any information storage and retrieval system without written permission from the author, except for the inclusion of brief quotations in a review.

International Standard Book Numbers
Paperbound: 978-1-888265-58-3
Clothbound: 978-0-7884-8836-8

The Engagements and Marriages in this book were extracted from available microfilm of the Manassas Gazette (M. G.) and Manassas Journal (M. J.) 1885-1910.

Carol Thompson Phillips
1998

**ABEL, Mattie Lee** – Jan. 25, 1907 M. J. – HONEYMOON IN JAIL – A special from Fredericksburg to the Washington Post, last Monday, says C. J. Martins of this city, who says he was married in Washington Saturday to Miss Mattie Lee Abel of Quantico arrived here Saturday night with his bride. Today he was arrested, charged with larceny of clothing from the Virginia Clothing House, where until recently he was employed.

Mayor Wallace fined him $25 and cost. Lacking funds, Martins went to jail for ninety days. Subsequently the bride paid the fine.

**ACHESON, Dr. H. W.** – Dec. 24, 1909 M. J. – Miss Correne J. Reeves, daughter of Mr. Henry W. Reeves, of Prince William county, Va., and Dr. H. W. Acheson, one of the leading veterinarians of Washington, D.C. were married Wednesday, Dec. 22, at 7:30 p.m., at St. Andrew's church, Washington, Rev. George Calvert Carter officiating.

The bride was escorted by her brother, Mr. Courtney Reeves, and was tastefully gowned in white messaline silk and carried a bouquet of violets and lilies of the valley.

**ADAMS, Marjorie Owen** – Jun. 11, 1909 M. J. – WARREN- Miss Marjorie Owen Adams, of Front Royal, and Frank L. Dunn, superintendent of the Crawford Woolen Mills, of Martinsburg, eloped to Hagerstown Tuesday in an automobile, and were married there by Rev. George B. Townsend of the Christian church.

Miss Adams left her home Monday evening, telling her parents she intended calling, and would shortly return. Instead she boarded a train for Shenanoah Junction, where she met Dunn. The couple went to Martinsburg and stopped at the home of Dunn's brother. At 2 o'clock Tuesday morning they started for Hagerstown, but near Williamsport the automobile broke down. The remainder of the journey was made by trolley. – Richmond Bulletin.

**ADRIAN, Edith** – Jan. 14, 1910 M. J.- LOUDOUN – Miss Edith Adrian and Mr. Frank Elliott, both of Ashburn, were married in Rockville Tuesday afternoon by the Rev. S. R. White, of the Baptist church, at the home of the minister.—Mirror, Jan. 7.

**ALEXANDER, J. R. H.** – Oct. 28, 1910 M. J.- LOUDOUN – Cards have been issued for the marriage of Miss Cora Lutz, daughter of Mr. and Mrs. S. S. Lutz, of Springwood, near Leesburg, to Mr. J. R. H. Alexander, attorney and mayor of Leesburg. The ceremony will be performed at Springwood November 2.—Alex. Gazette.

**ALLEN, Guy** – Jan. 25, 1907 M. J. – Mr. Guy Allen of Nokesville and Miss Nadine Davis, daughter of Mrs. A. P. Davis of this place, were married in Washington last week, Rev. D. L. Blakesmore officiating.

**ALLEN, William Lewis** – Nov. 5, 1 909 M. J. – Married at Warrenton, October 27, 1909, Mr. William Lewis Allen, of Prince William county, and Miss Laura C. Heflin, of Fauquier. Rev. J. L. Kibbler officiated.

**ALLENSWORTH, Maude Eleanor** – Nov. 25, 1910 M. J. – Miss Maude Eleanor Allensworth, daughter of Captain and Mrs. Walter S. Allensworth, was married Wednesday night to Mr. Ewell Walker, of Washington. Mr. Walker is a government employee of that city.

**ALLISON, Florida V.** – Dec. 24, 1909 M. J. – The following marriage licenses were issued this week at the clerk's office: Monday, Lewis M. Swartz, Culpeper county, and Miss Pearl L. Kelley, Fauquier county, Chas. N. Davis and Miss Virgie Wolfe, both of Prince William; Tuesday, John F. Donovan, Rockingham county and Miss Florida V. Allison, Loudoun county; Wednesday, Aubrey Flynn, Fauquier county, and Miss Annie L. Thomas, Prince William county; Thursday, Wm. E. Beahm, Rappahannock county, and Miss Edith G. Priest, Fauquier county; Geo. Spinks, Fauquier county, and Miss Bessie Baggott, Prince William county.

**AMIDON, Clymedia** - Mar. 1, 1907 M. J.- Mr. Quinton Hutchison and Miss Clymedia Amidon of Dumfries were married on Sunday.

**ANDERSON, Ford G.** – Feb. 25, 1910 M. J. – FAUQUIER – Mr. Ford G. Anderson and Miss Ethel Shirley of Warrenton, were married in Wilmington, Del., on Wednesday, Feb. 15, by the Rev. W. H. Laird of the Episcopal church. Mr. Anderson is a member of the well known firm of Nusbaum & Anderson, clothiers of this place, and Miss Shirley is the beautiful daughter of Sergeant J. W. Shirley, of this place.

**ANDERSON, Geneva T.** – Oct. 21, 1910 M. J. – FAIRFAX –Mr. Jos. L. Buckley and Miss Geneva T. Anderson were married by Rev. F. A. Strother, at the parsonage here, Wednesday morning. After a trip North, they will return to the home of the groom.

**ANDERSON, Irva** – Apr. 22, 1910 M. J. – Mr. Benjamin F. Matthews and Miss Irva Anderson, both of upper Prince William, were married Wednesday in the Baptist parsonage by Rev. T. D. D. Clark.

**ANDERSON, Lloyd** – Aug. 26, 1910 M. J. – FAUQUIER – Miss Menora Coons, the attractive daughter of Mr. and Mrs. J. A. Coons, of Warrenton, and Mr. Lloyd Anderson, a prosperous young business man of Culpeper, were married in Rockville, Md., on Monday last.

**ANDES, Miss** – Sept. 17, 1909 M. J. – Mr. Roy Heddings, of Midland, Va., and Miss Andes, of Michigan, were married Sunday morning at 8 o'clock, in the presence of a few friends, by Rev. A. Conner at his home near Manassas.

**ANKERS, Lelia V.** – Aug. 27, 1909 M. J. – LOUDOUN – Marriage licenses were issued in Leesburg this week to Mr. Robert Elmer Connon and Miss Goldie Kalb Brooks, of Clarke's Gap, and to William Lefevre and Lelia V. Ankers, of Lower Loudoun.

**ANKERS, Lelia V.** – Sept. 3, 1909 M. J.- LOUDOUN – Mr. William Lefever, of Ashburn and Miss Lelia V. Ankers, daughter of Mr. William Ankers, of Waxpool, were married at Mt. Hope Baptist church on Thursday of last week, Rev. G. W. Popkins officiating.

**ANTONSANTI, Louis** – Jan. 14, 1910 M. J. – FAUQUIER – Monday, at high noon, Jan. 3, Miss Nannie Jeffries, the pretty and accomplished daughter of Mrs. M. H. and J. P. Jefferies, late commonwealth's attorney of Fauquier, plighted her love to Louis Antonsanti, of Ponce, Porto Rico. The marriage was quietly solemnized at the rectory of the Trinity Episcopal church, Washington, by Rev. Richard P. Williams.

**ARMSTRONG, William** – Jun. 22, 1906 M. J. - Failing to overcome the objection of her parents, who, she said, had selected another man to be her husband, Miss Louisa M. McIntyre of Warrenton eloped to Washington Tuesday with William Armstrong, jr., of Norfolk, and the couple were married in the forenoon by Rev. J. B. McLaughlin, in the latter's office in the Columbian building, on Fifth street northwest. The bridegroom is a student in the Bethel Military Academy, near Warrenton, and it was there he made the acquaintance of the young lady who yesterday became his bride.

To the marriage license clerk at the city hall both of the parties gave their age as 22 years. The young lady is a daughter of Major

McIntyre, a well-known resident of Warrenton. When the ceremony was over she told the clergyman that her parents objected to the marriage because they had decided upon another man for her husband, but that she had made up her mind not to marry a man she did not love. Mr. and Mrs. Armstrong left Washington yesterday afternoon for Norfolk.

**ARNOLD, Claude E.** – Oct. 15, 1909 M. J. – A beautiful wedding was solemnized Oct. 6, at St. Margaret's church, St. Margaret's, Md., when Miss Ella M. Heymond, daughter of Mrs. Jane Heymond, of that place, became the bride of Mr. Claude E. Arnold, of Annapolis Junction. The church was lavishly decorated with wild heather and honeysuckle vines, the windows being banked and the chancel and chandeliers hung with the soft white blooms. As the last chord of the wedding march from Lohengrin sounded the bridesmaids, assembled in the vestibule, began singing sweetly together, "O, Perfect Love," and the whole party advanced slowly up the aisle, the bride leaning on the arm of her brother, Mr. Arthur P. Heymond, who gave her away, and attended by her maid of honor, Miss Nancy Byrd Turner, of King George, Va. They were met at the chancel by the groom and his best man, Mr. Maurice H. Arnold, and were made man and wife in the beautiful words of the Episcopal marriage service, read by the Rev. Alexander Galt, rector of the church. Then to the strains of Mendellsohn's march the party went out, making a lovely picture. The bride was gowned in white silk batiste with tulle veil and lilies of the valley and carried brides' roses. The maid of honor wore blue and carried pink roses. The bridesmaids were: Miss Alverta Arnold, of Baltimore, and Miss Clara Bell Kent, of Davidsonville, in white over green; Miss Jeannette MacMillan, of Baltimore, and Miss Bessie Turner, of King George, Va., in white over pink; Miss Laura Hanson, of Washington, and Miss Ada Moss, of Annapolis, in white over yellow, and Miss Marion Lewis, of Manassas, niece of the bride, as flower girl, in white. The ushers were: Mr. Paul Hines, of Annapolis Junction; Mr. Thornton Turner, of King George, Va., and Messrs. Thomas Arnold, Alex. Proskey, Corner Ridout and Thomas Corner, of Anne Arundel county. A reception for the bridal party was held at Mrs. Heymond's residence, immediately after which Mr. and Mrs. Arnold left for Washington, Richmond and other points. The gifts were many and handsome, and the two take with them the very loving wishes of a host of friends.

**ARNOLD, Sallie** – Jul. 1, 1910 M. J. – Mr. James Irving Arrington and Miss Sallie Arnold both of this county, were married on

Thursday last at the residence of the officiating minister, Rev. Dr. Hamner.

**ARRINGTON, James Irving** – Jul. 1, 1910 M. J. – Mr. James Irving Arrington and Miss Sallie Arnold both of this county, were married on Thursday last at the residence of the officiating minister, Rev. Dr. Hamner.

**ASHTON, Horace** – Jun. 18, 1909 M. J. – ALEXANDRIA -The marriage of Miss Ruth Ashton, daughter of Mr. Horace Ashton, and Dr. Llewellyn Powell, both of this city, was solemnized at 11 o'clock Tuesday morning at Christ Episcopal Church, in the presence of a large gathering of friends and relatives. The ceremony was performed by Rev. William J. Morton, rector. The bride was unattended, and was attired in a dark gray traveling gown and green hat. The groom had for his best man, Dr. William Syme, of Washington. Those serving as ushers were William G. Chapman, William G. Leadbeater, D. Edgar Snowden, of Washington; John Thornton Ashton, brother of the groom.

**BAGGOTT, Bessie** – Dec. 24, 1909 M. J. – The following marriage licenses were issued this week at the clerk's office: Monday, Lewis M. Swartz, Culpeper county, and Miss Pearl L. Kelley, Fauquier county, ; Chas. N. Davis and Miss Virgie Wolfe, both of Prince William; Tuesday, John F. Donovan, Rockingham county and Miss Florida V. Allison, Loudoun county; Wednesday, Aubrey Flynn, Fauquier county, and Miss Annie L. Thomas, Prince William county; Thursday, Wm.. E. Beahm, Rappahannock county, and Miss Edith G. Priest, Fauquier county; Geo. Spinks, Fauquier county, and Miss Bessie Baggott, Prince William county.

**BAGGOTT, Bessie** – Dec. 24, 1909 M. J. – Mr. George Spinks, of Fauquier county, and Miss Bessie Baggott, of Prince William county, were married yesterday noon at the parsonage of the M. E. church, South, by the pastor, Rev. W. T. Gover.

**BAILEY, Robert M.** - Oct. 26, 1906 M. J. – Married at Leonardtown, Md., Tuesday, Oct. 23, Miss Nellie Rae Maddox of this place to Mr. Robert M. Bailey.

**BAILEY, Robert M.** – Nov. 9, 1906 M. J. – From the St. Mary's (MD.) Gazette. A quiet marriage took place Tuesday evening last at the rectory of the M. E. Church, near Leonardtown, the contracting parties being Miss Nellie Rae Maddox of Manassas and Mr. Robt. M. Bailey of Kinsale, Va., the Rev. H. R. Miller officiating.

The groom is a prominent and successful business man of Kinsale, and the bride is one of Prince William's most charming and popular belles.

After the marriage, a reception was held at Moore's Hotel, where many of Mr. Bailey's St. Mary's friends had the pleasure of meeting his charming bride.

The happy couple left here Wednesday morning for Kinsale, their future home.

Our best wishes for a long and happy married life.

From the Northern Neck News.

Mr. Robert Bailey's large circle of friends here most cordially congratulate him on his marriage and wish for him and his fair bride all that is best in this life and the next. Mrs. Bailey is a sister of Mrs. Dr. Hammond and from Manassas, Prince William county.

**BAILEY, William E.** - Nov. 2, 1906 M. J. – Married on Tuesday last at the residence of the officiating minister, Rev. Robt. Smith, Mr. William E. Bailey and Miss Cora E. Smith, both of this county.

**BAKER, D. D.** – Mar. 22, 1907 M. J. – Mr. D. D. Baker, son of Mr. C. W. Baker of Orlando and Miss Ina McLinn of Loudoun were married in Washington on Thursday of last week.

**BALL, Murray L.** - Jan. 25, 1907 M. J. – Mr. Murray L. Ball of Fairfax county and Miss Lillian E. Breen of Prince William county were married Jan. 23, by Rev. J. K. Efird at the Lutheran parsonage here.

**BALL, Bessie Robena** – Dec. 17, 1909 M. J. – LOUDOUN – Mr. and Mrs. Samuel H. Ball, of Leesburg, announce the engagement of their daughter, Bessie Robena, to Mr. Joseph Milton Schue, of Parksely, Va., the wedding to take place Wednesday, Dec. 29, at the home of the bride.—News, Dec. 10.

**BALLARD, Robert T.** – Aug. 12, 1910 M. J. – FAIRFAX – Mr. Robt. T. Ballard, of Vienna, and Miss Blanche Sisson, of Legato (daughter of Mr. E. B. Sisson), were married in Atlantic City recently. They will reside in Vienna.

**BALLARD, Sargent I.** – Dec. 31, 1909 M. J. – On Wednesday evening at six o'clock, the home of Dr. and Mrs. B. F. Iden was the scene of a very pretty wedding, when Miss Pauline Elizabeth Iden became the bride of Mr. Sargent I. Ballard, of West Point, Mississippi. Miss Pauline Nicol, of Alexandria, and little Miss Jessie Adams, of Rectortown, who have been guests of the family this week, were the only ones to witness the ceremony outside of the immediate family. The bride was attired in a handsome traveling suit of blue cloth, with hat to match, and carried bride roses. Rev. Leslie F. Robinson, rector of Trinity Episcopal church, performed the ceremony and the bride was given away by her father.

The bridal party left on the evening train for Washington, passing through Manassas yesterday for an extended tour through the Southern states. After February 1$^{st}$ they will be in their future home in West Point.

**BANCROFT, Owen M.** – Jan. 14, 1910 M. J. – FAIRFAX – Mr. Owen M. Bancroft and Miss Bessie E. Stoneburner were married by Rev. F. A. Strother, at the parsonage of the M. E. church, South, on Wednesday last. Refreshments were served by the pastor and his good lady, after which the happy groom and his pretty bride went on their way rejoicing.

**BASCUE, Theo. M.** –Apr. 22, 1910 M. J. – LOUDOUN – Theo. M. Bascue and Minnie Willingham were married at the Methodist Parsonage, this place Wednesday, the 13$^{th}$ inst., Rev. D. L. Blakemore officiating. The bridal couple will make their home at Round Hill.

**BATEMAN, Amelia** – Jan. 14, 1910 M. J. – Mr. Jas. H. Cross, of Manassas and Miss Amelia Bateman,of Washington, were married last Friday in that city.

**BAYLISS, Elizabeth Virginia** – Oct. 21, 1910 M. J. – FAIRFAX – Miss Elizabeth Virginia Bayliss and Mr. Garnett T. Mayhugh, of Fairfax county, were married in Rockville Saturday.

**BEACH, Mary L.** – Dec. 31, 1909 M. J. – FAUQUIER – Marriage licenses were issued in Washington this week to Frederick M. Day and Mary L. Beach, both of Fauquier county. Also to Jos. M. Jacobs of Calverton and Miss Carrie B. Green of Midland, Va.

**BEAHM, William E.** – Dec. 24, 1909 M. J. – The following marriage licenses were issued this week at the clerk's office: Monday, Lewis M. Swartz, Culpeper county, and Miss Pearl L. Kelley, Fauquier county, Chas. N. Davis and Miss Virgie Wolfe, both of Prince

William; Tuesday, John F. Donovan, Rockingham county and Miss Florida V. Allison, Loudoun county; Wednesday, Aubrey Flynn, Fauquier county, and Miss Annie L. Thomas, Prince William county; Thursday, Wm. E. Beahm, Rappahannock county, and Miss Edith G. Priest, Fauquier county; Geo. Spinks, Fauquier county, and Miss Bessie Baggott, Prince William county.

**BEAHM, William E.** – Jan. 7, 1910 M. J. – At his resident on Christmas morning Rev. Dr. Hamner married Wm. E. Beahm of Washington, D.C., to Miss Edith G. Priest, of Prince William county. The young couple will reside in Washington, D. C.

**BEALES, Elmer L.** – Jul. 30, 1909 M. J. – LOUDOUN – Miss Genevieve Myers and Mr. Elmer L. Beales, of Hamilton, this county, were married at the residence of the bride in that town, on Wednesday evening, Rev. S. V. Hildebrand officiating.—News, July 22.

**BELL, Charles W.** – Jun. 25, 1909 M. J. – Mr. Chas. W. Bell, son of Mr. Geo. W. Bell, of Prince William, and Miss Lena Belle Brazewell, of Johnson City, Tenn., were married in the bride's home city Sunday, June 20. They are at present the guests of Mr. and Mrs. J. I. Randall, of Manassas. Mrs. Max Goldrose, Mrs. Randell's sister, who lives in Johnson city, accompanied the bride and groom to Manassas.

**BELL, Edward** – Jun. 8, 1906 M. J. - On the afternoon of Tuesday, June 5, 1906, there was a tastefully conducted marriage service celebrated at the beautiful home of the officiating minister, Rev. A. B. Carrington of Greenwich, Va.

The contracting parties were Miss Mamie Mayhugh, daughter of Mr. L. Mayhugh of Greenwich and Mr. Edward Bell of Washington, D. C.

Immediately after the ceremony the company was invited into the handsomely arranged dining room by Mrs. Carrington where light refreshments were served.

Beautiful flowers everywhere and a very handsomely attired bride and groom with a numerous following of pretty girls and admiring beaux helped to make the occasion very impressive.

The happy couple left on the evening train for Washington City, there future home.

**BELL, Essie** - Nov. 16, 1906 M. J. – Miss Essie Bell, daughter of Mr. G. W. Bell, was married on Wednesday last, at her father's home at

Sinclair's Mill, to Mr. J. I. Randall of this place, Rev. S. K. Cockrell officiating.

**BELL, Sadie** – Apr. 22, 1910 M. J. – Mr. Benjamin F. Wines and Miss Sadie Bell, both of Prince William county, were married Wednesday by Rev. J. N. Badger at his residence on Centre street.

**BERKLEY, Mary Pattison** – Jul. 23, 1909 M. J. – LOUDOUN – At the home of the bride, at Covington, Va., on Thursday, July 8, 1909, by Rev. F. P. Berkley, pastor of the Baptist church, were married Mr. Richard Conway Littleton, of Leesburg, and Miss Mary Pattison Berkley, daughter of the officiating minister. They left by the late train over the C. & O. for a short trip North, and upon their return will reside at Covington.—Mirror, July 16.

**BERRY, Dalias** – Nov. 11, 1910 M. J. – LOUDOUN – A quiet wedding occurred at the home of Mr. and Mrs. E. R. Swetnam, of Fairfax, on Wednesday evening, October 26, when their oldest daughter, Miss Roberta Randolph and Mr. Dalias Berry, son of the late Owens Berry, were united in marriage by the Rev. F. A. Strother.

**BERRY, Dallas** – Nov. 4, 1910 M. J. – FAIRFAX – Mr. Dallas Berry, of Ashgrove, and Miss Roberta R. Swetnam, daughter of Mr. and Mrs. E. R. Swetnam, were married Wednesday evening, at the home of the bride's parents, at Fairfax Station, Rev. F. A. Strother officiating.

**BEVERLEY, Harry** – Mar. 11, 1910 M. J. –Dr. and Mrs. Jones, of Alexandria, have announced the engagement of their daughter, Miss Bessie Jones to Mrs. Harry Beverley, of Thoroughfare. The wedding will take place the eighth of June.

**BEVERLEY, R. H. C.** – May 13, 1910 M. J. – FAUQUIER – Dr. and Mrs. T. Marshall Jones of Alexandria, have issued invitations to the marriage of their daughter, Miss Elizabeth Winter to Mr. R. H. C. Beverley, of Fauquier county. The marriage is to take place on May 25$^{th}$.

**BIRDSALL, Millard** – Jan. 7, 1910 M. J. – LOUDOUN – Miss Florence Peacock, daughter of Mr. H. B. Peacock, of Wheatland, this county, and Mr. Millard Birdsall, son of Mr. Eli Birdsall, of Purcellville, were married at the bride's home by Rev. W. B. Dorsey, of the Methodist church last week. After a short bridal tour South they will reside near Purcellville.—Mirror, Dec. 31.

**BLACKWELL, Eva Ashton** – Jan. 21, 1910 M. J. – FAUQUIER – A beautiful and interesting double wedding took place on the afternoon of Jan. 5 at Sunnyside, the home of Mr. and Mrs. Moore Carter Blackwell, when their daughter, Miss Eva Ashton Blackwell, was married to Mr. Warren W. Goodman of Montana, and their granddaughter, Miss Grayson McLean Blackwell, became the bride of Mr. Francis Boswell Talbott, of Maryland. The double ceremony was most impressively performed by Rev. Edwin S. Hinks. Mr. and Mrs. Goodman, after a trip through Mexico and California, will make their home in Montana. Mr. and Mrs. Talbott will reside in Calvert county, Maryland.

**BLACKWELL, Grayson McLean** – Jan. 21, 1910 M. J – FAUQUIER – A beautiful and interesting double wedding took place on the afternoon of Jan. 5 at Sunnyside, the home of Mr. and Mrs. Moore Carter Blackwell, when their daughter, Miss Eva Ashton Blackwell, was married to Mr. Warren W. Goodman of Montana, and their granddaughter, Miss Grayson McLean Blackwell, became the bride of Mr. Francis Boswell Talbott, of Maryland. The double ceremony was most impressively performed by Rev. Edwin S. Hinks. Mr. and Mrs. Goodman, after a trip through Mexico and California, will make their home in Montana. Mr. and Mrs. Talbott will reside in Calvert county, Maryland.

**BLAIR, William Richards** – Nov. 5, 1909 M. J. – LOUDOUN – Cards are out announcing the marriage of Miss Florence Lyon Smith, daughter of Mr. and Mrs. Charles G. Smith, of Washington to Dr. William Richards Blair, of Mount Weather. The ceremony took place at Hohenheim, on the mountains above Bluemont, the bride's home, Dr. Frank Sewell, of Washington, officiating. They will reside at Mount Weather.

**BODINE, Lera** – Nov. 4, 1910 M. J. – FAUQUIER – Mr. Owen McLearen and Miss Lera Bodine were married in Washington on the 15$^{th}$, landing in Catlett Sunday to be greeted by a shower of rice and many good wishes. We wish the young couple good luck and many happy years and we expect to hear more bells of the same kind in the near future.—Virginian.

**BOLEY, Cassie** - Jan. 18, 1907 M. J. – Mr. Gardner King of Nokesville and Miss Cassie Boley of Greenwich were married at the home of the bride's parents, Wednesday evening, Jan. 9, Rev. S. V. Hildebrand of Gainesville officiating.

**BOLEY, Cassie** – Jan. 18, 1907 M. J. – GREENWICH -The home of William Boley, near this place, was the scene of a very pretty wedding at 8 p.m., Jan. 9, when her daughter Cassie, became the bride of Mr. King of Nokesville. The marriage ceremony was performed by Rev. S. V. Hilderbrand of Gainesville in the presence of a few friends. The bride was becomingly attired in blue silk. The writer wishes them a happy journey through life.

**BOLLING, Mary** – Jan. 21, 1910 M. J. – The engagement of Dr. R. S. B. Shackelford, of Maynadier Sanitarium, near town, to Miss Mary Bolling, of Charlottesville, is announced. The wedding is expected to take place on the eighth of February, at the Episcopal church in Charlottesville.

**BOLLING, Mary Field** – Feb. 11, 1910 M. J. – The marriage of Dr. R. B. S. Shackelford, the popular young physician of this vicinity, to Miss Mary Field Bolling, of Charlesville, Va., took place in that town on Tuesday evening last, in Christ Church. The ceremony was performed by Rev. Harry Lee.

The bride wore a handsome gown of white messaline with silver and pearl trimmings. Her only attendant was her school girl sister, Miss Sallie Stuart Bolling, who wore an attractive gown of white organdie with green trimmings. The groom was attended by Dr. Archibald Cary Randolph, of Baltimore, as best man.

Following the ceremony a reception was given at the bride's home, which was attended by guests from a distance, relatives, and intimate friends of the bride and groom.

**BONDURANT, Elmo** – Jun. 18, 1909 M. J.- LOUDOUN – Miss Lydia Hixson and Mr. Elmo Bondurant, of Hampden-Sidney, Va., were married at the home of the bride's father, Mr. Nelson Hixson, Wednesday June 2.

**BOOKER, Samuel Edward** – Oct. 1, 1909 M. J. – CULPEPER – Mr. and Mrs. Charles Edward Smith have issued cards for the marriage of their daughter, Miss Mildred Earle Smith, to Mr. Samuel Edward Booker, the event to take place in Saint Stephen's church on Thursday, October 15th, at half past twelve o'clock.—Exponent, Sept.24.

**BORDEN, Emma C.** - Sept. 14, 1906 M. J. – Mr. J. Frank Bushong, son of Mr. M. J. Bushong of this place, and Miss Emma C. Borden of Tom's Brook were married on Wednesday last at the residence of the bride's parents. Mr. and Mrs. Bushong are spending their honeymoon at Niagara. Mr. J. Locke Bushong of this place was groomsman for his brother's wedding.

**BOULWARE, Ballard Preston** – Jul. 2, 1909 M. J. – LOUDOUN – Major B. W. Lynn has announced the engagement of his youngest daughter, Miss Mary Elizabeth Lynn, to Mr. Ballard Preston Boulware, of Richmond, Va. The Richmond Times Dispatch of Sunday contained a portrait of Miss Lynn, and in referring to the announcement says: "Miss Lynn is a charming type of a Virginia girl, and the announcement of her engagement to Mr. Boulware will be of wide interest."—Enterprise

**BOWEN, Walter** – Aug. 10, 1906 M. J. - Cards are out announcing the approaching marriage of Miss Janie, daughter of Capt. and Mrs. Jas. E. Herrell and Mr. Walter Bowen of Washington, formerly of Brentsville.

**BOWEN, Walter F.** – Sept. 7, 1906 M. J. – The marriage of Miss Jeanie S. Herrell, daughter of Capt. and Mrs. Jas. E. Herrell, to Mr. Walter F. Bowen will take place Saturday evening, Sept. 15, at seven o'clock at Trinity church, this place.

**BOWEN, Walter Fullerton** – Sept. 21, 1906 M. J. – PRETTY WEDDING AT TRINITY – Trinity Episcopal Church here was the scene of a very pretty marriage on Saturday last at 7 o'clock, when Miss Jeanie Shields Herrell, daughter of Captain and Mrs. James Edward Herrell, became the bride of Mr. Walter Fullerton Bowen of Brookland, D.C. The Rev. John McGill performed the ceremony.

The beautiful decorations were in goldenrod and candles, with yellow shades. Miss Julia Lewis had charge of the music and played with good expression the wedding marches and Mendelssohn's "Spring Song."

The maid of honor, Miss Elizabeth Herrell, and the bridesmaids, Misses Anna Taylor, Carrie Makely, Selina Taylor and Estelle Holden, wore white mull with golden girdles and yellow pon-pons in the hair. The maid of honor carried yellow chrysanthemums, and the brides maids goldenrod.

The groom was attended by Mr. Michael Stephan as best man, and the following gentlemen were ushers, Messrs. George Purcell, Robert Herrell, Clarence Faithfull and H. Kinzel Laws.

The groom is a son of the late Dr. P. B. Bowen and a grandson of Dr. Walter Hore, at one time a surgeon in the United States navy.

Among the out-of-town guests at the wedding were Mr. and Mrs. C. M. Eddington of Richmond, Miss May W. Hundley of Mount Laurel, Va.; Mr. C. M. Faithfull of Liberty, Mo.; Miss Anna Louise Forbes Taylor of Kinsale, Va.; Mr. H. C. Hammond of Wellsville, Ohio; Mr. M. Stephan of Baltimore; Mr. and Mrs. David Oertley of Brookland; Mrs. M. H. Bowen and Mr. W. W. Hore of Washington; Mrs. V. W.Duval of Hyattsville, Mrs. Horner Malone of Brookland, Misses Makeley of Alexandria; Mr. and Mrs. C. E. Jordan of Haymarket, Va.; Mr. and Mrs. Arthur Lee Henry of Stone House, Va.

**BOWMAN, D. F.** – Nov. 5, 1909 M. J. – Mr. D. F. Bowman and Mrs. Georgia Florance were married Wednesday evening at Clifton, Rev. J. K. Efird, performing the ceremony. The bridal couple left for a honeymoon trip through the Valley of Virginia.

**BRADFORD, Mary E.** – Jan. 14, 1910 M. J. – FAUQUIER – Miss Mary E. Bradford, of Warrenton, and Mr. Sanford J. Payne, of Flint Hill, Va., were married Dec. 29, 1909, at the home of Rev. V. H. Council, pastor of Orlean Baptist church. The bride wore a navy blue broadcloth gown. There were no attendants.

**BRADLEY, Myrtle** – Mar. 25, 1910 M. J. – Mr. Harry Coxen and Miss Myrtle Bradley, both of Washington, were married March 17th and are spending their honeymoon at the Fairfax home of Mr. W. H. Clark, the Southern agent at Manassas. Mr. Coxen, who is a cousin of Mrs. Clarke, is well known in Manassas.

**BRADY, Grace** – Dec. 9, 1910 M. J. – Mr. Lucian A. Davis, eldest son of Mrs. Ada Davis, of Manassas, and of the late Captain Lucian A. Davis, who commanded the gallant Company A, of the fourth Virginia Cavalry, and Miss Grace Brady, of Washington, were married in the National Capital on Friday last. The marriage came as a surprise to his many friends in Manassas, who had no thought that Mr. Davis' extreme diffidence had permitted him to yield to cupid's allurements.

**BRADY, Norman** - Dec. 21, 1906 M. J. – A marriage license was granted on Saturday last to Mr. Norman Brady and Miss Maud Nalls, both of this county.

**BRADY, Samuel** – Jun. 10, 1904 M. J. - Mr. Samuel Brady of Fairfax and Miss Hattie V. Crouch, daughter of Mr. and Mrs. Albert Crouch, of this county, were married yesterday at the residence of the officiating minister, Rev. Robert Smith of Manassas.

**BRAGG, William M.** – Feb. 4, 1910 M. J. – Invitations have been received here to the marriage of Mr. William M. Bragg, son of Mr. H. T. Bragg, of this town, to Miss Nannie Lucille Thompson, of Roanoke, Va. The ceremony is to take place at Trinity Methodist Church, Roanoke, on the fifteenth of this month. Mr. Bragg has the congratulations of this Haymarket friends.

**BRAGG, W. Magnese** – Feb.18, 1910 M. J. – Mr. W. Magnese Bragg, was married at Roanoke, Va., on Tuesday last to Miss Nannie Thomasson, of that city. Mr. Bragg, who is now a route agent for the Southern Express Company at Roanoke and who was formerly stationed here as assistant to Messrs. W. B. Rogers and F. E. Morris, is a son of Mr. and Mrs. H. R. Bragg, of Haymarket, and became very popular while here. Mr. C. C. Wenrich, of this place acted as best man for Mr. Bragg.

**BRANDT, Martha** – Dec. 21, 1906 M. J. – On Tuesday last a marriage license was granted Mr. Jas. P. R. Polley and Mrs. Martha Brandt, both of this county. The ceremony was performed by Rev. Dr. Hamner.

**BRAWNER, Charley Waugh** – Nov. 18, 1910 M. J. – Miss Charley Waugh Brawner, daughter of Mr. and Mrs. Charles E. Brawner, of Manassas, and Mr. Lee Cockrell Lloyd, of Kentucky and New York, were married at 4:30 o'clock, Wednesday, in Washington, D.C.

The ceremony, which was attended only by the immediate family, was performed at the church of the Good Shepherd, by the assistant rector, Rev. Ginon.

Mr. and Mrs. Lloyd left immediately after the ceremony for their future home in Jamestown, N.Y.

**BRAWNER, Harvey** – Jun. 8, 1906 M. J. - Mr. C. W. Embrey, for several years agent of the Southern railway at this place, and Miss

Harvey Brawner, daughter of Mr. P. D. Brawner of Broad Run, were married this week and passed through here on Wednesday on a northern tour.

**BRAWNER, Virginia Harvey** – Jun. 8, 1906 M. J. - A very pretty wedding took place Wednesday, June 6, at the home of Mrs. Mount, Thoroughfare, Va., the contracting parties being Miss Virginia Harvey Brawner of Broad Run, Va., and Mr. Charles William Embrey of Rockfish, Va. Rev. S. V. Hildebrand of Sudley Methodist church officiated.

The bride wore a very dainty gown of white and looked her prettiest. She was attended by her sister, Miss Susie Brawner of Manassas.

Only a few friends and the immediate family witnessed the ceremony, after which the bridal party left for Norfolk and vicinity.

Upon their return they will make their home at Rockfish, Va., where Mr. Embrey is in the employ of the Southern railroad.

**BRAZEWELL, Lena Belle** – Jun. 25, 1909 M. J. – Mr. Chas. W. Bell, son of Mr. Geo. W. Bell, of Prince William, and Miss Lena Belle Brazewell, of Johnson City, Tenn., were married in the bride's home city Sunday, June 20. They are at present the guests of Mr. and Mrs. J. I. Randall, of Manassas. Mrs. Max Goldrose, Mrs. Randell's sister, who lives in Johnson city, accompanied the bride and groom to Manassas.

**BREDRUP, Robena Olive** – May 13, 1910 M. J. – FAUQUIER – A marriage of unusual interest to their numerous friends here took place in Washington, on Monday last, the contracting parties being Miss Robena Olive Bredrup, of Richmond and Mr. Geo. B. Grayson, of Warrenton. The bride is the daughter of Mr. C. P. Bredrup. The ceremony was performed by the Rev. Mr. Shannon and was witnessed by a few intimate friends. Mr. and Mrs. Grayson will make their home in Washington.

**BREEDEN, Annie L.** – Jun. 10, 1910 M. J. – FAUQUIER - Prof. Harrison C. Hobart and Miss Annie L. Breeden were quietly married at the home of the bride's father Mr. John S. Breeden of Remington, at 11:30 Wednesday. The bridal couple left almost immediately after the ceremony for a month's stay at the seashore, after which they will make their home at Manassas.

**BREEN, Judie** - Jan. 25, 1907 M. J. – Miss Judie Breen and Mr. Frank Wells were married Jan. 9, 1907, at St. Joseph's Church and will make their future home at Bull Run.

**BREEN, Lillian E.** - Jan. 25, 1907 M. J. – Mr. Murray L. Ball of Fairfax county and Miss Lillian E. Breen of Prince William county were married Jan. 23, by Rev. J. K. Efird at the Lutheran parsonage here.

**BRENNEMAN, J. Irwin** – Dec. 10, 1909 M. J. – LOUDOUN – Miss Bertha Carpenter, daughter of W. J. Carpenter, of Mount Crawford, and Prof. J. Irwin Brenneman, of Ashburn, this county, were married at the home of the bride last week. They will reside at Ashburn.

**BRENTON, George C.** – Jun. 1, 1906 M. J. - Mr. George C. Brenton and Miss Daisy M. Bridwell, both of this place, were married in Washington on Monday last.

**BRIDGES, Bertha Alice** – Jul. 1, 1910 M. J. – LOUDOUN – The marriage of Miss Bertha Alice Bridges, daughter, of Mr. and Mrs. Benjamin Bridges, to Mr. Charles Emory Nelson, was beautifully solemnized at the residence of the bride's parents, in Washington, at 7:30 o'clock Wednesday evening.

**BRIDWELL, Albert L.** – Dec. 20, 1907 M. J. – On Thursday, Dec. 19, 1907, at Manassas, Va., Mr. Albert L. Bridwell and Miss Bessie E. Holmes of Prince William county, were united in marriage by Rev. T. D. D. Clark.

**BRIDWELL, Daisy M.** – Jun. 1, 1906 M. J. - Mr. George C. Brenton and Miss Daisy M. Bridwell, both of this place, were married in Washington on Monday last.

**BRIDWELL, William C.** – Nov. 4, 1910 M. J. – A marriage license was issued in Washington Monday to Mr. Wm. C. Bridwell and Mrs. Fannie Hower, of Manassas.

**BRILL, Harry** – Nov. 18, 1910 M. J. – Mr. Harry Brill, of Frederick county, and Miss Minnie M. Fetzer, of Prince William county were married on Wednesday, Nov. 16, 4:30 p.m., at the parsonage of Grace M. E. Church, south, Rev. W. T. Gover officiating. The bride wore a gray travelling suit and the groom conventional black.

They were attended by Miss Carried Fately, of Manassas, a cousin of the bride. After a short bridal trip they will go next Saturday to Mr. Brill's home in Frederick county, where they will reside.

**BRITTON, John** – Jan. 28, 1910 M. J. – FAUQUIER – The engagement of Miss Caroline Peyton Nelson, daughter of Mrs. Geo. W. Nelson, to Mr. John Britton, of Trenton, N. J., has been announced; the wedding to take place in the early summer.

**BROOKS, Goldie Kalb** – Aug. 27, 1909 M. J. – LOUDOUN – Marriage licenses were issued in Leesburg this week to Mr. Robert Elmer Connon and Miss Goldie Kalb Brooks, of Clarke's Gap, and to William Lefevre and Lelia V. Ankers, of Lower Loudoun.

**BROOKS, Lawrence** – Sept. 17, 1909 M. J. – Mrs. Helen Davis surprised her friends here recently by her marriage in Washington to Mr. Lawrence Brooks, of New York, a prominent business man. They are now in Connecticut on their bridal trip and expect to return next week.

**BROOKS, Mary E.** – Jun. 15, 1906 M. J. – Mr. Ambrose F. Higgins and Miss Mary E. Brooks, both of Washington, D. C., were united in holy matrimony on Monday last, June 11, by Rev. J. K. Efird at the Lutheran Parsonage.

**BROWN, Grace S.** – Jan. 7, 1910 M. J. – FAIRFAX – Mrs. Grace S. Brown and Henry C. Ryer, of Falls Church, were married on Christmas day at the home of the bride in Washington, Rev. W. S. O. Thomas, of Falls Church, officiating.

**BROWN, W. V.** – May 10, 1907 M. J. – Mr. W. V. Brown and Mrs. Lena Rainer, both of Manassas, were married yesterday.

**BROWNING, Irma** – Aug. 13, 1909 M. J. – CULPEPER – Miss Irma Browning, of Culpeper, became the bride of Rev. W. M. Edwards, pastor of the Methodist church at Culpeper, Wednesday, August 4. The ceremony was performed at the home of the bride, Rev. E. W. Winfrey, officiating.

**BRYANT, Media F.** – Nov. 18, 1910 M. J. –A marriage license was issued Wednesday to Mr. Hezekiah Reid and Mrs. Media F. Bryant, of Hoadley.

**BUBB, Abram M. C.** – Nov. 11, 1910 M. J. – A current issue of a Wilmington, De., paper contains the following interesting announcement; Rev. George L. Wolfe, pastor of the First Methodist Protestant Church, received a letter requesting him to announce the marriage he performed on August 17, last, when he united in wedlock at his residence, Abram M. C. Bubb, of Woodbridge, Va., and Miss Anna J. Neufer, of Prince William county, Virginia.

**BUCHANAN, Lephia** – Nov. 4, 1910 M. J. – Rockville, Md., Nov. 2. Being unable to furnish $2,000 bail, Otto Linaweaver, who was married here Saturday afternoon under the name of Owen La Monta to Miss Lephia Buchanan, daughter of A. C. Buchanan, of Craigsville, Va., was committed to jail to await the action of the grand jury.

The offense with which Linaweaver is charged is that he swore falsely in giving his name as La Monta in making application for marriage license and in stating that he had not been divorced. The man's divorced wife, who was Miss Nellie Neville, of Washington, testified that she and Linaweaver were married in Rockville in July, 1907, by Rev. Thomas H. Campbell, pastor of the Baptist church, and that he was married under the name of Linaweaver. The court records were produced to corroborate the statement. Mrs. Linaweaver said she was granted a divorce from him in June of this year. Deputy Clerk of the Circuit Court Bowman testified that Linaweaver swore, in making application for the license last Saturday, that his name was La Monta and that he had never been divorced.

Linaweaver is a son of J. L. Linaweaver, of Manassas, Va. He lived in Washington several years and several weeks ago he represented himself as a palmist. Mr. Buchanan said the young man conducted himself in an exemplary manner in Craigsville, praying and participating in a revival in progress there. He was allowed to visit the Buchanan home.

When Linaweaver was arrested he had only about $2, but his bride had about $20. Linaweaver had with him a ticket showing that he had pawned two of the girl's rings in Alexandria, one of which, her father said, was valuable. Mr. Buchanan took the tickets with the intention of redeeming the rings on his way back home. He said he and his daughter would leave for their home tonight.—Baltimore Sun.

**BUCKLEY, Joseph L.** – Oct. 21, 1910 M. J. – FAIRFAX – Mr. Jos. L. Buckley and Miss Geneva T. Anderson were married by Rev. F. A. Strother, at the parsonage here, Wednesday morning. After a trip North, they will return to the home of the groom.

**BUCKLEY, Rush** – May 6, 1910 M. J. – CLIFTON – Mr. Rush Buckely, our popular young mail-carrier, and Miss Ella Wilt, were married Saturday returning Monday night to be welcomed by a merry crowd from Clifton, who serenaded them.

**BULLARD, Lelia** – Oct. 7, 1910 M. J. – Marriage license was issued Wednesday in Washington to Mr. Oscar S. Woody and Miss Lelia Bullard. Miss Bullard is one of the most popular young ladies of Clifton. Mr. Woody, who has made Clifton his home for a number of years, is connected with the mail service between New York and London. They will make Clifton their home.

**BUSHONG, J. Frank** - Sept. 14, 1906 M. J. – Mr. J. Frank Bushong, son of Mr. M. J. Bushong of this place, and Miss Emma C. Borden of Tom's Brook were married on Wednesday last at the residence of the bride's parents. Mr. and Mrs. Bushong are spending their honeymoon at Niagara. Mr. J. Locke Bushong of this place was groomsman for his brother's wedding.

**BUSHONG, J. Locke** – Aug. 5, 1910 M. J. – There was celebrated at Cedar church, which was artistically decorated in potted plants and ferns, Wednesday afternoon at two o'clock, one of the prettiest wedding of the mid-summer season, the participating parties being Miss M. Gladys Dinges, the very pretty and attractive daughter of Mr. and Mrs. Wm. H. Dinges, of "Ripple," Frederick county, and Mr. J. Locke Bushong of Manassas, Va.

The bridal party entered and left the church to the strains of Mendelssohn's wedding march, which was beautifully rendered by Miss Nellie Dinges, sister of the bride, who also played "Hearts and Flowers" during the ceremony.

The bride was handsomely gowned in white messaline satin trimmed in embroidered net with tulle veil, held in place by maidenhair fern and orange blossoms, and carried a shower bouquet of bride's roses. The bride was attended by her two sisters, Misses Edna and Vista Dinges, who were becomingly attired in blue messaline silk and wore large black picture hats, carrying bouquets of white asters.

The ceremony was performed by the bride's pastor, Rev. A. G. Link, of Strasburg, Va. The groom was attended by Messrs. Byron F. Hixson, of Washington, D.C., and Fred D. Maphis, of Strasburg, Va. Messrs. H. Kinzel Laws, of Front Royal, Va., and Clinton C. Rhodes, of Rockland, Va., acting as ushers.

The groom is a successful young business man of Manassas, Va., and is well known and honored by all who know him. He is the youngest son of Mr. and Mrs. Mahlon Bushong of that place.

After the ceremony the bridal party returned to the hospitable home of the bride where a delicious luncheon was served. Later the bride and groom were driven to the station at Vauchluse, where amid a shower of rice and with the best wishes of their friends, they boarded the eastbound train for a trip to the cities and seaside resorts.

Many handsome and useful presents including cut glass, silverware and linen were received by the happy couple.

Among the visiting guests were Misses Nellie B. Lupton, of Winchester, Va.; Rebekah S. Kilmer, of Martinsburg, W. Va., and Messrs. Mahlon Bushong, of Manassas, Va.; J. Frank Bushong, of Toms Brook, Va., and J. J. Boehin, of Roanoke, Va.

**BUSHONG, Joseph Locke** – Jul. 22, 1910 M. J. – Cards are out announcing the approaching marriage of Mr. Joseph Locke Bushong and Miss Mary Gladys Dinges at Cedar Cliff Presbyterian church, Vaucluse, Va., Wednesday afternoon Aug. 3, 1910, at 2 o'clock. On this happy event we can congratulate the bride as well as the groom.

**BUTLER, Bertha E.** – Sept. 2, 1910 M. J. – FAUQUIER – Miss Bertha E. Butler and Mr. Irvin Fox were married at the home of the bride's father, Mr. Daniel Butler, of Meetz, Saturday, August 20, at 5 p.m. The wedding was a very quiet one, only the immediate family and a few friends being present. The couple leaves for their home near Greenwich, Va.

**BUTLER, Lieut.** – Apr. 12, 1907 M. J. – Miss Janie A. Williams of Mississippi, who, with her parents, visited Mr. J. B. T. Thornton in 1905, and a niece of Congressman John Sharp Williams, was married Wednesday, April 3, to Lieut. Butler.

**CALDWELL, Virginia Prudence** – Jul. 1, 1910 M. J. – LOUDOUN – Mr. James Ludwell Lake, son of Rev. I. B. Lake, was married to Miss Virginia Prudence Caldwell on Wednesday, June 15th, at Upperville, Va.

**CALLAWAY, Elizabeth Sue** – Oct. 22, 1909 M. J. – Among those who attended the marriage of Miss Elizabeth Sue Callaway and Mr. Gustavus A. Hutchison on Thursday of this week, at Maryville, Tenn., were Mr. Robert A. Hutchison and little daughter, Ruth, Miss Isabella Holden and Miss Susan Hutchison.

CALLAWAY, Elizabeth Sue – Nov. 5, 1909 M. J. – We are publishing this week an interesting account of the Hutchison-Callaway nuptials which was received last week from Tennessee too late to appear in Friday's paper.

At the New Providence Presbyterian church in Maryville Thursday night, Oct. 21, was solemnized a wedding of much interest to Knoxville friends and relatives when Miss Elizabeth Sue Callaway became the bride of Mr. G. A. Hutchison, of Hickory Grove, Va. A special car took the Knoxville party over to Maryville for the wedding, and a large and brilliant assemblage witnessed the church ceremony. Rev. Joseph Calhoun, D. D., said the impressive ring service to an accompaniment of organ music, charmingly rendered by Mrs. Bartlett. In the personnel of the wedding party were Miss Annie Belle Callaway, maid of honor; Misses Isabelle and Susan Hutchison, Mary Belle Harrison and Beatrice Rutherford, bridesmaids; Mr. James B. Carson, best man; Messrs. Jos. and Thos. Callaway, A. M. Hill and Thos. C. Carson, ushers.

A color scheme of white and yellow characterized the details of the wedding arrangements, the several maids appearing in either white or yellow costumes and carrying arm bouquets of chrysanthemums of like shades. The bride's gown was a lovely creation of white satin, fashioned princess, and she carried a shower bouquet of bride's roses.

The church was decorated with a bank of palms and lighted by candles.

Following the ceremony a reception was tendered at the home of the bride's father, Mr. James Callaway, for members of the bridal party, relatives, out of town guests and intimate friends. The cutting of the wedding cake and its many favors were features of the occasion.

The bride is a niece of Mr. and Mrs. J. L. Callaway, Mrs. J. S. Callaway and Mr. and Mrs. J. B. Carson, of Knoxville. Mr. Hutchison is a son of Mr. and Mrs. Westwood Hutchison, of Manassas, and a nephew of Mr. H. G. Hutchison, of Vonore, Tenn.

The many handsome gifts of linen, silver and cutglass attest the popularity of the contracting parties.

Among the out of town guests were Mr. and Mrs. Jno. Callaway, Mrs. J. B. Carson, Mrs. J. S. Callaway, Mr. and Mrs. Thos. Callaway, Misses Sue, Carrie, Elizabeth, and Julia Callaway and Mr. and Mrs. Boyton, of Knoxville; Mrs. H. G. Hutchison and Mr. and Mrs. W. S. Harrison, of Vonore; Miss Lavinia Ish, of Chattanooga; Mr. and Mrs. R. A. Hutchison, of Manassas, Va.

**CALVERT, Alfonso** – Jun. 10, 1904 M. J. - Mr. Alfonso Calvert and Miss Annie Leona Sabine were married at the Greenwood Baptist church, this county, on Sunday, June 5.

**CALVERT, D. J.** – Apr. 12, 1907 M. J. – Mr. D. J. Calvert of Dumfries and Miss Nora Sutherland were married in Washington on Wednesday last.

**CAMMACK, Frank A.** – Jan. 14, 1910 M. J. – CULPEPER – The home of Mr. and Mrs. Somerville J. White was the scene of a very quiet home wedding last Wednesday at 1 p.m. when the oldest daughter, Flossie Elizabeth, was given in marriage to Mr. Frank A. Cammack, of Washington, D. C., Rev. Thomas F. Grimsley, officiating. None witnessed the ceremony save the immediate relatives of the bride and groom. Immediately after the ceremony the couple left via C. & O. for Richmond, from where they will extend their tour to Florida, returning about Feb. 1, to make their home in Washington, D. C.

**CAMMANN, H. Schuyler** – Jun. 17, 1910 M. J. – Mr. and Mrs. Hamilton Fairfax, of New York city, have announced the engagement of their daughter, Miss Katharine Van Ransslear Fairfax to H. Schuyler Cammann, of that city. Mr. and Mrs. Fairfax formerly resided in Loudoun county, Virginia, and is a brother of Henry Fairfax, of Oakhill, and a son of the late Col. Jno. W. Fairfax of Neabsco, this county.

**CANNON, Oswold** – Feb. 4, 1910 M. J. – CULPEPER – Mr. Oswold Cannon and Miss Rosa Hitt were married at the home of the bride Wednesday 26.—Exponent.

**CARNEY, Quenton A.** – Apr. 22, 1910 M. J. – Mr. Quenton A. Carney and Miss Frances S. Rison, both of Dumfries, were married Tuesday in Washington.

**CARPENTER, Bertha** – Dec. 10, 1909 M. J. – LOUDOUN – Miss Bertha Carpenter, daughter of W. J. Carpenter, of Mount Crawford, and Prof. J. Irwin Brenneman, of Ashburn, this county, were married at the home of the bride last week. They will reside at Ashburn.

**CARPENTER, Grace** – Feb. 25, 1910 M. J. – CULPEPER – Mr. J. F. Carpenter, of Brandy, Va., announces the marriage of his daughter, on Feb. 12th, Grace, to Mr. John E. Layman, of Roanoke. They will be at the home to their many friends after the 18th of February at 905 Patterson avenue, Roanoke, Va.—Exponent, Feb. 18.

**CARRICO, Ella M.** – Mar. 18, 1910 M. J.- Rev. T. D. D. Clarke performed the ceremony which united in marriage Mr. James N. Williams, of Washington, and Miss Ella M. Carrico, of Prince William county, on Wednesday, at the Baptist Parsonage.

**CARSON, Mr.** – Jan. 7, 1910 M. J. – The engagement of Miss Lucile Jordan, youngest daughter of Mr. and Mrs. C. E. Jordan to Mr. Carson, of Chicago, is announced, and the marriage is to take place in February, in Panama, where the family have spent several winters.

**CARTER, Dulany F.** – Jan. 21, 1910 M. J. – FAUQUIER –Mr. Dulany F. Carter, of Marshall, Fauquier county, and Miss Clara Lickey, of Round Hill, this county, were married recently in Washington.

**CARTER, Harry** – Nov. 4, 1910 M. J. – Mr. Harry Carter, one of Occoquan's most popular young men, was married in Washington on Wednesday last to Miss Hattie Shepperd, of Fairfax. They returned from their bridal trip on Saturday evening where a large crowd awaited them with an old time serenade. The young couple have the best wishes of the entire community for their future happiness.

**CARTER, Harry C.** – Oct. 28, 1910 M. J. –Marriage license was issued in Washington yesterday to Mr. Harry C. Carter, of this county, and Miss Harriet V. Shepherd, of Fairfax.

**CARTER, Harry C.** – Nov. 4, 1910 M. J. –FAIRFAX – A marriage license was issued in Washington Wednesday to Henry C. Carter, of Prince William county, and Harriet V. Shepherd, of Fairfax county—Rev. Jno. W. Smith officiating.

**CARTER, Samuel Henley** – Nov. 19, 1909 M. J. – FAUQUIER – Miss Francis Lee Flemming, daughter of Mr. and Mrs. Richard Bland Lee Flemming, on Monday afternoon was married at her home, near The Plains, in Fauquier county, to Mr. Samuel Henley Carter. Rev. John H. Norwood performed the ceremony. Only the immediate families of the bride and bridegroom were present. Miss Mary Flemming attended her sister as maid of honor.

**CARVER, Elizabeth** – Mar. 18, 1910 M. J. – FAIRFAX – A very pretty wedding took place in Wake Forest, N. C., when Miss Elizabeth Carver became the bride of M. D. Hall superintendent of the schools of Fairfax county. Congressman Carlin was Mr. Hall's best man. Immediately after the ceremony Mr. and Mrs. Hall left to spend their honeymoon in Jacksonville and Cuba.

**CARVER, Elizabeth McDonald** – Mar. 4, 1910 M. J. – FAIRFAX – Mrs. Octavia J. Shell, of Wake Forest, N. C., has issued invitations to the marriage of her daughter, Elizabeth McDonald Carver, to Col. M. D. Hall, Division Superintendent of Schools for Fairfax county, Va., on Wednesday, March 9th.

**CASSELL, Lloyd T.** – Dec. 16, 1910 M. J. – Among the marriage licenses issued in Washington Wednesday was that of Mr. Lloyd T. Cassell and Miss Amanda B. Cowne, both of Calverton. Mrs. Cowne has relatives in this county, and the groom is well known here.

**CATHER, Cordelia L.** – Dec. 30, 1910 M. J. – Mr. Hamilton Swart and Miss Cordelia L. Cather were married in Washington yesterday. The bride is a sister of Mr. W. H. Cather, of Manassas, and the groom a well-to-do farmer of near Sudley, in this county.

**CATLETT, Pauline** – Aug. 19, 1910 M. J. – Miss Pauline Catlett, nineteen years old, of Buckton, Va., and Mr. S. B. Stonnell, of Occoquan, were married Wednesday afternoon in Washington by Rev. D. C. McLeod. The wedding marked the culmination of a romance and elopement, in which the bride's love for her sweetheart overcame her parents' opposition to the match.

Although young Stonnell is the only son of Mr. S. B., a wealthy farmer, near Occoquan, who owns 2,000 acres of land in the Old Dominion, the parents of Miss Catlett are said to have selected another man for their son-in-law, and did not look with favor on the suit of the young farmer.

But Cupid, not to be outdone by parental objection, put into the head of young Stonnell the notion of visiting Washington, instead of Front Royal, and when the suggestion was made to Miss Catlett she concurred.

**CHADWELL, India** – Sept. 23, 1910 M. J. – FAUQUIER – Marriage licenses were issued in Washington on Thursday to the following Fauquier couples: Joseph B. Pulliam and Carolyn Spicer, both of Remington; Benjamin Gordon, of Markham, and India

Chadwell, of Hume; Joseph A. Jeffries, of Warrenton, and Sallie Thompson, of Washington.

**CHAMBERLAIN, Edward Matthews** – Dec. 3, 1909 M. J. – LOUDOUN – Mr. and Mrs. James Moses, of New York, have issued cards for the marriage of their daughter, Vera McFarland, to Mr. Edward Matthews Chamberlain, of Paeonian Springs, this county. The ceremony will take place in St. Thomas' church in New York, on Dec. 1. Miss Helen Meeks, of Paeonian, will be maid of honor.

**CHARLTON, Edith** – Apr. 1, 1910 M. J. – Miss Edith Charlton, whose articles on Domestic Science have been of so much interest to our readers, was married to Mr. George A. Salisburg, at Crawford, Nebraska, on March 26, 1910.

**CHESHER, James R.** – Feb. 4, 1910 M. J. –Mr. Jas. R. Chesher and Miss Bettie Patterson, both of Prince William county, were married in Washington Wednesday.

**CHISOLM, George** – Nov. 26, 1909 M. J. – Yesterday morning, at 10 o'clock, Miss Leo A. Lynch became the bride of Mr. George Chisolm, of Washington, at the home of the bride on Centre street. Father Patrick performed the ceremony. The bridal party left on the twelve o'clock train for an extensive tour through the Southern states.

**CLAGETT, Gertrude Dulaney** – Jul. 1, 1910 M. J. – LOUDOUN – Miss Gertrude Dulaney Clagett, daughter of Mrs. Wm. B. Clagett, and Mr. Richard Dulany Hall were married at the home of the bride's mother, in Washington, at high noon on Wednesday. The happy couple is well known and has many friends in Loudoun.—Enterprise.

**CLAGETT, J. Mack** – Jun. 11, 1909 M. J. – LOUDOUN – Mr. J. Mack Clagett, a well known stockman and farmer, of Clarke county, and Mrs. Lillian Timberlake were married in New York on Tuesday. Mrs. Clagett was formerly Miss Lillian Somer, of New York, and her first husband was Shelby Timberlake of Clarke.-Enterprise.

**CLARK, Bessie** – Aug. 10, 1906 M. J. - Miss Bessie Clark and Mr. Walter Holland were married here on Wednesday last.

**CLARK, Fannie** – Feb. 1, 1907 M. J. – Dr. W. R. Tulloss and Miss Fannie Clark of The Plains were married in Washington last

Tuesday evening. After a short tour they will return to his home in Haymarket.

**CLARKE, Sarah Gertrude** – Dec. 10, 1909 M. J. – CULPEPER – On Wednesday, December 1$^{st}$, at the home of her parents, Mr. and Mrs. W. D. Clarke, Miss Sarah Gertrude Clarke was married to Mr. Oliver C. Taylor, of Pennsylvania. Mr. and Mrs. Taylor will spend their honeymoon in Pittsburg with his relatives, and in Newark N. J., with Mrs. and Mrs. Jennings. Mrs. Jennings was Miss May Clarke. Miss Sallie Clarke is a beautiful girl, who is much beloved by those who know her for bright and amiable disposition.

**CLARKSON, Hugh T.** – Sept. 17, 1909 M. J. – The marriage of Miss Mary C. Jolliffe to Mr. Hugh T. Clarkson is announced to take place in October at the home of the bride's aunt, Mrs. Elizabeth Crenshaw, Baltimore. One of the most pleasant social events of the past few weeks was a linen shower, given Miss Jolliffe by Miss DePauw. About twenty-five guests were present and the young bride-elect received quite a number of pretty gifts. Mr. Clarkson is the son of Dr. H. M. Clarkson, and is with the C. P. Telephone Co., of Washington. The young couple have many warm and interested friends here.

**CLARKSON , Hugh Thompson** – Oct. 22, 1909 M. J. – The marriage of Miss Mary C. Joliffe, daughter of the late Mr. and Mrs. William H. Joliffe, of Baltimore, to Mr. Hugh Thompson Clarkson, of Haymarket, Va., took place at noon yesterday at the home of the bride's aunt, Mrs. Nathaniel Bacon Crenshaw, on Lake avenue.

Rev. Chas. A. Hensel, rector of the Protestant Episcopal church of the Redeemer, performed the ceremony, which was followed by the reception for the members of the two families and intimate friends.

The bride was given in marriage by her cousin, Mr. Benjamin T. Moore. Her gown of heavy corded white silk, with a trimming of old lace, and tulle veil, caught with orange blossoms, was the same her mother had worn at her wedding. The bride of yesterday also wore ornaments of old family pearls. Her bouquet was of bride roses and maidenhair ferns.

The maid of honor was Miss Marion B. Wyatt, who wore a gown of embroidered white crepe de china a white picture hat trimmed with plumes and carried a shower bouquet of pink chrysanthemums. Two little cousins of the bride, Elizabeth Joliffe McElroy, were flower girl and ribbon bearer. Little Miss McElroy wore white and carried a basket of white flowers tied with blue ribbons.

The groom was attended by his brother, Mr. Walter Clarkson, of Philadelphia, as best man.

Later in the afternoon Mr. and Mrs. Clarkson left for an extended trip South. On their return they will live in Laurel, Maryland.

Among the guest at the wedding were: Dr. and Mrs. H. M. Clarkson, of Haymarket, Va., parents of the groom; Gen. and Mrs. W. Robinson, of Raleigh, N.C.; Mr. and Miss Gilless, of Washington; Mr. Charles Keyser, of Haymarket, Va.; Mr. Thomas Clarkson, of Laurel, Md.; Miss Katherine Crenshaw, of Philadelphia.—Baltimore Sun.

**CLARKSON, Jean** – Jul. 27, 1906 M. J. - Dr. and Mrs. H. M. Clarkson announce the marriage of their daughter, Jean, to Gen. Thomas Ross Robertson of North Carolina at St. Paul's Church, Haymarket, Tuesday, August 7, at 6 o'clock. No cards except to friends at a distance.

**CLARKSON, Jean** – Jul. 27, 1906 M. J. - A special dispatch from Wilmington, N.C., to the Richmond Times Dispatch says:

Friends in this city have received invitations to a marriage that is of much importance to society and the military of the State. They are to the wedding of Adjutant-General Thomas Ross Robertson of the North Carolina National Guard, and Miss Jean Clarkson, daughter of Dr. and Mrs. Henry Mazyck Clarkson of Haymarket, Va., the event to be celebrated Thursday, August 7th, in St. Paul's Church, Haymarket.

General Robertson is of Charlotte, N.C., and is delightfully remembered in Wilmington, as he has been in attendance upon a number of encampments at Wrightsville, near here, and was always prominent in the social functions attendant upon the encampments.

The Raleigh (N.C._ Observer of a recent date says:

Wedding invitations have been received by friends which will be read with interest and pleasure in North Carolina, where the groom-to-be is a prominent lawyer and a leading figure in the North Carolina National Guard.

The invitation reads as follows:

Dr. and Mrs. Henry Mazyck Clarkson request the honor of your presence at the marriage of their daughter,
    Jean,
      to
General Thomas Ross Robertson,
Tuesday, August the seventh,
nineteen hundred and six;

at six o'clock,
Saint Paul's Church,
Haymarket, Virginia

General Robertson is now a citizen of Charlotte, where he is a prominent attorney. He has long been a member of the military force of the State, captain of his home company, colonel of the First Regiment, and serving during the Spanish-American War when his company went to Cuba, now Adjutant-General of the North Carolina National Guard, appointed by Governor Glenn. He is a clever and popular gentleman and his bride-elect is a charming lady of Virginia, a member of one of the most prominent and influential families in the State. It will be of special interest to the people of Raleigh to know that after the first of October General and Mrs. Robertson will make Raleigh their home.

There will go to the happy event some of the most prominent people in North Carolina, among these Governor Glenn and a large number of officers of the North Carolina National Guard.

**CLARKSON, Jean** – Aug. 10, 1906 M. J. - The marriage of Miss Jean Clarkson and General Thomas Ross Robertson took place in St. Paul's church, Haymarket, Tuesday, Aug.7, at 6 p.m. The ceremony was impressively performed by the rector, Rev. Cary Gamble. The bride is the youngest daughter of who Dr. and Mrs. H. M. Clarkson and is one of the most attractive and popular young women in the neighborhood. Gen. Robertson is a distinguished lawyer of Charlotte, N. C., as well as Adjutant-General of the state troops.

The church was beautifully decorated by the bride's friends, the color scheme being white and green ablaze with the mellow radiance of white lights. The wedding marches as well as other music, were finely rendered by Miss Norton Tyler. The matron of honor, Mrs. Thomas B. Clarkson, wore a gown of white crepe de chene and carried white roses. The bride's maids, Misses Fanny White, Hallie Meade, May Beverly, Belle Price, Florence Gilliss and Mary Price were gowned in white organdie trimmed net lace and carried large bouquets of pink roses. The order of entering the church was unique and pretty, the matron of honor and bride's maids came from the vestry room and walking down the aisle with the bride at the church door, there, preceded by the ushers, Mr. Alexander B. Andrews, Jr., Col. Westcott Robertson, Mr. Hugh Clarkson, Major Joseph T. Cannon, Capt. Wm. R. Robertson and Mr. Lee M. Clarkson, they came up the circle followed by the bride on the arm of her father by whom she was given away.

The bride's gown was an exquisite white fabric, imported from China by a relative in the Navy. If was made princess with train and elbow sleeves, the yoke made of thread lace. The Tulle veil was beautifully arranged with orange blossoms, her flowers were a shower bouquet of bride roses and she looked a typical and lovely bride.

The bridegroom with his best man, Gen. Francis A. Macon, came from the vestry room and met the bride at the chancel. Gen. Robinson, the best man and ushers were in full evening dress with boutonnieres of white gardenias. The bridal party was very imposing as it passed up the aisle and the beautiful tableau and the chancel steps of " fair women and brave men" is one that will long be remembered by all present. Mrs. Clarkson, the bride's mother wore black "feau de soie" with duchess lace, Mrs. Robert Lee Reading of California, sister of the bride, wore her own wedding dress of white crepe de chene and looked very handsome.

An elaborate luncheon was given before the wedding at the bride's home to the bridal party, relatives and a few friends.

The presents were numerous and handsome. Among those from a distance present were Mrs. Hugh Thompson of New York the bride's aunt, Mrs. Reading, Miss Love and Mr. Breckinridge of Washington, Mrs. Charles Phelps of Baltimore, Mrs. Samuel Claggett of Frederick county, M. D. and Mr. Hugh Thompson of New York.

Gen. and Mrs. Robertson left on the evening train for an extended tour South.

**CLARKSON, Walter Beaumont** – Feb. 4, 1910 M. J. – The marriage of Mr. Walter Beaumont Clarkson, of Philadelphia, son of Dr. H. M. Clarkson, of this town, to Miss Anna Elise Reid, took place on January the thirty-first in Washington, D. C., of which city the bride was a resident. The ceremony was performed by Rev. Robert Talbot.

**CLAYTON, Louise Adelaide** – Jun. 8, 1906 M. J. - Announcement has been made of the coming marriage of Mr. M. Otho Efird, son of Rev. J. K. Efird of this place, to Miss Louise Adelaide Clayton of Florence, S. C. The bride is a daughter of Hon. Wm. F. Clayton, a prominent South Carolina lawyer. After June 25 Mr. and Mrs. M. Otho Efird will be at home to their Manassas friends at the Lutheran parsonage here.

**CLAYTON, Louise Adelaide** – Jun. 22, 1906 M. J. - On June 14, 1906, in the city of Florence, S.C., at the First Baptist church at the hour of 6 p.m., was witnessed perhaps one of the most beautiful weddings ever witnessed in that city. The church was beautifully decorated, the music was grand and the bridal party both men and women the handsomest and loveliest that ever assembled for a like occasion.

Promptly at 6 o'clock Mrs. N. W. Hicks at the organ accompanied by Mrs. J. W. Ragsdale on the violin struck up the grand processional, and from the two aisles came the charming ribbon girls, dressed in the colors pink and white, Misses Ruth Darr and Annie Joe Timons on the left and Misses Mirand Waters and Alma Muldrow on the right, they were followed by the ushers Messrs. P. J. Maxwell and M. A. Wisnant on the left and Charles Commander and John Webster on the right; then followed the flower girls scattering roses and daisies, little Miss Sarah Oliver and Miss Marion Clayton, a niece of the bride. After these had reached their stations the bridal party entered, the bridesmaids and maid of honor on the left all handsomely gowned in white chiffon over white silk, carrying large bouquets of pink carnations. The first to enter were Miss Katie Clayton and Mr. J. N. Sweeney and in succession were Miss Inez Bowen and Mr. Robt. Tomlinson, Miss Ethel Ford and Mr. Sandborn Chase, Miss Mattie Anthony and Mr. J. B. Clayton, Miss Nannie Hodges and Albert Reldrow and Miss Jessie Timmons and Gedney Brown. These were followed on the left by Miss Julia Florence Clayton, maid of honor, beautifully costumed in a dress of white mouline over white taffeta, carrying a bunch of pink bridesmaid roses. Miss Julia is the twin sister of the bride and very much like her in appearance. On the right Mrs. Robbie Chase, dame of honor, in a beautiful dress of ecru net over white taffeta with a bouquet of pink roses; behind these came the bride, Miss Louise Adelaide Clayton, leaning on the arm of her father, Hon. W. F. Clayton. Her dress was of white crepe de chene over white taffeta, with a bouquet of white bride's roses and lilies of the valley. Miss Clayton is considered quite a beauty and upon this occasion with her flowing veil looked even lovelier than usual. On the right came the groom, Mr. Milton Otho Efird, leaning upon the arm of his brother, Charles E. Efird. At the chancel the father turned the bride over to her future husband and before the Rev. Mr. Will Oliver, the talented, popular and loved rector the couple stood until made man and wife.

From the church the bridal party and guests repaired to the home of Hon. W. F. Clayton where a delicious repast was served, Mrs. J. W. Ragsdale and Mrs. W.A. Wisnant presiding over the punch bowl while Mrs. John A. Chase and Miss Robbie Chase acted as hostesses and received the guests.

The presents were both numerous, handsome and valuable coming from Virginia where the groom's parents reside at Manassas to Georgia and Florida where relatives of both the bride and groom reside. After a short stay the bride and groom left under a shower of rice and good wishes for their bridal tour, which includes New York, Philadelphia, Washington and Baltimore, with a visit to the groom's parents at Manassas, returning to Florence about July 1 which will be their future home.

**CLEMENT, Small A.** – Feb. 25, 1910 M. J. – CULPEPER – Win.Taliaferro, of Rapidan, has issued invitation to the marriage of his daughter, Miss Agnes Marshall Taliaferro to Small A. Clement, Ensign, United States Navy. The ceremony is to take place on Wednesday, Feb. 23$^{rd}$, in St. Paul Episcopal church, Oakland, Cal., where his is stationed.

**CLIFTON, Zoa Langdon** – Jun. 18, 1909 M. J. – Adjacent to the picturesque village of Occoquan, above the rushing mill-race that hurls its turbulent waters back into its mother steam, Occoquan River, yet hidden in a miniature amphitheater among the wooden hills, lies Rattlesnake Camp. A bubbling spring, a collection of gleaming tents, a long deal table and a roaring camp fire that throws its fitful gleam athwart the rippling surface of the stars and stripes stretched high up between two trees, and the picture is complete, except for the throng of young folk, moving in and out among the tents in noisy, care free confusion, which adds to the scene the one lacking touch of color and life.

In this charming spot occurred a wedding on last Tuesday at noon, which carried the mind of the spectator back to the fabled village of Arcadia. The contracting parties were Miss Zoa Langdon Clifton, of Baltimore, and Mr. Wm. Elisha Sweet, of Erie, Pa. Rev. F. L. Robinson, rector of Trinity Church, Manassas, performed the ceremony. Miss Bertha S. Austin, of Baltimore, was the only attendant, and Mr. G. Raymond Ratcliffe gave away the bride.

The ceremonies were ushered in with Lohengrin's Wedding March, sung by the assembled campers, and the bride and groom to be stood before the rustic altar, under the star spangled banner, to be united in the holy bonds of wedlock. The beautiful, solemn words of the marriage ceremony were unaccompanied by the customary strains of the pipe organ, but the murmur of the hidden waters floated upward, mingled with the gentle crooning of the wind among the tree-tops, while silvery bird notes wove threads of melody into the woof of the semi-silence—and Nature played an obbligato.

The bride was attired in an Empire gown of snowy linen, elaborately hand embroidered, and the bridesmaid, Miss Austin, wore a green gown cut Empire.

Those present to witness the ceremony were Mrs. G. Raymond Ratcliffe, of Manassas, who is chaperoning the party, Mrs. A. A. Hynson, of Occoquan, Misses Elizabeth Myer, of Washington, Norma V. Round, of Manassas, Margaret E. Newman, of Waynesboro, Pa., Martha P. Hall, of Binghampton, N.Y., and Bertha S. Austin, of Baltimore; Messrs. G. Raymond Ratcliffe, of Manassas, Wm. Edward Austin, of Baltimore, Joseph Parker, of Baltimore, Thomas Clarke, of Washington, W. Willis Davies, of Manassas, Reid Hynson, of Occoquan, and Drs. J. C. Reichley, of York, Pa., Frank Hornbaker, of Occoquan and J. Marye Lewis, of Manassas. These, with the exception of the Occoquan guests, and Dr. Lewis and Mr. Davies, of Manassas, comprise the regular camping party at Rattlesnake Camp.

**CLINE, Walter A.** - Feb. 22, 1907 M. J. – Mr. and Mrs. W. F. Hale announce the marriage of their daughter, Miss Fleeta Anna, to Mr. Walter A. Cline Thursday morning, March 14, at eleven o'clock.

**CLINE, Walter A.** – Mar. 15, 1907 M. J. – The home of Mr. and Mrs. William F. Hale, near Nokesville, was the scene of a beautiful wedding on Thursday, when Miss Fleta A. Hale became the bride of Mr. Walter A. Cline of Washington.

The ceremony was performed by Rev. M. G. Early, while Miss Edna D. Miller played the wedding march.

Miss Fannie Keagy of Harrisonburg was bridesmaid, and Mr. W. C. Long of Harrisonburg was best man.

Mr. and Mrs. Cline left in the afternoon for a short bridal trip, which will include Norfolk. Upon their return, they will reside in Washington, where Mr. Cline is in business.

About fifty guests witnessed the ceremony, including Messrs. S. B. Van Nest, Geo. M. Oyster, W. H. Cline, Walter Hooker and J. F. Moller of Washington, Misses Lena and Annie L. Cline and Mr. Harry Cline of Falls Church, and Mr. Westwood Hutchison of Manassas.

Immediately after the ceremony, the dining hall was thrown open, where a splendid lunch was served.

**CLOUD, Lillie** – Feb. 4, 1910 M. J. – CULPEPER – Laurel Mills, Jan. 24.—Mr. Henry Sours and Miss Lillie Cloud eloped to Hagerstown, Md. last Tuesday and were married. When they returned to Kimball a heavy snow had fallen and as they had several miles to walk before getting to the house of Mr. Fox a brother-in-law of the groom they started but found the snow too deep for the bride to walk. Mr. Sours left her at a farm house and went for a buggy and when he came back he could not find his bride for sometime as he could not tell the house at which he had left her.

**COCKE, William R. C.** – Oct. 15, 1909 M. J. – Miss Alice Watts Du Bose and Dr. William R. C. Cocke, both of Charlottesville, were married at noon yesterday at the home of the bride's uncle and aunt, Dr. and Mrs. George Du Bose, 2903 Q street northwest, Washington. The ceremony was performed by Rev. Dr. Lloyd, of Alexandria, bishop elect of Virginia, in the presence of a large company of relatives and friends of the bride and bridegroom, including a party of 30 who went to Washington from Virginia.

**COCKERILLE, Coleman** – Jul. 30, 1909 M. J. – Mr. Coleman Cockerille, of Washington, and Miss Monnie Elizabeth Marsteller, daughter of Mr. S. A. Marsteller, of this county, were married Monday afternoon of last week at Rockville, Md., by Rev. Dr. Packard in the presence of an aunt of the bride and a few friends. After the ceremony they left for a wedding trip, which will include visits to Niagara, Toronto, New York and Atlantic City. On their return they will reside at 1364 Kenyon street, N. W., Washington.

**COLBERT, Frank** – Jun. 4, 1909 M. J. – Mr. Frank Colbert and Miss Rosa Robinson, both of Manassas, were married Wednesday, May 26, at the Methodist Parsonage by Mr. W. T. Gover.

**COLE, Howard Elton** – Aug. 20, 1909 M. J. – LOUDOUN – Mr. and Mrs. Charles A. English of Leesburg, have announced the engagement of their daughter, Miss Myra Gardner English, to Mr. Howard Elton Cole, of the Peoples National Bank. The wedding will take place in Leesburg during the autumn.

**COLE, Howard Elton** – Oct. 29, 1909 M. J. – LOUDOUN – Mr. and Mrs. Charles Albert English, of Leesburg, have issued invitations for the marriage of their daughter, Myra Gardner, to Mr. Howard Elton Cole, of the Peoples National Bank. The wedding will take place in St. James Episcopal church, in Leesburg, on Wednesday, Nov. 3, at 3 o'clock in the afternoon. No cards in the town or county.

**COLE, Howard Elton** – Nov. 12, 1909 M. J. – A lovely marriage was solemnized by Rev. W. H. Burkhardt at the Episcopal church, in Leesburg, on Wednesday evening, Nov. 3, according to the beautiful ceremony of that church, when Miss Myra Gardner, the accomplished daughter of Mr. Chas. A. English, was made the wife of Mr. Howard Elton Cole.

The church was beautifully decorated for the happy occasion and the sweet-toned organ in solemn melody gave forth notice of the approaching nuptials. A large crowd was in attendance attesting the general popularity of the contracting parties.

Mr. Hubert T. Plaster was best man and Mrs. E. F. Concklin, of Washington, was matron of honor. The ushers were Mr. C. Albert English, brother of the bride; Mr. Edgar Littleton, of the Fairfax National Bank; Mr. J. R. H. Alexander, mayor of Leesburg, and Dr. Jno. A. Gibson.

**COLE, Stockton W.** – Nov. 25, 1910 M. J. – FAUQUIER – Rev. Stockton W. Cole, of Remington, and Miss Fannie Price were married Monday afternoon at 5 o'clock, at the residence of the bride's father, Hon. J. M. Price, of Bealeton. There were only the family and a few intimate friends present when Rev. T.P. Brown, pastor of the Bealeton Baptist church, united them in marriage. The bridal couple took the evening train for a short trip north, after which they will attend the General Baptist Association at Roanoke and be back to their future home in Remington by the 1$^{st}$ of December or perhaps sooner. This is a marriage that will meet with the hearty approval of all that know the contracting parties. Miss Price is a young woman, who besides having her full share of womanly charms and graces, is such a splendid church worker, so talented as an organist and in all that will make her an ideal helpmate for a pastor, that Rev. Cole is to be congratulated. And Mr. Cole, who has charge of seven churches in Fauquier, Culpeper and Rappahannock is a Christian worker that deserves just such a wife. We can pay him no higher nor more deserved compliment.

**COLVIN, Thomas L.** – Sept. 17, 1909 M. J. – Mr. Thos. L. Colvin, of Washington, and Miss Irva H. Davis, daughter of Mrs. A. P. Davis, Manassas, were married in Washington last Monday.

**COMPTON, Earl** – Jul. 29, 1910 M. J. – A marriage license was issued in Washington Monday to Mr. Earl Compton, of Fairfax county, and Miss Lillie M. Stephens, of Fauquier county.

**COMPTON, Robert F.** – Jul. 8, 1910 M. J. – The engagement of Miss Mary Barbour Rixey, daughter of the late Hon. John F. Rixey, who represented the Eighth District in congress, to Dr. Robert F. Compton, is announced. The wedding will be celebrated at the home of the bride's mother near Charlottesville. Dr. Compton is a member of the medical faculty of the University of Virginia.

**COMPTON, Robert F.** – Oct. 28, 1910 M. J.- The marriage of Miss Mary Barbour Rixey, daughter of the late Congressman John F. Rixey and niece of Rear Admiral Rixey, to Dr. Robert F. Compton will take place on Tuesday, November $8^{th}$, at the home of Miss Rixey's mother, near Charlottesville. Dr. Compton is a member of the faculty of the University of Virginia.

**COMPTON, Robert French** – Nov. 11, 1910 M. J. – Mrs. John F. Rixey, widow of the late Congressman Rixey, of the Eighth district, has issued cards for the wedding of her daughter, Miss Mary Barbour Rixey, to Dr. Robert French Compton, which is to take place on the afternoon of November 8, at "Gowan Lee," the home of Rixey, near Charlottesville.

**CONKLIN, Edward Franklin** – Jun. 11, 1909 M. J. – LOUDOUN – Miss Frances Edwards Marlow, daughter of Mrs. Marlow and the late Edward Grandison Marlow, and Edward Franklin Conklin, of Washington, were married Tuesday in St. James' Episcopal Church, Leesburg, by Rev. William H. Burkhardt.—Alex. Gazette.

**CONNER, Elizabeth K.** - Feb. 8, 1907 M. J. – Miss Elizabeth K. Conner, daughter of Rev. Abraham Conner and Mrs. Conner, was married January $29^{th}$ to Mr. Milton Hottle of Ohio. The ceremony was performed by Rev. William Conner of Newport News, brother of the bride. The bride was beautifully attired in a gown of white mull.

Immediately following the ceremony a wedding supper was given at the parents' home for the relatives of both bride and bridegroom.

Mr. and Mrs. Hottle left for a Northern trip. They will make their future home in Ohio.

**CONNON, Robert Elmer** – Aug. 27, 1909 M. J. – LOUDOUN – Marriage licenses were issued in Leesburg this week to Mr. Robert Elmer Connon and Miss Goldie Kalb Brooks, of Clarke's Gap, and to William Lefevre and Lelia V. Ankers, of Lower Loudoun.

**COONS, Menora** – Aug. 26, 1910 M. J. – FAUQUIER – Miss Menora Coons, the attractive daughter of Mr. and Mrs. J. A. Coons, of

Warrenton, and Mr. Lloyd Anderson, a prosperous young business man of Culpeper, were married in Rockville, Md., on Monday last.

**CORNELL, William** – Nov. 11, 1910 M. J. – LOUDOUN – Mr. Wm. Cornell, of Fairfax, and Miss Virginia Redmond, of Loudoun, were married in the parlors of the Leesburg Inn on Thursday, by Rev. J. H. Wiltshire.

**CORNWELL, Daisy M.** – Apr. 1, 1910 M. J. – Mr. Jas. Russell and Miss Daisy M. Cornwell, both of Canova, were married at high noon yesterday at the home of the bride, by Rev. T. D. D. Clark, pastor of the Manassas Baptist church. Mr. and Mrs. B. C. Cornwell, of Manassas, were present at the ceremony.

**CORNWELL, Willie** - Dec. 28, 1906 M. J.- Married, Dec. 23, at the home of the bride by Rev. J. K. Efird, Mr. Willie Cornwell and Miss Laura Riley, both of this county.

**COWNE, Amanda B.** – Dec. 16, 1910 M. J. – Among the marriage licenses issued in Washington Wednesday was that of Mr. Lloyd T. Cassell and Miss Amanda B. Cowne, both of Calverton. Mrs. Cowne has relatives in this county, and the groom is well known here.

**COXEN, Harry** – Mar. 25, 1910 M. J. – Mr. Harry Coxen and Miss Myrtle Bradley, both of Washington, were married March 17th and are spending their honeymoon at the Fairfax home of Mr. W. H. Clark, the Southern agent at Manassas. Mr. Coxen, who is a cousin of Mrs. Clarke, is well known in Manassas.

**CRAGG, Thomas Mark** – Jul. 22, 1910 M. J. – FAIRFAX – Miss Mabel Isabelle Hunter, daughter of Mr. and Mrs. John C. Hunter, of Accotink, and Thomas Mark Cragg, of Alexandria, were married at the Washington street Methodist Episcopal Church South Thursday night, July 7th, by the Rev. Harry M. Canter, pastor.

**CRAWFORD, Angus MacDonald** – Jun. 18, 1909 M. J. - ALEXANDRIA – Mr. Angus MacDonald Crawford, of San Antonio, Tex., son of Dr. Angus Crawford of the Theological Seminary, near Alexandria, and Miss Elizabeth Lewis Worthington, daughter of Mr. and Mrs. George V. Worthington, formerly of this city, but now of Washington, were married Saturday night at Christ church, Georgetown.

**CRAWFORD, Dellie W.** – Jun. 24, 1910 M. J.- Mr. Dellie W. Crawford and Miss Edith M. Harris, both of this county, were married by Rev. J. K. Efird at the Lutheran parsonage on Monday, June 20$^{th}$.

**CREAMER, Margaret Ada** – Jun. 24, 1910 M. J. – Mrs. Anna E. Spies, of this place, attended the wedding of Mr. Edward Emerentia Spies and Miss Margaret Ada Creamer in Washington on Wednesday last.

**CRITTENDEN, William J.** – Dec. 9, 1910 M. J. – On Thursday night, of last week, as the guests were gathering at The Prince William Hotel to take part in the dance to be given under the auspices of The Manassas Orchestra, a telegram was received by Mr. Lucas, proprietor to the hotelry, requested that he have a minister on hand upon the arrival of train No. 44 due at Manassas 6:35 o'clock.

There were no further details, but Mr. Lucas, inferring that a marriage was on hand rang up Dr. Hervin U. Roop, of Eastern College, and asked him to officiate in the prospective wedding.

Upon the arrival of the train Dr. William J. Crittenden, of Orange, accompanied by Miss Mary Mason, repaired at once to the hotel parlor where they were quietly married. After taking supper, and receiving the congratulations of the host and others, the happy couple boarded the 8:10 o'clock train for Washington and Baltimore.

**CROSBY, Luna E.** - Oct. 5, 1906 M. J. – Mr. W. E. McCoy and Miss Luna E. Crosby - both of this county were married last Wednesday at the residence of the bride's parents, near Bristow. Rev. J. K. Efird, officiating.

**CROSS, James H.** – Jan. 14, 1910 M. J. – Mr. Jas. H. Cross, of Manassas and Miss Amelia Bateman, of Washington, were married last Friday in that city.

**CROSS, Pemmie Tim** – Feb. 15, 1907 M. J. – From the Alexandria Gazette of Saturday. On Wednesday afternoon Pemmie Tim Cross of Manassas and Miss Julia M. D. Maddox of Washington, went to Rockville, Md., after obtaining a marriage license went to the Catholic church rectory, where they met Rev. Father Rosensteel of Forest Glen. Father Rosensteel told the young couple that he could not marry them because they did not have any letter of identification from the home parish of either.

The couple left, stating that they would get such letters and return as soon as possible.

**CROSS, Wilmer.** – Oct. 5, 1906 M. J. – Miss Eva Hunt, daughter of Mr. S. W. Hunt of Woolsey, and Mr. Cross of Fairfax were married at the Little River Baptist church on Wednesday last, Rev. T. D. D. Clark officiating.

**CROSS, Wilmer B.** - Oct. 19, 1906 M. J. – The wedding of Mr. Wilmer B. Cross of Fairfax county and Miss Eva Hunt, daughter of Mr. Silas Hunt of "The Oaks," Prince William county, was one of the prettiest seen for some time in Prince William. The wedding was at high noon, Wednesday, Oct. 3, at Little River Church, Rev. T. D. D. Clark of Manassas performing the ceremony.

The church was most tastefully decorated with flowers and palms and as the bride and groom, with their attendants, marched up the aisle to Hymen's favorite melody, magnificently rendered by Miss Robena Hay of Ashburn, Va., the scene resembled enchantment rather than reality.

After the ceremony the bride, groom and guests repaired to "The Oaks," where a sumptuous repast was served.

Miss Miller of Washington, who was maid of honor, Miss Day, and Miss Harris attended the bride, Mr. Eppa Hunt was best man and Messrs. John Lefevre, C. S. Hutchison and I. A. House were ushers.

Mr. and Mrs. Cross expect to leave shortly for Washington state where they will reside.

**CROUCH, Frank** – Apr. 1, 1910 M. J. – Mr. Frank Crouch and Miss Rebecca Sayres, both of this county, were married Wednesday by Rev. Dr. Hamner at his residence on East Main street.

**CROUCH, Hattie V.** – Jun. 10, 1904 M. J. - Mr. Samuel Brady of Fairfax and Miss Hattie V. Crouch, daughter of Mr. and Mrs. Albert Crouch, of this county, were married yesterday at the residence of the officiating minister, Rev. Robert Smith of Manassas.

**CROUCH, Inez** – Feb. 18, 1910 M. J. – Mr. Wm. Harris and Inez Crouch, both of this county, were married in Washington City on Tuesday last.

**CROUCH, Inez** – Feb. 18, 1910 M. J. – Mr. Williams Harris and Miss Inez Crouch left for Washington Sunday returning on Tuesday evening as bride and groom. We wish them a happy journey through life.

**CROUCH, Leonora** – Jul. 10, 1896 M. G. - Marriage licenses were granted this week to Mr. Geo. E. Hayth and Miss Maria A. Sayers, and Mr. G. W. Robinson and Miss Leonora Crouch, daughter of Mr. Elias Crouch—all of this county.

**CROUCH, Mary Anna** – Mar. 25, 1910 M. J. –Mr. Wade Hampton Rogers, one of the first boys of Manassas, who has been living in Washington state for twenty-one years, spent Saturday and Sunday with his niece, Mrs. R. S. Hynson, on his way to Washington, where he was united in marriage with Miss Mary Anna Crouch, Wednesday. When a boy Mr. Rogers was student at Ruffner Public School, under Mr. Wm. R. Will, the school's first male principal, who is now professor in Brand-Stratton Business College, Baltimore.

**CULLEN, William W.** – Sept. 16, 1910 M. J. – Miss M. Lillian Saffer, daughter of Mr. and Mrs. F. E. Saffer, of Manassas, Va., and Mr. Wm. W. Cullen, son of Mr. and Mrs. N. J. Cullen, of Paeonion Springs, Loudoun county, Va., were married Wednesday, Sept. 14, at 3 p.m. at the home of the bride's parents by Rev. W. T. Gover.

The couple were attended by Miss Beatrice Biebetheiser, of Baltimore, Md., and Mr. Harry A. Cullen, a brother of the groom.

The bride was attired in a blue traveling suit, hat and gloves to match.

The couple left for an extended trip north accompanied by their attendants. Upon their return they will reside at 2015 S st., n.w., Washington. Will be at home to their many friends after Oct. 1st.

**CURTIS, Miss** – Sept. 16, 1910 M J. – FAUQUIER – Mr. Will Edmonds, of The Grove, and Miss Curtis, of Deep Run were married August 24th in Grove Baptist church by the pastor, Rev. C. W. Brooks.

**CUSHING, Katherine** – Mar. 18, 1910 M. J. – Miss Katherine Cushing, daughter of Mr. and Mrs. Robert B. Cushing, of near Wellington, became the bride of Mr. James R. White, a prominent druggist of Dublin, Montgomery county, Va., on Monday morning, Rev. Dr. Hammer performing the ceremony. The young couple left for Washington on the Branch train. They will be at home in Dublin, Va., after March 24th.

**DALEY, Edward A.** – Aug. 31, 1906 M. J. - Married on Tuesday last at the Church of the Holy Comforter, Washington, D.C. Miss Lillian W. Spindle of Bristow, to Mr. Edward A. Daley of Brooklyn, N.Y.

**DANDRIDGE, Edmund Pendleton** – Oct. 15, 1909 M. J.- Miss Mary Robertson Lloyd, eldest daughter of the bishop coadjutoe-elect of Virginia and Mrs. A. S. Lloyd, and Rev. Edmund Pendleton Dandridge, of Lewisburg, W. Va., were married last Friday at Christ Episcopal Church, Alexandria. The ceremony was performed by the bride's father, assisted by Bishop Peterkin, of West Virginia.

**DARLINGTON, Elizabeth** – Jun. 17, 1910 M. J. – The Herndon Observer, announces the engagement of Miss Elizabeth Darlington, daughter of Mr. J. J. Darlington, of Washington, to Dr. Charles Augustus Simpson, of the same city.

**DAVIES, Madie W.** – Nov. 22, 1901 M. J. - On Thursday morning last another beautiful wedding took place in our town. On this occasion Mr. E. Humphrey Hibbs and Miss Madie W. Davies were the contracting parties.

Trinity church was beautifully decorated with palms, ferns, chrysanthemums and other rare plants, and quite a crowd was in attendance, as Mrs. Dr. Wolfe took her place at the organ. Promptly at 10 o'clock the bridal party entered the church, the four ushers, Messrs. E. B. Giddings, J. Jenkyn, Will W., and Hawes Thornton Davies, preceding the bridal couple, and were met at the alter by Rev. W. H. K. Pendleton, the rector of Trinity church, who, in the beautiful and impressive ceremony of the Episcopal church, the twain were made one, the meanwhile Mrs. Wolfe playing softly at the organ.

The bride is a handsome blonde and was beautifully attired in navy blue broadcloth with hat to match. She was given away by her uncle, Mr. J. B. T. Thornton.

The groom is a prominent business man of the town and a member of the firm of Hibbs. & Giddings.

Mr. and Mrs. Hibbs were the recipients of many congratulations and beautiful presents. Among the latter was a deed for a valuable town lot from her uncle, Mr. J. B. T. Thornton.

The bridal party left on train No. 14 for a Northern tour and will probably attend the New York horse show.

Congratulations and best wishes are tendered them by THE JOURNAL.

**DAVIES, William Willis** – Jun. 3, 1910 M. J. – Cards are out announcing the coming marriage of Mr. William Willis Davies and Miss Nora Vera Round, eldest daughter of Mr. Geo. C. Round of this place, at Trinity Episcopal church, Wednesday evening, June 15, at 6:30. Owing to the wide acquaintance of both families, no invitations have been issued in the county.

**DAVIES, William Willis** – Jun. 17, 1910 M. J. – Because of the wide acquaintance of the contracting parties, and the prominence of the families connected, the marriage of Miss Norma Vera Round and Mr. William Willis Davies is of unusual interest to the society of Manassas and vicinity. The wedding took place Wednesday evening, June 15, at 6:30 o'clock at Trinity Episcopal church, of this place, the former rector, Rev. F. L. Robinson, officiating.

The church was beautifully decorated with palms, ferns and pink roses banked around the altar—the color scheme being green, pink, and white. "O Promise Me" well sung by Miss Florence Hall of Brookville, Pa., preceded the wedding march from Lohengrin, played by Miss Mabel Bennett, cousin of the bride, of Washington, assisted by Miss Charlotte Smith of Manassas. The ushers, Hon. R. Ewell Thornton of Fairfax; H. Thornton Davies, John J. Davies, of Culpeper; William Harold Lipscomb, L. Frank Pattie and George C. Round, Jr., preceded Miss Ruth Althea Round, sister of the bride. Miss Round, as maid of honor, was attired in a gown of pink satin messaline and a picture hat. She was followed by Miss Emily Maitland Round, youngest sister of the bride, who was dressed in white over pink, and carried a large basket of flowers which she spread in the path of the bride.

The bride, dressed in an elaborate gown of white crepe meteor with pearl and renaissance lace trimmings and a tulle veil caught with lilies of the valley, approached the altar on the arm of her father, Hon. George Carr Round. They were met at the chancel by the groom and his uncle, Judge J. B. T. Thornton, who served as best man.

After a beautiful and an impressive ceremony the bridal party passed out of the church to the strains of Mendelssohn's wedding march.

A reception to the relatives and out of town guests was held at the home of the bride's parents during the evening, the success of which was largely due to the efforts of Miss Althea E. Loose, cousin of the bride, and an instructor in the Harrisonburg Normal School.

After a short trip to various points in the East, Mr. and Mrs. Davies will return to Manassas for permanent residence, in a new dwelling which will be erected during the summer.

The bride is an Alumna of Goucher College and the Barnard Hospital of Baltimore, Md., and has held for several years the position of Sanitary Supervisor of the former institution. The bride's mother is a native of London, Canada. Through her, the bride is $13^{th}$ in descent from the lawyer-poet of Scotland, Sir Richard Maitland, after whom the Maitland Club of Glasgow was named; and through her she is likewise descended from Colonel Richard Blood, one of Cromwell's fighters immortalized by Sir Walter Scott. Through her father she is $9^{th}$ from Caleb Carr, the Quaker Governor of Rhode Island and traces descent from the Hopkins and Church families which furnished a Signer of the Declaration of Independence, Stephen Hopkins, and the hero of the King Phillips' War, Capt. Benjamin Church. The bride is a Daughter of the Revolution through Bartram Round, a lieutenant in the Scituate Hunters of Rhode Island and through his wife, Alce Wilkinson, she is $9^{th}$ in descent from Lawrence Wilkinson, a lieutenant in the army of Charles I, who, in Browning's Americans of Royal Descent, Pedigree LXXII is given as $16^{th}$ from King Edward I of England and as descended from the Royal Houses of France and Spain.

The groom received his education in William and Mary College and the University of Virginia. He is connected with the Health Office of the District of Columbia. His is of an old and prominent family of Virginia. His grandfather, Major W. W. Thornton, was the first superintendent of schools in the county, and served in the Prince William cavalry of the Confederate army. His father was of a well-known English family. Born in England and educated at Christ College, Oxford, he came to Virginia in his early manhood and at once took an active interest in our public questions. The groom's present family is identified with the affairs of the state and are prominent in business circles.

Many relatives and friends were in attendance at the wedding, among them—Mrs. R. Ewell Thornton and Miss Helen Moore of Fairfax; Mrs. Harriet I. Davies and her sister, Miss Lelia Green, from Aden; Miss Grace Abbott from Ilion, N.Y.; Dr. Jac Reichley of York, P.; Dr. Frank Hornbaker of Occoquan; Mrs. Dr. Noland of Loudoun, and Miss Martha P. Hall from Binghamton, N.Y. Among Washingtonians were—Dr. Maitland C. Bennett and wife, Dr. Harrison M. Bennett, Dr. Charles B. Chamberlin and wife, Mr. H. F. Tompkins and wife, Misses Alice and Catharine Boorman and Mrs. L. Adelia Pine, the sister of Mr. Round, The following were present from Baltimore—Mrs. Clara F. Hanneman, Miss Florence Hall, Dr. Wisner and wife, Miss Edith Rickert and Miss Bertha Austin.

With the happy couple now on their beautiful honeymoon go the best wishes of a large circle of friends who will welcome their return.

**DAVIS, Alton A.** - Dec. 17, 1909 M. J. – A marriage license was issued in Washington Tuesday to Alton A. Davis and Miss Elsie L. Perry, both of Prince William, and the young people were united in marriage by Rev. C. W. Whitmore.

**DAVIS, Charles N.** – Dec. 24, 1909 M. J. – Mr. Chas. N. Davis and Miss Virgie Wolfe, of near Hoadley, were married Wednesday at the home of Rev. W. M. Smoot, of near Occoquan, who performed the ceremony.

**DAVIS, Charles N.** – Dec. 24, 1909 M. J. – The following marriage licenses were issued this week at the clerk's office: Monday, Lewis M. Swartz, Culpeper county, and Miss Pearl L. Kelley, Fauquier county, Chas. N. Davis and Miss Virgie Wolfe, both of Prince William; Tuesday, John F. Donovan, Rockingham county and Miss Florida V. Allison, Loudoun county; Wednesday, Aubrey Flynn, Fauquier county, and Miss Annie L. Thomas, Prince William county; Thursday, Wm., E. Beahm, Rappahannock county, and Miss Edith G. Priest, Fauquier county; Geo. Spinks, Fauquier county, and Miss Bessie Baggott, Prince William county.

**DAVIS, Eppa** – Mar. 18, 1910 M. J. – Mr. Eppa Davis and Miss Sarah E. Davis, both of Prince William county, were united in marriage Monday by Rev. J. K. Efird at the Lutheran Parsonage.

**DAVIS, Fannie** - Jan. 4, 1907 M. J. – Mr. Monk Mills and Miss Fannie Davis, daughter of Mr. Richard Davis, both of lower Prince William, were married on Wednesday last.

**DAVIS, Helen** – Sept. 17, 1909 M. J. – Mrs. Helen Davis surprised her friends here recently by her marriage in Washington to Mr. Lawrence Brooks, of New York, a prominent business man. They are now in Connecticut on their bridal trip and expect to return next week.

**DAVIS, Hunter** – Nov. 22, 1901 M. J. - The marriage of Miss Marguerite Selecman to Rev. Hunter Davis was celebrated at the home of the bride's father, Mr. W. R. Selecman in Washington, D. C., on Thursday last. The bride was charmingly attired in pearl grey silk crepe de cline over pearl grey taffeta silk and carried white bride roses.

The house was beautifully decorated with palms and chrysanthemums. A wedding breakfast followed the ceremony, which was performed by Rev. W. F. Locke of Front Royal, Va. The guests numbered 85 persons. The presents were beautiful and numerous. Among those who attended from Occoquan were: Dr. C. Lee Starkweather, Mr. Edwin Cockrell, Mr. and Mrs. Daniel W. Ritterbusch, Mr. and Mrs. R. C. Hammill and son Perry and Miss Rowena Selecman.

**DAVIS, Irva H.** – Sept. 17, 1909 M. J. – Mr. Thos. L. Colvin, of Washington, and Miss Irva H. Davis, daughter of Mrs. A. P. Davis, Manassas, were married in Washington last Monday.

**DAVIS, Lemuel J.** – Jun. 11, 1909 M. J.– Mr. Lemuel J. Davis and Miss May Wolfe, of upper Prince William, were married last Wednesday.

**DAVIS, Lizzie** – Jul. 8, 1910 M. J. – A marriage license was granted in Washington on Tuesday to Mr. Robert Waite and Miss Lizzie Davis, both of this county.

**DAVIS, Lucien** - Dec. 28, 1906 M. J. – Mr. Lucien Davis and Miss Myrtle Mills, both of lower Prince William, were married on Monday last, Elder Smoot officiating.

**CORRECTION** – Jan. 4, 1907 - The announcements of two weddings were given us last Friday morning , just before going to press, and in some way the names were gotten wrong.

FAIRFAX-MILLS – Mr. Lucien Fairfax (not Davis) and Miss Myrtle Mills, daughter of Mr. Richard Mills, were married on the 24th, Elder Smoot officiating.

**DAVIS, Lucian A.** – Dec. 9, 1910 M. J. – Mr. Lucian A. Davis, eldest son of Mrs. Ada Davis, of Manassas, and of the late Captain Lucian A. Davis, who commanded the gallant Company A, of the fourth Virginia Cavalry, and Miss Grace Brady, of Washington, were married in the National Capital on Friday last. The marriage came as a surprise to his many friends in Manassas, who had no thought that Mr. Davis' extreme diffidence had permitted him to yield to cupid's allurements.

**DAVIS, Nadine** – Jan. 25, 1907 M. J. – Mr. Guy Allen of Nokesville and Miss Nadine Davis, daughter of Mrs. A. P. Davis of this place, were married in Washington last week, Rev. D. L. Blakesmore officiating.

**DAVIS, Sarah E.** –Mar. 18, 1910 M. J. – Mr. Eppa Davis and Miss Sarah E. Davis, both of Prince William county, were united in marriage Monday by Rev. J. K. Efird at the Lutheran Parsonage.

**DAY, Frederick M.** – Dec. 31, 1909 M. J. – FAUQUIER – Marriage licenses were issued in Washington this week to Frederick M. Day and Mary L. Beach, both of Fauquier county. Also to Jos. M. Jacobs of Calverton and Miss Carrie B. Green of Midland, Va.

**DAYMUDE, Alice J.** – Oct. 7, 1910 M. J. – LOUDOUN – Mr. Jas. M. Lane and Miss Alice J. Daymude, both of Lower Loudoun, were married in the parlors of the Leesburg Inn Wednesday morning, Rev. J. H. Wiltshire, of the Baptist church, officiating. –The Mirror

**DEANE, Charles Russe** – Jun. 11, 1909 M. J. – FAUQUIER – Mrs. G. H. Sublett, of Warrenton, announces the engagement of her daughter Eliza Lawrason, to Chas. Russe Deane, formerly of Albermarle county. The wedding will take place in October.—Alex. Gazette

**DEARMONT, William A.** - Jan. 11, 1907 M. J. – From the Alexandria Gazette. The marriage Tuesday of William A. Dearmont, the well known turf-man and steeplechase rider of White Post, Clarke county, and Miss Sallie Rixey, daughter of Hon. John F. Rixey, member of Congress from the Eight Virginia district, of Culpeper, was solemnized at 4:30 o'clock Tuesday at the Presbyterian manse at Strasburg, Rev. A. C. Link, officiating. The bride and groom took the 5 o'clock train on the Southern Railway for Washington, on their wedding trip. They are to make their home at "Dearmont Hall," in Clarke county.

The bride is well known in society in Virginia and Washington.
**CORRECTION-** Jan. 18, 1907 – The announcement of the marriage of Miss Sallie Rixey, in last week's JOURNAL from the Alexandria Gazette, stated that she was the daughter of Hon. John F. Rixey, member of Congress from the Eighth district. Miss Rixey is the daughter of Mr. Thomas P. Rixey a brother of the Congressman.

**DECATUR, Annie E.** – Nov. 12, 1909 M. J. – Mr. and Mrs. Wilson Decatur, of Stafford county, announce the approaching marriage of their daughter, Miss Annie E. Decatur, to Geo. McQuinn, of Washington. The ceremony will take place on Wednesday, Nov. 10, at Salem M. E. church, 3:30 p. m.

**DELK, Owington Gordon** – Apr. 8, 1910 M. J. – At the home of the bride Wednesday morning at 9 o'clock Miss Lena Francis Tulloss, daughter of Dr. W. R. Tulloss, of Haymarket, was quietly married to Mr. Owington Gordon Delk, of Smithfield, Va., in the presence of the immediate family and a few friends. The ceremony was performed by Rev. R. Gamble See, pastor of the Presbyterian church, of Marshall, Va.

The bride was attired in a handsome traveling costume of champagne cloth with hat and gloves to match. Mr. and Mrs. Frank B. Simpson, of Smithfield, were among those present from a distance. The groom is a brother of Mrs. Simpson.

The bridal party took the morning train for a wedding tour which will include New York, Niagara and other points North. They will reside in Smithfield.

**DEMORY, Oscar** – Aug. 17, 1906 M. J. - The marriage of Mr. Oscar Demory and Miss Hattie Shackelford took place at the home of the bride near Broad Run, Va., Wednesday, Aug. 15$^{th}$, at 4 p. m., Rev. Mr. Hollis officiating.

**DEVERS, Alfred** – Jul. 23, 1909 M. J.- A marriage license was issued in Washington Tuesday to Alfred Devers, of Alexandria, and Annie M. Hutchison, of Prince William county.

**DICKERSON, Ora** – Oct. 8, 1909 M. J.- Mr. John K. O'Neil, son of Mr. and Mrs. Dennis O'Neil, and Miss Ora Dickerson, of Burnleys, Va., were married last week at the home of the bride.

**DINGES, Mary Gladys** – Jul. 22, 1910 M. J. – Cards are out announcing the approaching marriage of Mr. Joseph Locke Bushong and Miss Mary Gladys Dinges at Cedar Cliff Presbyterian church, Vaucluse, Va., Wednesday afternoon Aug. 3, 1910, at 2 o'clock. On this happy event we can congratulate the bride as well as the groom.

**DINGES, M. Gladys** – Aug. 5, 1910 M. J. – There was celebrated at Cedar church, which was artistically decorated in potted plants and ferns, Wednesday afternoon at two o'clock, one of the prettiest wedding of the mid-summer season, the participating parties being Miss M. Gladys Dinges, the very pretty and attractive daughter of Mr.

and Mrs. Wm. H. Dinges, of "Ripple," Frederick county, and Mr. J. Locke Bushong of Manassas, Va.

The bridal party entered and left the church to the strains of Mendelssohn's wedding march, which was beautifully rendered by Miss Nellie Dinges, sister of the bride, who also played "Hearts and Flowers" during the ceremony.

The bride was handsomely gowned in white messaline satin trimmed in embroidered net with tulle veil, held in place by maidenhair fern and orange blossoms, and carried a shower bouquet of bride's roses. The bride was attended by her two sisters, Misses Edna and Vista Dinges, who were becomingly attired in blue messaline silk and wore large black picture hats, carrying bouquets of white asters.

The ceremony was performed by the bride's pastor, Rev. A. G. Link, of Strasburg, Va. The groom was attended by Messrs. Byron F. Hixson, of Washington, D.C., and Fred D. Maphis, of Strasburg, Va. Messrs. H. Kinzel Laws, of Front Royal, Va., and Clinton C. Rhodes, of Rockland, Va., acting as ushers.

The groom is a successful young business man of Manassas, Va., and is well known and honored by all who know him. He is the youngest son of Mr. and Mrs. Mahlon Bushong of that place.

After the ceremony the bridal party returned to the hospitable home of the bride where a delicious luncheon was served. Later the bride and groom were driven to the station at Vauchluse, where amid a shower of rice and with the best wishes of their friends, they boarded the eastbound train for a trip to the cities and seaside resorts.

Many handsome and useful presents including cut glass, silverware and linen were received by the happy couple.

Among the visiting guests were Misses Nellie B. Lupton, of Winchester, Va.; Rebekah S. Kilmer, of Martinsburg, W. Va., and Messrs. Mahlon Bushong, of Manassas, Va.; J. Frank Bushong, of Toms Brook, Va., and J. J. Boehin, of Roanoke, Va.

**DODD, Thomas Franklin** – Jun. 25, 1909 M. J. – FAIRFAX - Mrs. Orion Triplett, of Fairfax county, has issued invitations to the marriage of her daughter, Miss Catherine Louise Smith, to Dr. Thomas Franklin Dodd, of Stuarts Draft, son of Mr. and Mrs. George Y. Dodd, of Braddock Heights. The wedding will take place Wednesday evening, June 30, at 8:30 o'clock, in Christ Church.—Alex. Gazette.

**DODGE, Sarah Katrina.** – Dec. 15, 1905 M. J. - Mr. and Mrs. Howard P. Dodge announce to their friends in Manassas the marriage of their daughter, Miss Sarah Katrina, and Mr. Charles Willoughby

Hardy on December 10. Mr. and Mrs. Hardy will live in Spencer, Idaho.

**DONOVAN, John F.** – Dec. 24, 1909 M. J. – The following marriage licenses were issued this week at the clerk's office: Monday, Lewis M. Swartz, Culpeper county, and Miss Pearl L. Kelley, Fauquier county, Chas. N. Davis and Miss Virgie Wolfe, both of Prince William; Tuesday, John F. Donovan, Rockingham county and Miss Florida V. Allison, Loudoun county; Wednesday, Aubrey Flynn, Fauquier county, and Miss Annie L. Thomas, Prince William county; Thursday, Wm. E. Beahm, Rappahannock county, and Miss Edith G. Priest, Fauquier county; Geo. Spinks, Fauquier county, and Miss Bessie Baggott, Prince William county.

**DOWNS, Minnie C.** – Jul. 2, 1909 M. J. – FAUQUIER – Wm. McLean Heyl, and Miss Minnie C. Downs, both of Marshall, were married in Washington Thursday.—Fredericksburg Free Lance, June 26.

**DU BOSE, Alice Watts** – Oct. 15, 1909 M. J. – Miss Alice Watts Du Bose and Dr. William R. C. Cocke, both of Charlottesville, were married at noon yesterday at the home of the bride's uncle and aunt, Dr. and Mrs. George Du Bose, 2903 Q street northwest, Washington. The ceremony was performed by Rev. Dr. Lloyd, of Alexandria, bishop elect of Virginia, in the presence of a large company of relatives and friends of the bride and bridegroom, including a party of 30 who went to Washington from Virginia.

**DULANY, Eva Randolph** – Jul. 16, 1909 M. J. – LOUDOUN – Mr. and Mrs. Richard Hunter Dulany, of Grafton Hall, have announced the engagement of their daughter, Miss Eva Randolph Dulany, to Dr. Archibald Cary Randolph, of Willwood.

**DULANY, Eva Randolph** – Apr. 29, 1910 M. J. – At Grafton Hall, Fauquier county, at noon Tuesday, Miss Eva Randolph Dulany, daughter of Mr. and Mrs. Richard Hunter Dulany, of Grafton Hall, was married to Dr. Archibald Cary Randolph, of Baltimore, formerly of Clarke county. The bride is a very attractive girl, and has been for several seasons a favorite at Greenbrier White Sulphur Spring. These springs were formerly owned by her father and were sold a few months ago. She is a niece of Mrs. Robert Neville, of Washington. The pair will live in Baltimore.

**DULLEY, Bessie L.** – Jul. 27, 1906 M. J. - Mr. Allen S. Wolfe and Miss Bessie L. Dulley both of Washington, D.C., were united in marriage by Rev. J. K. Efird at the Lutheran parsonage, Manassas, Va., July 21, 1906.

**DUNCAN, Etta** – Sept. 3, 1909 M. J. – FAUQUIER – Miss Etta Duncan, of Fauquier county, and Mr. John Ambler Smith, of Washington, were married recently. The bride is a granddaughter of Colonel John Matthew Monroe. Mr. Smith is the youngest son of John Ambler Smith, who was in Congress for several years.

**DUNN, Frank L.** – Jun. 11, 1909 M. J. – WARREN- Miss Marjorie Owen Adams, of Front Royal, and Frank L. Dunn, superintendent of the Crawford Woolen Mills, of Martinsburg, eloped to Hagerstown Tuesday in an automobile, and were married there by Rev. George B. Townsend of the Christian church.

Miss Adams left her home Monday evening, telling her parents she intended calling, and would shortly return. Instead she boarded a train for Shenanoah Junction, where she met Dunn. The couple went to Martinsburg and stopped at the home of Dunn's brother. At 2 o'clock Tuesday morning they started for Hagerstown, but near Williamsport the automobile broke down. The remainder of the journey was made by trolley. – Richmond Bulletin.

**DYER, Edith**– Dec. 28, 1906 M. J. – Mr. Rosier Fairfax and Miss Edith Dyer, both of this county, were married here on Christmas day, Rev. T. D. D. Clark performing the ceremony.

**CORRECTION** – Jan. 4, 1907 –The announcements of two weddings were given us last Friday morning, just before going to press, and in some way two of the names were gotten wrong.

FAIRFAX-DAVIS – On Christmas day Mr. Rosier Fairfax and Miss Edna Davis (not Miss Dyer) were married, Rev. T. D. D. Clark of this place performing the ceremony.

**EASTER, Gray H.** – Nov. 5, 1909 M. J. – LOUDOUN – Miss Grace Whaley, daughter of W. F. Whaley, of Loudoun, and Gray H. Easter, of Washington, were married Tuesday by Rev. George Cummings, of the Presbyterian church. The bride was attended by her sister, Miss Orra Whaley, and the groom by Richard Swindell, of Washington.

**EASTHAM, Blanche Byrd** – Dec. 10, 1909 M. J. – CULPEPER – The marriage of Miss Blanche Byrd Eastham, of Culpeper, to Mr. Eilbeck Grasty, of Orange took place at the residence of the bride's sister, Mrs. Byrd Leavell, at 3072 Q. street Northwest, Washington, D.C., at 2:30 o'clock Tuesday afternoon.

**ECKHART, Clara** - Nov. 9, 1906 M. J.- Miss Clara Eckhart, daughter of Mrs. A. Davis, was married in Washington on Tuesday last to Mr. Wm. G. Johnson of that city.

**ECKHART, Lillian** – Dec. 23, 1910 M. J. – Mr. Allen Ernest Tate and Miss Lillian Eckhart, of Washington, were married in that city last week. Miss Eckhart was formerly a resident of Manassas, her mother being the owner of the hotel Maine in this place which burned some years ago while she was the hostess.

**EDMONDS, Will** – Sept. 16, 1910 M. J. – FAUQUIER – Mr. Will Edmonds, of The Grove, and Miss Curtis, of Deep Run were married August 24th in Grove Baptist church by the pastor, Rev. C. W. Brooks.

**EDWARDS, W. M.** – Aug. 13, 1909 M. J. – CULPEPER – Miss Irma Browning, of Culpeper, became the bride of Rev. W. M. Edwards, pastor of the Methodist church at Culpeper, Wednesday, August 4. The ceremony was performed at the home of the bride, Rev. E. W. Winfrey, officiating.

**EFIRD, M. Otho** – Jun. 8, 1906 M. J. - Announcement has been made of the coming marriage of Mr. M. Otho Efird, son of Rev. J. K. Efird of this place, to Miss Louise Adelaide Clayton of Florence, S. C. The bride is a daughter of Hon. Wm. F. Clayton, a prominent South Carolina lawyer. After June 25 Mr. and Mrs. M. Otho Efird will be at home to their Manassas friends at the Lutheran parsonage here.

**EFIRD, Milton Otho** – Jun. 22, 1906 M. J. - On June 14, 1906, in the city of Florence, S.C., at the First Baptist church at the hour of 6 p.m., was witnessed perhaps one of the most beautiful weddings ever witnessed in that city. The church was beautifully decorated, the music was grand and the bridal party both men and women the handsomest and loveliest that ever assembled for a like occasion.

Promptly at 6 o'clock Mrs. N. W. Hicks at the organ accompanied by Mrs. J. W. Ragsdale on the violin struck up the grand processional, and from the two aisles came the charming ribbon girls, dressed in the colors pink and white, Misses Ruth Darr and Annie Joe Timons on the left and Misses Mirand Waters and Alma Muldrow on the right, they were followed by the ushers Messrs. P. J. Maxwell and M. A. Wisnant on the left and Charles Commander and John Webster on the right; then followed the flower girls scattering roses and daisies, little Miss Sarah Oliver and Miss Marion Clayton, a niece of the bride. After these had reached their stations the bridal party entered, the bridesmaids and maid of honor on the left all handsomely gowned in white chiffon over white silk, carrying large bouquets of pink carnations. The first to enter were Miss Katie Clayton and Mr. J. N. Sweeney and in succession were Miss Inez Bowen and Mr. Robt. Tomlinson, Miss Ethel Ford and Mr. Sandborn Chase, Miss Mattie Anthony and Mr. J. B. Clayton, Miss Nannie Hodges and Albert Reldrow and Miss Jessie Timmons and Gedney Brown. These were followed on the left by Miss Julia Florence Clayton, maid of honor, beautifully costumed in a dress of white mouline over white taffeta, carrying a bunch of pink bridesmaid roses. Miss Julia is the twin sister of the bride and very much like her in appearance. On the right Mrs. Robbie Chase, dame of honor, in a beautiful dress of ecru net over white taffeta with a bouquet of pink roses; behind these came the bride, Miss Louise Adelaide Clayton, leaning on the arm of her father, Hon. W. F. Clayton. Her dress was of white crepe de chene over white taffeta, with a bouquet of white bride's roses and lilies of the valley. Miss Clayton is considered quite a beauty and upon this occasion with her flowing veil looked even lovelier than usual. On the right came the groom, Mr. Milton Otho Efird, leaning upon the arm of his brother, Charles E. Efird. At the chancel the father turned the bride over to her future husband and before the Rev. Mr. Will Oliver, the talented, popular and loved rector the couple stood until made man and wife.

From the church the bridal party and guests repaired to the home of Hon. W. F. Clayton where a delicious repast was served, Mrs. J. W. Ragsdale and Mrs. W.A. Wisnant presiding over the punch bowl while Mrs. John A. Chase and Miss Robbie Chase acted as hostesses and received the guests.

The presents were both numerous, handsome and valuable coming from Virginia where the groom's parents reside at Manassas to Georgia and Florida where relatives of both the bride and groom reside. After a short stay the bride and groom left under a shower of rice and good wishes for their bridal tour, which includes New York, Philadelphia, Washington and Baltimore, with a visit to the groom's parents at

Manassas, returning to Florence about July 1 which will be their future home.

**ELLIOTT, Frank** – Jan. 14, 1910 M. J.- LOUDOUN – Miss Edith Adrian and Mr. Frank Elliott, both of Ashburn, were married in Rockville Tuesday afternoon by the Rev. S. R. White, of the Baptist church, at the home of the minister.—Mirror, Jan. 7.

**ELLIS, Maude D.** – Dec. 30, 1910 M. J. – Mr. Noah Mayhugh and Miss Maude D. Ellis, daughter of Mr. and Mrs. Jas. B. Ellis, of Gainesville, were married at the home of the bride's parents, on 21$^{st}$ instant, the Rev. Homer Welsh, pastor of the Gainesville M. E. church, officiating. Miss Grace Ellis was maid of honor and Mr. James V. Ellis, of Washington, was best man. Miss Mandy Ellis and Mr. Bruce Sinclair were waiters. The ceremony was performed in the presence of a large company of relatives and friends.

The parlor was decorated beautifully with evergreens. The bride was gowned in a princess of white silk. After the wedding ceremony a sumptuous supper was served. Mr. and Mrs. Mayhugh are well known residents of Gainesville, and their numerous friends wish them much happiness and success in life.

**EMBREY, Charles William** – Jun. 8, 1906 M. J. - A very pretty wedding took place Wednesday, June 6, at the home of Mrs. Mount, Thoroughfare, Va., the contracting parties being Miss Virginia Harvey Brawner of Broad Run, Va., and Mr. Charles William Embrey of Rockfish, Va. Rev. S. V. Hildebrand of Sudley Methodist church officiated.

The bride wore a very dainty gown of white and looked her prettiest. She was attended by her sister, Miss Susie Brawner of Manassas.

Only a few friends and the immediate family witnessed the ceremony, after which the bridal party left for Norfolk and vicinity.

Upon their return they will make their home at Rockfish, Va., where Mr. Embrey is in the employ of the Southern railroad.

**EMBREY, C. W.** – Jun. 8, 1906 M. J. - Mr. C. W. Embrey, for several years agent of the Southern railway at this place, and Miss Harvey Brawner, daughter of Mr. P. D. Brawner of Broad Run, were married this week and passed through here on Wednesday on a northern tour.

**EMBREY, Murry A.** – Nov. 9, 1906 M. J. – Married at the home of the bride's parents, near Garrisonville, Stafford county, Mr. Murry A. Embrey and Miss Bertha A. Halpenny, Saturday evening, November 3, the bride's father, Rev. J. Halpenny, officiating. Mr. and Mrs. Embrey will reside in Stafford.

**EMBRY, Lilly** – Sept. 3, 1909 M. J. – FAUQUIER – Miss Lilly Embry and Mason Glascock both of Marshall, Va., drove to Warrenton on Wednesday and were married by Rev. F. R. Boston.

**ENGLISH, Alvin** – Jul. 1, 1910 M. J. –Miss Lillie Lowe, daughter of Mr. M. C. Lowe, of Fayman, and Mr. Alvin English, of Stafford county, were married on Thursday last.

**ENGLISH, Myra Gardner** – Aug. 20, 1909 M. J. – LOUDOUN – Mr. and Mrs. Charles A. English of Leesburg, have announced the engagement of their daughter, Miss Myra Gardner English, to Mr. Howard Elton Cole, of the Peoples National Bank. The wedding will take place in Leesburg during the autumn.

**ENGLISH, Myra Gardner** – Oct. 29, 1909 M. J. – LOUDOUN – Mr. and Mrs. Charles Albert English, of Leesburg, have issued invitations for the marriage of their daughter, Myra Gardner, to Mr. Howard Elton Cole, of the Peoples National Bank. The wedding will take place in St. James Episcopal church, in Leesburg, on Wednesday, Nov. 3, at 3 o'clock in the afternoon. No cards in the town or county.

**ENGLISH, Myra Gardner** – Nov. 12, 1909 M. J. – A lovely marriage was solemnized by Rev. W. H. Burkhardt at the Episcopal church, in Leesburg, on Wednesday evening, Nov. 3, according to the beautiful ceremony of that church, when Miss Myra Gardner English, the accomplished daughter of Mr. Chas. A. English, was made the wife of Mr. Howard Elton Cole.

The church was beautifully decorated for the happy occasion and the sweet-toned organ in solemn melody gave forth notice of the approaching nuptials. A large crowd was in attendance attesting the general popularity of the contracting parties.

Mr. Hubert T. Plaster was best man and Mrs. E. F. Concklin, of Washington, was matron of honor. The ushers were Mr. C. Albert English, brother of the bride; Mr. Edgar Littleton, of the Fairfax National Bank; Mr. J. R. H. Alexander, mayor of Leesburg, and Dr. Jno. A. Gibson.

**ENNIS, Ada V.** – Jul. 16, 1909 M. J. – A marriage license was issued in Washington Wednesday to Melvin C. Gray, of Nokesville, and Miss Ada V. Ennis, of Catlett.

**ENNIS, Claude** – Apr. 29, 1910 M. J. – Mr. James H. Pearson, of Belvoir, Fauquier county, and Miss Claude Ennis, daughter of Mr. Thos. E. Ennis, of near Buckhall were united in marriage Wednesday at the home of the bride's parents. Rev. J. F. Britton performed the ceremony, immediately after which the bride and groom, accompanied by the bride's sister, Miss Maud Ennis, left for Belvoir.

**ENNIS, Nelson L.** – Nov. 22, 1901 M. J. - Married, at the Southern Methodist parsonage, in Manassas, Nov. 14, 1901, by Rev. W. G. Hammond, Mr. Nelson L. Ennis and Miss Mollie Renner, all of Prince William county, Va.

**EVANS, E. D.** - Dec.10, 1909 M. J. – FAIRFAX – A license was issued by the county clerk on Wednesday to E. D. Evans, of Shenandoah county, and Bertie F. Lindamood, of Clifton, after which they repaired to the parsonage of the M. E. church, South, where they were united in marriage by Rev. F. A. Strother.—Herald, Dec. 3.

**EVANS., E. K.** – Aug. 3, 1906 M. J. - Miss Pearl Kincheloe, daughter of Mr. D. E. Kincheloe of Buckhall was married on Monday last to Mr. E. K. Evans of the same neighborhood. The ceremony took place in Washington, Rev. D. L. Blakemore officiating.

**EVANS, W. H.** – Dec. 20, 1907 M. J. – Mr. W. H. Evans and Miss Roxie Whitmer were married yesterday at the Lutheran parsonage, Rev. J. K. Efird, officiating.

**EWING, Augusta M.** – Jan. 14, 1910 M. J. – LOUDOUN – Charles Ashby Williams, farmer and business man, of Middleburg, Loudoun county, and Miss Augusta M. Ewing were married Tuesday afternoon at the home of the bride's brother-in-law, Silas Cather, in Winchester, by Rev. H. M. Richardson, of the United Brethren church.

**FAIR, Delia F.** – Mar. 18, 1910 M. J. – It may be of interest to note that the Mrs. Delia F. Fair, who yesterday became the bride of Mr. Joseph Nelson, is the widow of the late Charles Fair, an account of whose tragic death is given on the first page of this issue. Mr. Nelson, her present husband, lost his last wife about five weeks ago.

**FAIR, Delia F.** – Mar. 18, 1910 M. J. – Mr. Joseph Nelson and Mrs. Delia F. Fair, both of lower Prince William, were married yesterday at the Lutheran Parsonage by Rev. J. K. Efird.

**FAIRFAX, Katharine Van Rasslear** – Jun. 17, 1910 M. J. – Mr. and Mrs. Hamilton Fairfax, of New York city, have announced the engagement of their daughter, Miss Katharine Van Ransslear Fairfax to H. Schuyler Cammann, of that city. Mr. and Mrs. Fairfax formerly resided in Loudoun county, Virginia, and is a brother of Henry Fairfax, of Oakhill, and a son of the late Col. Jno. W. Fairfax of Neabsco, this county.

**FAIRFAX, Lucien** - Dec. 28, 1906 M. J. – Mr. Lucien Davis and Miss Myrtle Mills, both of lower Prince William, were married on Monday last, Elder Smoot officiating.

**CORRECTION** – Jan. 4, 1907 - The announcements of two weddings were given us last Friday morning, just before going to press, and in some way the names were gotten wrong.

FAIRFAX-MILLS – Mr. Lucien Fairfax (not Davis) and Miss Myrtle Mills, daughter of Mr. Richard Mills, were married on the 24th, Elder Smoot officiating.

**FAIRFAX, Willie** – Jan. 14, 1910 M. J. – A marriage license was issued last week in Leesburg to Mr. Willie Fairfax, of this county, and Miss Ospah Halley, of Loudoun.

**FERGUSON, Anna Louise** – Jun. 3, 1910 M. J. – The marriage of Mr. William Thomas Clagget Rogers of Leesburg, a present resident of Haymarket, to Miss Anna Louise Ferguson of Belmont, Loudoun county, is announced to take place on Tuesday evening of next week, at the Episcopal Chapel, Belmont. The ceremony will be performed by Rev. Mr. Burkhardt, Rector of St. James church, Leesburg.

**FERGUSON, Anna Louise** – Jun. 17, 1910 M. J. – LOUDOUN – One of the most beautiful weddings ever seen took place in the historic Belmont Chapel, near Leesburg, on Tuesday afternoon, when Miss Anna Louise Ferguson became the bride of Mr. W. T. C. Rogers, Rev. W. H. Burkhardt, of Leesburg, performed the ceremony.

**FERGUSON, Bettie** – Nov. 18, 1910 M. J. – One of the most interesting weddings in the history of Fairfax county occurred on Tuesday last at the home of Mr. Pickton Thomas, near Fairfax

Courthouse, when his sister, Mrs. Bettie Ferguson, became the bride of Mr. William M. Martin, of Fauquier.

The groom, who owned up to the advanced age of eighty, and who gave his bride's as the same, is the only surviving member of the jury which served on the famous John Brown trial previous to the Civil War.

Promptly at 2 o'clock the aged couple, preceded by two charming little flower girls, entered the beautifully decorated room, where the impressive ceremony was performed by Eld. J. N. Badger, of Manassas. The bride, who looked almost girlish and shy, wore a dress of black cloth and carried a bunch of white chrysanthemums.

Following the ceremony a sumptuous wedding dinner was served, shortly after which the happy couple left for their future home a few yards distant where the bride had lived all alone for a number of years. Their many friends wish them much happiness in the remaining years of their life. Quite a number of relations and friends were present, among whom were Elder J. N. Badger and wife and Mrs. B. J. Holden, of Manassas, Va.

**FERNEYHOUGH, Robert F.** – Oct. 28, 1910 M. J. – FAUQUIER – The wedding of Miss Margaret Hutton, the daughter of Mr. and Mrs. Henry I. Hutton, to Dr. Robert E. Ferneyhough which was celebrated Wednesday afternoon in the Baptist church in Warrenton, was one of wide interest in Virginia, as both the bride and groom are prominently related throughout the state. It was perhaps the most brilliant affair of the fall season in Warrenton. –Democrat.

**FETZER, Minnie M.** – Nov. 18, 1910 M. J. – Mr. Harry Brill, of Frederick county, and Miss Minnie M. Fetzer, of Prince William county were married on Wednesday, Nov. 16, 4:30 p.m., at the parsonage of Grace M. E. Church, south, Rev. W. T. Gover officiating. The bride wore a gray travelling suit and the groom conventional black. They were attended by Miss Carrie Fately, of Manassas, a cousin of the bride. After a short bridal trip they will go next Saturday to Mr. Brill's home in Frederick county, where they will reside.

**FEWELL, Emma** – Jan. 21, 1910 M. J. – Wednesday afternoon at four o'clock, at her home on Battle street, Miss Emma Fewell, daughter of the late E. N. Fewell, became the bride of Mr. A. H. Harrell, who recently bought the grocery business of E. N. Fewell & Company, in which he was formerly a partner, and which is now conducted in his name. Rev. T. D. D. Clark, pastor of the Baptist church, performed the ceremony. The marriage was quietly consummated, only the immediate family being present.

**FEWELL, William F.** – Aug. 19, 1910 M. J. – A marriage license was issued in Washington Tuesday to Mr. William F. Fewell, of The Plains and Miss Josephine Haley, of Broad Run.

**FLEMING, Virginia** – Sept. 17, 1909 M. J. – LOUDOUN – Mr. William T. Lee, of Bluemont, Loudoun county, and Miss Virginia Fleming, of Landmark, Fauquier county, were married at the residence of Mrs. Lutie Carruthers, Round Hill, on Thursday last, by Rev. I. B. Lake, D. D., pastor of the Baptist Church of Upperville. They will reside near Bluemont.—Mirror, Sept. 10.

**FLEMMING, Francis Lee** – Nov. 19, 1909 M. J. – FAUQUIER – Miss Francis Lee Flemming, daughter of Mr. and Mrs. Richard Bland Lee Flemming, on Monday afternoon was married at her home, near The Plains, in Fauquier county, to Mr. Samuel Henley Carter. Rev. John H. Norwood performed the ceremony. Only the immediate families of the bride and bridegroom were present. Miss Mary Flemming attended her sister as maid of honor.

**FLETCHER, Gilbert** – May 20, 1910 M. J. – FAUQUIER – Mr. Gilbert Fletcher and Miss Bertie Wigfield, both of Bethel, were married in Washington, D. C., on Tuesday last, by the Rev. J. B. McLaughlin, Mr. and Mrs. Fletcher are both well known in Warrenton, and the Democrat extends to the young couple congratulations, and wishes for them years and years of happiness.

**FLETCHER, Mauzy** – Jul. 2, 1909 M. J. – FAUQUIER- Miss Mauzy Fletcher and Curell Elgin Tiffany were married at the home of the bride Tuesday, June 28$^{th}$, at high noon, in the presence of the immediate family. Miss Fletcher is the second daughter of T. N. Fletcher. She is also well known in the society of Baltimore and Washington, where she had visited. Mr. Tiffany is the cashier of Fauquier National Bank. Mr. and Mrs. Tiffany left on the noonday train for Baltimore, after which they will go North on a short trip.— Times Dispatch.

**FLORANCE, Georgia** – Nov. 5, 1909 M. J. – Mr. D. F. Bowman and Mrs. Georgia Florance were married Wednesday evening at Clifton, Rev. J. K. Efird, performing the ceremony. The bridal couple left for a honeymoon trip through the Valley of Virginia.

**FLORENCE, Mabel** – Oct. 29, 1909 M. J. – FAIRFAX - Mr. C. H. Wine, of this place (Clifton), and Miss Mabel Florence, of Manassas, were married last week at Manassas. We wish them a long, happy prosperous life. Mr. Wine's new and commodious dwelling is being erected by Mr. Evans, of Manassas, and will soon be ready for occupancy.

**FLORANCE, Robert H.** – Jan. 7, 1910 M. J. – On Jan. 5, 1910, at the Baptist parsonage, Mr. Robert H. Florance and Miss Lillian C. Hoffman, of Prince William county, were united in marriage by Rev. T. D. D. Clark. The bride and groom left Manassas at 12:50 for a brief visit to Richmond after which they will return to their home near Gainesville. The kind wishes of a host of friends will attend them as they take up the duties of the new life upon which they have entered. Mr. Florance is a brother of the popular young pharmacist, Mr. J. A. Florance, until recently identified with the drug business of Mr. Walter Shannon. Mrs. Florance is the worthy and charming daughter of Mr. Wm. H. Hoffman, of the Catharpin neighborhood.

**FLYNN, Aubrey** – Dec. 24, 1909 M. J. – The following marriage licenses were issued this week at the clerk's office: Monday, Lewis M. Swartz, Culpeper county, and Miss Pearl L. Kelley, Fauquier county, Chas. N. Davis and Miss Virgie Wolfe, both of Prince William; Tuesday, John F. Donovan, Rockingham county and Miss Florida V. Allison, Loudoun county; Wednesday, Aubrey Flynn, Fauquier county, and Miss Annie L. Thomas, Prince William county; Thursday, Wm. E. Beahm, Rappahannock county, and Miss Edith G. Priest, Fauquier county; Geo. Spinks, Fauquier county, and Miss Bessie Baggott, Prince William county.

**FOLLEN, Annie D.** – Apr. 29, 1910 M. J. – A marriage license was issued in Washington last week to Orin A. Wright, of Oakton, Prince William county, and Mrs. Anna D. Follen, of Warrenton.

**FOLLEN, Nannie** – Apr. 22, 1910 M. J. – FAUQUIER – Mr. Orin Wright, of Fairfax and Mrs. Nannie Follen, of this place were quietly married in Washington on Monday last. They returned to Warrenton on Tuesday and spent several days here after which they left for their future home in Fairfax.—Democrat, April 16th.

**FORSYTH, Josephine** – Apr. 29, 1910 M. J. – Mr. Wm. V. Robertson, of Rockville, Md., and Miss Josephine Forsyth were quietly married at the bride's parents near Haymarket, on Thursday, April 21$^{st}$, at 5:30 p.m., Rev. Homer Welsh officiating.

**FOSTER, Margaret Mitchell** – Jan. 14, 1910 M. J. – LOUDOUN – Announcement has been made of the engagement of Miss Margaret Mitchell Foster, daughter of Capt. and Mrs. J. W. Foster, of Leesburg, to Thomas Francis Green, of Richmond. The wedding will take place at the home of the bride on Wednesday, Jan. 12.

**FOSTER, Margaret Mitchell** – Jan. 21, 1910 M. J. – LOUDOUN – The marriage of Miss Margaret Mitchell Foster, daughter of Capt. and Mrs. J. W. Foster, of Leesburg, to Mr. Thomas Francis Green, of Richmond, took place at St. James Episcopal church on Tuesday evening at 7:49, Rev. W. H. Burkhardt, assisted by Rt. Rev. Robert A. Gibson, bishop of Virginia, officiating. By reason of a recent death in the family of the groom, the wedding was a very quiet one, only the immediate relatives of the contacting parties being present, and no reception followed. After the ceremony the bridal party left on a special train. Mr. and Mrs. Green will make an extended trip to Florida, after which they will reside in Richmond where Mr. Green is prominently engaged in the real estate business.—Mirror, Jan. 14.

**FOX, Irvin** – Sept. 2, 1910 M. J. – FAUQUIER – Miss Bertha E. Butler and Mr. Irvin Fox were married at the home of the bride's father, Mr. Daniel Butler, of Meetz, Saturday, August 20, at 5 p.m. The wedding was a very quiet one, only the immediate family and a few friends being present. The couple leaves for their home near Greenwich, Va.

**FREE, Mabel** – Oct. 12, 1906 M. J. – Mr. and Mrs. W. R. Free, Jr., announce the marriage of their daughter Mabel to Mr. J. Claude Herrell of Kings Mountains, N.C., in St. Anns Memorial Chapel, Nokesville, this county, on Tuesday evening, 30$^{th}$ inst., at seven o'clock. No formal invitations will be extended in the village or its immediate vicinity.

**FREE, Mable Gertrude** - Nov. 2, 1906 M. J. – St. Ann's Memorial chapel at Nokesville, this county, was the scene of a pretty wedding at 7:30 o'clock, when Mr. J. Claude Harrell, assistant to the auditor of the Charlotte division of the Southern Railway Company, with headquarters at King's Mountain, N.C., and Miss Mabel Gertrude, daughter of Mr. W. R. Free, Jr., senior member of the mercantile establishment of W. R. Free, Jr., & Co., of Nokesville, were made man and wife.

Miss Lila Jonas, cousin of the bride, was maid of honor and Mr. J. E. Hall of Afton, Va., an intimate friend of the bridegroom, was bestman.

The bride was gowned in Princess embroidered net over white taffeta; wore a tulle veil with a coronet of lilies of the valley, and carried a prayer-book to which was attached a shower of white violets entwined with ribbon. Her only jewel was a handsome pearl pendant, a present from the bridegroom.

Miss Jonas was becomingly attired in pink organdie over pink silk, and carried a bouquet of pink chrysanthemums.

The Rev. Dr. John McGill, rector of the church, performed the ceremony.

Promptly at the appointed hour the doors of the chapel were thrown open by the ushers, Messrs. Harvey Jonas of Charleston, S.C., and George Madena of King's Mountain, N.C., and the wedding party entered in the following order. The ushers, the flower girls, Misses Mattie and Thelma Nash of Manassas, the former wearing white over pink silk and the latter white organdie over blue silk and each bearing in her arms a huge bouquet of white chrysanthemums; and lastly the bride, accompanied by her father and attended by her maid of honor, who were met at the altar by the bridegroom and his best man.

As the wedding party proceeded up the aisle of the church the organ sounded forth the strains of Mendelsshon's wedding march under the touch of Mrs. Harvey Williams of High Point, N.C., an intimate friend of the bride.

After giving away of the bride by her father, the rector, in a graceful manner proceeded with the marriage ceremony including the ring feature.

The church was tastefully festooned in evergreens and jardinieres of ferns and palms; together with other fragrant potted plants, were much in evidence.

Immediately after the ceremony the wedding party were driven to White Hall, the home of the bride's parents, where an informal reception was held and a beautiful luncheon served.

The bride was the recipient of many handsome and valuable presents from friends both near and far, including a check in a liberal sum from her father. At eleven o'clock the happy pair boarded at train amidst a shower of rice and old slippers, coupled with the hearty good wishes of all for an extended tour in the land of orange blossoms and flowers, their chief objective points being Tampa, Jacksonville and St. Augustine, Fla.

**FRENCH, Sanford William** – Oct. 29, 1909 M. J. – LOUDOUN – Mr. and Mrs. W. W. Orrison, of Ashburn, have issued cards for the marriage of their daughter, Agnes Elizabeth, to Dr. Sandford William French, of New York. The wedding will take place in the Presbyterian church, at Ashburn, on Wednesday, Oct. 27, at 2 o'clock.

**FRENCH, Sanford William** – Nov. 5, 1909 M. J. – LOUDOUN – Miss Agnes Elizabeth Orrison, daughter of Mr. and Mrs. W. W. Orrison, of Ashburn, Loudoun county, and Dr. Sanford William French, of New York city, were married Wednesday afternoon in the Presbyterian church at Ashburn, by Rev. Dr. Nelms, of the church of the Ascension. The bride wore a handsome gown of messaline satin, draped princess style, trimmed with lace and pearls, and a tulle veil fastened with orange blossoms. She was given away by her brother, Mr. Foster Orrison, and her matron of honor was Mrs. Harry Rider Sanford and the bridesmaid Miss Ruby Orrison. The ushers were Messrs. William A. Woodruff, of New York, and Lieut. Charles A. Fair, U. S. N., of Washington. After a reception at the bride's home Doctor and Mrs. French left for an extended tour North. Returning they will reside in Washington.—Mirror, Oct. 29.

**GARNER, Pearl** – Jun. 24, 1910 M. J. – Miss Pearl Garner, daughter of Mr. Newton Garner, of this place, and Mr. Warren Hutchinson, were married in Alexandria on Saturday last. The young couple have the best wishes of the community for their future happiness.

**GARRETT, J. Alfred** – Dec. 31, 1909 M. J. – LOUDOUN – Rev. J. Alfred Garrett, son of Capt. W. E. Garrett, of Leesburg, and Miss Katharine Custis Wise, of Norfolk were married a the home of the bride in Norfolk, on Wednesday afternoon, Rev. Dr. A. J. Fristoe officiating. We extend your best wishes to the young couple.

**GARRISON, Gertrude** – Nov. 11, 1910 M. J. –Mr. Philip P. Weber and Miss Gertrude Garrison, of Independent Hill, were married at the Lutheran parsonage by Rev. J. K. Efird, November 9, 1910.

**GERMAN, Belle** – Apr. 15, 1910 M. J. – Mr. M. E. Whip, who formerly lived in Manassas, and Miss Belle German, of Marshall, Va., were married in Marshall Sunday afternoon. Mr. Whip is a tie and lumber inspector for the Baltimore & Ohio Railway Co., with headquarters at Mt. Vernon, Indiana.

**GHEEN, Joseph E.** – Mar. 11, 1910 M. J. – A marriage license was issued in Washington yesterday to Mr. Jos. E. Gheen, of Prince William, and Miss Ida B. Putnam, of Culpeper county.

**GIBSON, Annie** – Nov. 18, 1910 M. J. – Mr. Joseph Turner, of Culpeper, and Miss Annie Gibson, daughter of Mrs. Fannie Gibson, of Hickory Grove, were married yesterday at Aldie, Loudoun county. The bride is a niece of former Mayor T. O. Taylor, of this place.

**GIBSON, W. Preston** – Oct. 12, 1906 M. J. – Cards are out announcing the marriage of Mr. W. Preston Gibson, brother to Mrs. R. S. Hynson of this place, to Miss Alice Nutt Wise of Leesburg.

**GILKESON, Carlisle H.** – Aug. 20, 1909 M. J. – FAUQUIER – Miss Elizabeth Smith, daughter of Mr. A. J. Smith, and Prof. Carlisle H. Gilkeson, of French Camp, Miss., were married in the Presbyterian church, Bealeton, Va., on August 4$^{th}$, at 8:30 a. m. The church was tastefully decorated in green with white flowers. Mrs. H. E. Guthrie sister of the groom, was matron of honor. The bride entered the church with the maid of honor, her sister, Miss Eleanor G. Smith. These were joined in front of the pulpit by the groom and the best man, Mr. Samuel F. Gilkeson, who entered the building by the rear door. The wedding march was played by Miss Marian Smith, of Fauquier Springs. The ceremony was performed by Rev. L. F. Harper, the pastor of the bride, using the ring ceremony. After the ceremony the bridal party drove to "Pleasant Hill," the home of Mr. and Mrs. Smith, where a delightful reception was held. The happy couple left amidst at shower of rice on the 10:20 train for Montreal, Canada. They will make their home in French Camp, Miss., where Prof. Gilkeson is teaching.

The guests from a distance were Mr. and Mrs. Guthrie, of Louisiana, Mr. Sam. F. Gilkeson, of Augusta county, Va., Mrs. Sampson and Miss Sampson of West Virginia, Miss Bettie Gilkeson, of Mississippi, Miss Emma Shannon, of Manassas, Va., Mr. and Mrs. Walter Smith, of Fairfax county, Mr. Philip Smith, of Tennessee, Miss Margaret Smith, of Manassas.—Democrat, Aug. 14.

**GILLISS, Charles James** – May 25, 1906 M. J. – Cards are out announcing the marriage of Miss Esther May, daughter of Capt. and Mrs. John R. Rust to Mr. Chas. James Gilliss June 12 at 5:30 p.m. at St. Paul's Church, Haymarket. Mr. Gilliss has charge of the bureau of silk industry, Agricultural Department.

**GILLISS, Charles James** – Jun. 22, 1906 M. J. - Miss Esther May Rust, daughter of Capt. John R. and Mrs. Nannie A. Rust of Wayside, near Haymarket, who a few years ago moved from the Valley of Virginia, where they numbered among their relatives the Marshalls, the Ashbys and others, was married on the afternoon of the 12th of June at 5:30 o'clock, to Mr. Charles James Gilliss of Washington D.C., son of the late Col. James Gilliss, U.S. Army and grandson of Commodore Gillis, U.S. navy. The ceremony was solemnized at St. Paul's church, Haymarket, which was tastefully decorated with evergreens, potted plants and cut flowers. The Rev. C. W. S. Hollis of the Presbyterian church, the bride's pastor, officiated, assisted by Rev. W. W. Gillis, brother of the groom, and Rev. Cary Gamble, rector of St. Paul's.

The bride was gowned in white crepe de chien en princesse, her veil being caught up by orange blossoms and she carried in her hand a bunch of bride roses. her maid of honor, Miss Florence S. Gillis, sister of the groom, was attired in white point d'es prit, and carried sweet peas. The groom's best man was Mr. Robert A. Rust, brother of the bride. Mr. Walter Gilliss of New York, Mr. Jno. D. Rust of Fairfax and Messrs. Walter B. and Hugh T. Clarkson of Washington city were the ushers.

Miss Hallie Meade presided at the organ and rendered the wedding marches from Mendelssohn and Lohengrin.

The newly-wedded pair drove to Manassas and there took the train for Philadelphia and Cape May, and on their return they will reside at Beaumont, the recently built country home of the groom.

The wedding presents were numerous and costly.

A very pleasant reception was tendered the bridal party at the hospitable home of the bride's parents, at which there were present among others from abroad, Mrs. Jas. Gilliss, Misses Julia and Helen Gillis, Mrs. Edward Stellwagen and Miss Stellwagen, Miss Dolly Loud and Mr. Aleck N. Breckenridge of Washington, D.C.; Gen. T. R. Robertson, of Charlotte, N. C. ; Miss Kathryn McKay, Greenville, Va., Miss Virginia McKay, Cumberland, Md.; Miss Elizabeth Jones, Culpeper, Va.; Miss Elizabeth Rust, Front Royal, Va.; Mrs. Caldwell, New York; Messrs. Ashby Rust, Thomas McKay, Miss Lou Marshall, Miss LeHew, Mrs. Leach, Mrs. Johnston and Miss Johnston of Warren Co, Va.

**GLASCOCK, Mason** – Sept. 3, 1909 M. J. – FAUQUIER – Miss Lilly Embry and Mason Glascock both of Marshall, Va., drove to Warrenton on Wednesday and were married by Rev. F. R. Boston.

**GLASCOCK, Silas D.** – Jun. 22, 1906 M. J. - A marriage license was issued in Washington Saturday to Silas D. Glascock of Marshall, and Lillie L. Utterback of Haymarket.

**GLASS, Dorothy Beatrice** – Jan. 21, 1910 M. J. – FAUQUIER – On Saturday, Jan. 1, one of the prettiest weddings ever seen in Toronto took place at the residence of Mr. and Mrs. Chester Glass, New York, in Spadina Road (rented temporarily), when their only daughter, Dorothy Beatrice, and Dr. Harry Hyland Kerr, Washington, D. C., son of Dr. and Mrs. James Kerr, of Warrenton, Va., were married. The Venerable Archdeacon Cody, St. Paul's church, officiated. Dr. and Mrs. Kerr will reside at 1742 N. street N. W., Washington, D. C., where a house has been presented as a wedding gift.—Virginian, Jan. 13.

**GOLD, Bessie V.** – May 3, 1907 M. J. – Mr. Wilson N. Wenrich of this place and Miss Bessie V. Gold, daughter of Mr. and Mrs. William H. Gold of Hagerstown, Md., were married at high noon on Tuesday last at the home of the bride, Rev. J. Spangler Keiffer of Zion Reformed church, conducting the ceremony. The bride was attired in a beautiful blue silk costume.

Miss May Wenrich and Mr. Charles C. Wenrich, sister and brother of the groom, and a large number of the relatives and friends of the bride were present.

After the ceremony a dinner was served, and on reaching here that evening, the groom's parents gave a reception.

The bride, who is one of the most popular young ladies of Hagerstown, was the recipient of many beautiful presents and the groom was the recipient of a handsome token of esteem from the dramatic club of Bull Run Council.

**GOODE, Mr.** – May 6, 1910 M. J. – The home of Mr. and Mrs. C. B. Holtzclaw was the scene of a very pretty wedding when Miss Payne, of Orlean, and Mr. Goode were married, Rev. Mr. Brad officiating.

**GOODMAN, Warren W.** – Jan. 21, 1910 M. J. – FAUQUIER – A beautiful and interesting double wedding took place on the afternoon of Jan. 5 at Sunnyside, the home of Mr. and Mrs. Moore Carter Blackwell, when their daughter, Miss Eva Ashton Blackwell, was married to Mr. Warren W. Goodman of Montana, and their granddaughter, Miss Grayson McLean Blackwell, became the bride of

Mr. Francis Boswell Talbott, of Maryland. The double ceremony was most impressively performed by Rev. Edwin S. Hinks. Mr. and Mrs. Goodman, after a trip through Mexico and California, will make their home in Montana. Mr. and Mrs. Talbott will reside in Calvert county, Maryland.

**GORDON, Benjamin** – Sept. 23, 1910 M. J. – FAUQUIER – Marriage licenses were issued in Washington on Thursday to the following Fauquier couples: Joseph B. Pulliam and Carolyn Spicer, both of Remington; Benjamin Gordon, of Markham, and India Chadwell, of Hume; Joseph A. Jeffries, of Warrenton, and Sallie Thompson, of Washington.

**GOUGH, Joseph** – Dec. 3, 1909 M. J. – Mr. Joseph Gough and Miss Eliza Reeves, both of this county, were married in Manassas last week.

**GRAFTON, W.** – Oct. 28, 1910 M. J. – FAUQUIER – Miss Nanette Peyton, daughter of Mr. and Mrs. Robt. Peyton, of "Edenburne," near The Plains, and Mr. W. Grafton, of Washington, were married on Wednesday, at the home of the bride.

**GRASTY, Eilbeck** – Dec. 10, 1909 M. J. – CULPEPER – The marriage of Miss Blanche Byrd Eastham, of Culpeper, to Mr. Eilbeck Grasty, of Orange took place at the residence of the bride's sister, Mrs. Byrd Leavell, at 3072 Q. street Northwest, Washington, D.C., at 2:30 o'clock Tuesday afternoon.

**GRAY, George D.** – Jan. 14, 1910 M. J. – Mr. George D. Gray, of Nokesville and Miss Dell M. Haymarker were married in Washington on Wednesday, December 15th. The bride was attired in a traveling dress of blue with hat to match. Her only attendant was his sister, Miss Rosie Gray. Mr. Edgar Gray was best man. They returned to the groom's home and spent several days.

**GRAY, Hazel** – Jan. 14, 1910 M. J. – FAUQUIER –Miss Hazel Gray, youngest daughter of Mr. and Mrs. Tom Gray, and Mr. Nicholas Nolan, both of Meetze, Va., were married at the Methodist parsonage in Warrenton, Wednesday, Dec. 29, Rev. J. L. Kibler, offciating. The bride wore a London smoke-colored suit, lace waist and a large white picture hat and veil and made a most charming bride. Mr. Nolan is a popular and industrious young man of this county. Their many friends wish them both a happy married life.—Democrat, Jan. 8

**GRAY, Maud B.** – May 13, 1910 M. J. – A marriage license was issued in Washington Wednesday to Mr. Daniel H. Griffith, of Manassas, Va., and Miss Maud B. Gray, of Page, Va.

**GRAY, Melvin C.** – Jul.16, 1909 M. J. – A marriage license was issued in Washington Wednesday to Melvin C. Gray, of Nokesville, and Miss Ada V. Ennis, of Catlett.

**GRAY, Minerva** – Oct. 26, 1906 M. J.- Married, Wednesday, Oct. 17, at Ewell Chapel, Rev. Cary Gamble officiating, Mr. Chas. Brower McIntosh to Miss Minerva Gray, eldest daughter of Mr. Turner Gray, of Fauquier. A beautiful wedding supper was served them at Mr. Peter Polen's.

**GRAYSON, George B.** – May 13, 1910 M. J. – FAUQUIER – A marriage of unusual interest to their numerous friends here took place in Washington, on Monday last, the contracting parties being Miss Robena Olive Bredrup, of Richmond and Mr. Geo. B. Grayson, of Warrenton. The bride is the daughter of Mr. C. P. Bredrup. The ceremony was performed by the Rev. Mr. Shannon and was witnessed by a few intimate friends. Mr. and Mrs. Grayson will make their home in Washington.

**GRAYSON, T. Keller** – Oct. 1, 1909 M. J. – A pretty but quiet wedding took place in the quaint little town of Buckland, Prince William county, Tuesday morning, September 28$^{th}$ at 10 o'clock, when Miss Angie Sanders and Mr. T. Keller Grayson, of New Baltimore, were married at "The Willows," the home of the bride's father, Mr. W. W. Sanders. Rev. Mr. Council, of Warrenton performed the ceremony.

The bride was becomingly attired in a handsome suit of blue broadcloth with hat and gloves to match. She was unattended, and only relatives were present. The house was prettily decorated, the couple standing during the ceremony under a bower of autumn leaves and a bell of golden rod and ferns. A wedding breakfast was served, after which Mr. and Mrs. Greyson left for an extended tour North. They will reside in New Baltimore, where they will be "at home" to their friends after October fifteenth.

**GREEN, Carrie B.** – Dec. 31, 1909 M. J. – FAUQUIER – Marriage licenses were issued in Washington this week to Frederick M. Day and Mary L. Beach, both of Fauquier county. Also to Jos. M. Jacobs of Calverton and Miss Carrie B. Green of Midland, Va.

**GREEN, Thomas Francis** – Jan. 14, 1910 M. J. – LOUDOUN – Announcement has been made of the engagement of Miss Margaret Mitchell Foster, daughter of Capt. and Mrs. J. W. Foster, of Leesburg, to Thomas Francis Green, of Richmond. The wedding will take place at the home of the bride on Wednesday, Jan. 12.

**GREEN, Thomas Francis** – Jan. 21, 1910 M. J. – LOUDOUN – The marriage of Miss Margaret Mitchell Foster, daughter of Capt. and Mrs. J. W. Foster, of Leesburg, to Mr. Thomas Francis Green, of Richmond, took place at St. James Episcopal church on Tuesday evening at 7:49, Rev. W. H. Burkhardt, assisted by Rt. Rev. Robert A. Gibson, bishop of Virginia, officiating. By reason of a recent death in the family of the groom, the wedding was a very quiet one, only the immediate relatives of the contacting parties being present, and no reception followed. After the ceremony the bridal party left on a special train. Mr. and Mrs. Green will make an extended trip to Florida, after which they will reside in Richmond where Mr. Green is prominently engaged in the real estate business.—Mirror, Jan. 14.

**GREEN, Willard** - Nov. 22, 1901 M. J. – Mr. Willard Green, one of Maj. Sylvester's bluecoats, who was appointed on the Metropolitan police force less than a year ago, and who is attached to the Eighth precinct station, has been the recipient of many congratulations from his brother officers and other friends during the past two or three days.

Miss Mable M. Kincheloe was the name of his bride. She is a Virginia belle, nineteen years of age, the daughter of Mr. W. W. Kincheloe, a wealthy merchant of Prince William county, who resides near Manassas. Mr. Green had known Miss Kincheloe for three years or more prior to coming to Washington, but his attentions to the young lady were not appreciated by her parents, who objected on the ground that she was too young to make a matrimonial venture. The young lady came to Washington about two months ago to pursue her studies, and here she found it possible to frequently see the man of her choice.

On Saturday Mr. Green secured a day's leave of absence. There was no session at the business college where Miss Kincheloe was a pupil that day, and they decided to take a trip to Baltimore. On the way the romance was agreed to. In Baltimore they met a friend, and in short order a marriage certificate was procured. It took but a few minutes to have the ceremony performed by Rev. D. Guthree, a Presbyterian minister and after a short honeymoon spent in the Monumental City Mr. and Mrs. Green returned to Washington, and are living happily at 624 Rhode Island avenue northwest.—Washington Post of Tuesday.

**GRIFFIN, William** – Jan. 25, 1907 M. J. – Miss Cora Hottle, daughter of Mr. J. S. Hottle of Limstrong and William Griffin of Hardware, W. Va., were married in Alexandria county, Thursday, Jan. 17, 1907.

**GRIFFITH, Daniel H.** – May 13, 1910 M. J. – A marriage license was issued in Washington Wednesday to Mr. Daniel H. Griffith, of Manassas, Va., and Miss Maud B. Gray, of Page, Va.

**GRIFFITH, Pearl** – Sept. 9, 1910 M. J. – Miss Pearl Griffith, for some time a most efficient clerk with Hynson & Co., was married on Wednesday last at 11 a.m., by Rev. W. T. Gover, at the residence of the bride's parents, Mr. and Mrs. Benjamin Griffith, to M. J. J. Haley, of Alexandria.

The bride wore a beautiful costume of white. Her going away dress was dark blue.

The bridal party left on No. 10 Wednesday for Washington, Norfolk, Newport News and Danville.

They will make their future home in Alexandria.

**GROFF, R. L.** – Dec. 20, 1907 M. J. – Miss Lula McLain Merchant of this place, was married on Friday last to Mr. R. L. Groff of Washington.

**HALE, Fleeta Anna** - Feb. 22, 1907 M. J. – Mr. and Mrs. W. F. Hale announce the marriage of their daughter, Miss Fleeta Anna, to Mr. Walter A. Cline Thursday morning, March 14, at eleven o'clock.

**HALE, Fleta A.** – Mar. 15, 1907 M. J. – The home of Mr. and Mrs. William F. Hale, near Nokesville, was the scene of a beautiful wedding on Thursday, when Miss Fleta A. Hale became the bride of Mr. Walter A. Cline of Washington.

The ceremony was performed by Rev. M. G. Early, while Miss Edna D. Miller played the wedding march.

Miss Fannie Keagy of Harrisonburg was bridesmaid, and Mr. W. C. Long of Harrisonburg was best man.

Mr. and Mrs. Cline left in the afternoon for a short bridal trip, which will include Norfolk. Upon their return, they will reside in Washington, where Mr. Cline is in business.

About fifty guests witnessed the ceremony, including Messrs. S. B. Van Nest, Geo. M. Oyster, W. H. Cline, Walter Hooker and J. F. Moller of Washington, Misses Lena and Annie L. Cline and Mr. Harry Cline of Falls Church, and Mr. Westwood Hutchison of Manassas.

Immediately after the ceremony, the dining hall was thrown open, where a splendid lunch was served.

**HALE, John T.** – Oct. 22, 1909 M. J. – A marriage license was issued in Washington on Oct. 13 to John T. Hale, of Dumfries, and Anna Patterson, of Prince William.

**HALEY, Josephine** – Aug. 19, 1910 M. J. – A marriage license was issued in Washington Tuesday to Mr. William F. Fewell, of The Plains and Miss Josephine Haley, of Broad Run.

**HALEY, M. J. J.** – Sept. 9, 1910 M. J. – Miss Pearl Griffith, for some time a most efficient clerk with Hynson & Co., was married on Wednesday last at 11 a.m., by Rev. W. T. Gover, at the residence of the bride's parents, Mr. and Mrs. Benjamin Griffith, to M. J. J. Haley, of Alexandria.

The bride wore a beautiful costume of white. Her going away dress was dark blue.

The bridal party left on No. 10 Wednesday for Washington, Norfolk, Newport News and Danville.

They will make their future home in Alexandria.

**HALL, M. D.** – Mar. 4, 1910 M. J. – FAIRFAX – Mrs. Octavia J. Shell, of Wake Forest, N. C., has issued invitations to the marriage of her daughter, Elizabeth McDonald Carver, to Col. M. D. Hall, Division Superintendent of Schools for Fairfax county, Va., on Wednesday, March 9th.

**HALL, M. D.** – Mar. 18, 1910 M. J. – FAIRFAX – A very pretty wedding took place in Wake Forest, N. C., when Miss Elizabeth Carver became the bride of M. D. Hall superintendent of the schools of Fairfax county. Congressman Carlin was Mr. Hall's best man. Immediately after the ceremony Mr. and Mrs. Hall left to spend their honeymoon in Jacksonville and Cuba.

**HALL, Richard Dulany** – Jul. 1, 1910 M. J. – LOUDOUN – Miss Gertrude Dulaney Clagett, daughter of Mrs. Wm. B. Clagett, and Mr. Richard Dulany Hall were married at the home of the bride's mother, in Washington, at high noon on Wednesday. The happy couple is well known and has many friends in Loudoun.—Enterprise.

**HALLEY, Ospah** – Jan. 14, 1910 M. J. – A marriage license was issued last week in Leesburg to Mr. Willie Fairfax, of this county, and Miss Ospah Halley, of Loudoun.

**HALPENNY, Bertha A.** – Nov. 9, 1906 M. J. – Married at the home of the bride's parents, near Garrisonville, Stafford county, Mr. Murry A. Embrey and Miss Bertha A. Halpenny, Saturday evening, November 3, the bride's father, Rev. J. Halpenny, officiating. Mr. and Mrs. Embrey will reside in Stafford.

**HAMILTON, Susan** – Jun. 11, 1909 M. J. – FAUQUIER – Miss Susan Hamilton, daughter of Mr. Hugh Hamilton, and Mr. Richard Washington Hilleary, were married at "Scotis," the home of the bride, near Warrenton, on Tuesday evening at eight o'clock.

**HAMILTON, Susan Fitzhugh** – Jun. 11, 1909 M. J. – FAUQUIER – The marriage of Miss Susan Fitzhugh Hamilton, daughter of Mr. Hugh Hamilton, county treasurer of Fauquier county, and Richard Hilleary, of Warrenton, took place Tuesday afternoon at the home of the bride. Rev. Edwin S. Hinks, rector of St. James' Episcopal church, officiated.

**HARDY, Charles Willoughby** – Dec. 15, 1905 M. J. - Mr. and Mrs. Howard P. Dodge announce to their friends in Manassas the marriage of their daughter, Miss Sarah Katrina, and Mr. Charles Willoughby Hardy on December 10. Mr. and Mrs. Hardy will live in Spencer, Idaho.

**HARPER, Elizabeth Edmonds** – Nov. 25, 1910 M. J. – LOUDOUN – The marriage of Miss Elizabeth Edmonds Harper, daughter of the late Robert Harper, of Leesburg and Washington, and Dr. Walter Gordon Trow, of Southern Virginia, took place Wednesday evening at 8 o'clock, at Metropolitan church, Washington. Rev. Paul Hickok performed the ceremony and the bride was escorted and given in marriage by her brother, Mr. Bernard F. Harper. Her sister, Miss Roberta Wallace Harper, was her only attendant. Dr. Earl Clark, brother-in-law of the bridegroom, was best man. Messrs. Harry F.

Harper, J. William Harper and Leslie Holt were the ushers. Following the ceremony a reception was held in the home of the bride's mother, Mrs. R. W. Harper, in Park road, for the bridal party and out-of town guest. The young couple will make their future home at Hallwood, Va.

**HARRELL, A. H.** – Jan. 21, 1910 M. J. – Wednesday afternoon at four o'clock, at her home on Battle street, Miss Emma Fewell, daughter of the late E. N. Fewell, became the bride of Mr. A. H. Harrell, who recently bought the grocery business of E. N. Fewell & Company, in which he was formerly a partner, and which is now conducted in his name. Rev. T. D. D. Clark, pastor of the Baptist church, performed the ceremony. The marriage was quietly consummated, only the immediate family being present.

**HARRELL, J. Claude** - Nov. 2, 1906 M. J. – St. Ann's Memorial chapel at Nokesville, this county, was the scene of a pretty wedding at 7:30 o'clock, when Mr. J. Claude Harrell, assistant to the auditor of the Charlotte division of the Southern Railway Company, with headquarters at King's Mountain, N.C., and Miss Mabel Gertrude, daughter of Mr. W. R. Free, Jr., senior member of the mercantile establishment of W. R. Free, Jr., & Co., of Nokesville, were made man and wife.

Miss Lila Jonas, cousin of the bride, was maid of honor and Mr. J. E. Hall of Afton, Va., an intimate friend of the bridegroom, was best man.

The bride was gowned in Princess embroidered net over white taffeta; wore a tulle veil with a coronet of lilies of the valley, and carried a prayer-book to which was attached a shower of white violets entwined with ribbon. Her only jewel was a handsome pearl pendant, a present from the bridegroom.

Miss Jonas was becomingly attired in pink organdie over pink silk , and carried a bouquet of pink chrysanthemums.

The Rev. Dr. John McGill, rector of the church, performed the ceremony.

Promptly at the appointed hour the doors of the chapel were thrown open by the ushers, Messrs. Harvey Jonas of Charleston, S.C., and George Madena of King's Mountain, N.C., and the wedding party entered in the following order. The ushers, the flower girls, Misses Mattie and Thelma Nash of Manassas, the former wearing white over pink silk and the latter white organdie over blue silk and each bearing in her arms a huge bouquet of white chrysanthemums; and lastly the bride, accompanied by her father and attended by her maid of honor, who were met at the altar by the bridegroom and his best man.

As the wedding party proceeded up the aisle of the church the organ sounded forth the strains of Mendelsshon's wedding march under the touch of Mrs. Harvey Williams of High Point, N.C., an intimate friend of the bride.

After giving away of the bride by her father, the rector, in a graceful manner proceeded with the marriage ceremony including the ring feature.

The church was tastefully festooned in evergreens and jardinieres of ferns and palms; together with other fragrant potted plants, were much in evidence.

Immediately after the ceremony the wedding party were driven to White Hall, the home of the bride's parents, where an informal reception was held and a beautiful luncheon served.

The bride was the recipient of many handsome and valuable presents from friends both near and far, including a check in a liberal sum from her father. At eleven o'clock the happy pair boarded at train amidst a shower of rice and old slippers, coupled with the hearty good wishes of all for an extended tour in the land of orange blossoms and flowers, their chief objective points being Tampa, Jacksonville and St. Augustine, Fla.

**HARRIS, Edith M.** – Jun. 24, 1910 M. J. - Mr. Dellie W. Crawford and Miss Edith M. Harris, both of this county, were married by Rev. J. K. Efird at the Lutheran parsonage on Monday, June 20$^{th}$.

**HARRIS, William** – Feb. 18, 1910 M. J. – Mr. Wm. Harris and Inez Crouch, both of this county, were married in Washington City on Tuesday last.

**HARRIS, Williams** – Feb. 18, 1910 M. J. – Mr. Williams Harris and Miss Inez Crouch left for Washington Sunday returning on Tuesday evening as bride and groom. We wish them a happy journey through life.

**HARRISON, Eva May** – Jan. 7, 1910 M. J. – FAIRFAX – Miss Eva May Harrison and Edward Clinton Utterback, of Clifton station, were married at Rockville, Md., Monday afternoon by the Rev. W. D. Keene, pastor of the Southern Methodist church, at the home of the minister.—Herald, Dec. 31.

**HARRISON, Ernest P.** – Sept. 23, 1910 M. J. – FAIRFAX – Mr. Ernest P. Harrison and Miss Bettie K. Swetnan were married

Wednesday evening at the home of Mrs. Jennie Swetnan, the bride's mother, at Burke, Rev. Burnley Harrison, the groom's brother, performing the ceremony.

**HAYMARKER, Dell M.** – Jan. 14, 1910 M. J. – Mr. George D. Gray, of Nokesville and Miss Dell M. Haymarker were married in Washington on Wednesday, December 15$^{th}$. The bride was attired in a traveling dress of blue with hat to match. Her only attendant was his sister, Miss Rosie Gray. Mr. Edgar Gray was best man. They returned to the groom's home and spent several days.

**HAYTH, George E.** – Jul. 10, 1896 M. G. - Marriage licenses were granted this week to Mr. Geo. E. Hayth and Miss Maria A. Sayers, and Mr. G. W. Robinson and Miss Leonora Crouch, daughter of Mr. Elias Crouch—all of this county.

**HEDDINGS, Roy** – Sept. 17, 1909 M. J. – Mr. Roy Heddings, of Midland, Va., and Miss Andes, of Michigan, were married Sunday morning at 8 o'clock, in the presence of a few friends, by Rev. A. Conner at his home near Manassas.

**HEDRICK, W. P.** – Jul. 10, 1896 M. G. – There appeared in a communication from Nokesville to the Warrenton Virginian, this week, the following concerning the marriage of Miss Kincheloe and Mr. Hedrick:
Mr. W. P. Hedrick and Miss Lillie, daughter of Mr. and Mrs. W. W. Kincheloe, of Brentsville, were married in Washington on last Wednesday. It was one of the old fashioned runaways. Her parents opposed the bands so strongly that they thought best to runway. So on Tuesday evening at about 11 o'clock accompanied by his cousins, Mr. John Hedrick and Miss Lillie Laws, they drove within a mile of Brentsville, there taking a buggy—the brave knight drove to her house and at a given signal with hat and shoes in hand, she quickly responded and then the drive for Washington began which was made in about six hours. The groom is a prosperous young man of our town and we heartily congratulate him and wish him much happiness.

**HEFLIN, Eva** – Sept. 16, 1910 M. J. – FAUQUIER – A pleasant surprise to all their friends was to learn on Friday that Mr. A. M. Roberts and Miss Eva Heflin, both of The Plains, had been married in Washington Thursday. They returned to Warrenton Saturday and drove to The Plains, which will hereafter be their home.—Virginian.

**HEFLIN, Laura C.** – Nov. 5, 1 909 M. J. – Married at Warrenton, October 27, 1909, Mr. William Lewis Allen, of Prince William county, and Miss Laura C. Heflin, of Fauquier. Rev. J. L. Kibbler officiated.

**HEINEKEN, Averick Parker** – Oct. 12, 1906 M. J. – Miss Averick Parker Heineken, daughter of Mr. C. A. Heineken of Haymarket, was married on Tuesday last to Mr. Walter Lann of Aberdeen, Miss.

**HEINEKEN, Averick Parker** – Oct. 12, 1906 M. J. – We are please to record the marriage of Mr. Walter Lann and Miss Averick Parker Heineken, second daughter of our prominent and highly esteemed fellow-citizen, Mr. C. A. Heineken, at "Mill Park" on Tuesday evening, October ninth, Rev. Cary Gamble, rector of St. Paul's Church, Haymarket, officiating.

On account of the recent bereavement in the family, the wedding took place quietly at home in the conservatory amidst a mass of palms and flowering plants, the effects of many candles making the whole scene a very impressive one. Only immediate members of the family and a few friends were present. We were pleased to greet the Right Rev. Dr. Robert A. Gibson, bishop of the diocese, on the occasion. The bride wore a very becoming dress of white crepe de chine, the veil being held in place by orange blossoms and carried brides roses and lilies of the valley and was given away by her father.

Miss Emma Heineken, the youngest sister of the bride, wearing white silk mull and carrying white carnations, was maid of honor, and Herman Heineken, brother of the bride, best man.

The couple left for a trip North followed by the best wishes for their future happiness by those present. Their home will be in Aberdeen, Miss., where Mr. Lann is one of the leading business men.

**HEINEKEN, Christian A.** – Apr. 8, 1910 M. J. Mr. Christian A. Heineken and Mrs. Charlotte J. Jordan, both of Haymarket, were quietly married in Washington Wednesday of this week.

**HEISTAND, Florance G.** – Nov. 4, 1910 M. J. – FAIRFAX – A marriage license was issued by the County Clerk on the 18th inst., to Robert H. Rice and Florance G. Heistand.––Herald.

**HENRY, William Alexander** – Sept. 7, 1906 M. J. – [Reprinted from the Washington Star of June 21, 1906, by request] The marriage of Miss Fannie Stuart Lee, daughter of Mr. William F. Lee of Manassas, Va., and Mr. William Alexander Henry of Ontario, Canada, took place at Mount Vernon Place Church last evening 8 o'clock, the Rev. William French Locke performing the ceremony. The bride wore a very becoming gown of Paris muslin, elaborately trimmed with lace and insertion, and carried a shower bouquet of bride roses and lilies of the valley. After the ceremony a luncheon was served at the home of the bride's cousin, Mrs. Clinton R. Tucker, 645 C street, northwest. At a late hour the couple left for a tour through Canada, stopping by way of Niagara.

Mr. Henry was not met during the encampment here as published at the time, but has been a friend of the family for several years.

**HERNDON, Alidion** – May 13, 1910 M. J. – Mr. Wallace E. Partlow and Miss Alidion Herndon, both of Prince William county, were married yesterday at the Lutheran parsonage by Rev. J. K. Efird, the pastor.

**HERNDON, Hattie M.** – Sept. 17, 1909 M. J. – Mr. Everett P. Robertson, of Bristow and Miss Hattie M. Herndon, of Nokesville, were married last week in Washington.

**HERRELL, J. Claude** – Oct. 12, 1906 M. J. – Mr. and Mrs. W. R. Free, Jr., announce the marriage of their daughter Mabel to Mr. J. Claude Herrell of Kings Mountains, N.C., in St. Anns Memorial Chapel, Nokesville, this county, on Tuesday evening, 30th inst., at seven o'clock. No formal invitations will be extended in the village or its immediate vicinity.

**HERRELL, Janie** – Aug. 10, 1906 M. J. - Cards are out announcing the approaching marriage of Miss Janie, daughter of Capt. and Mrs. Jas. E. Herrell and Mr. Walter Bowen of Washington, formerly of Brentsville.

**HERRELL, Jeanie S.** – Sept. 7, 1906 M. J. – The marriage of Miss Jeanie S. Herrell, daughter of Capt. and Mrs. Jas. E. Herrell, to Mr. Walter F. Bowen will take place Saturday evening, Sept. 15, at seven o'clock at Trinity church, this place.

**HERRELL, Jeanie Shields** – Sept. 21, 1906 M. J. – PRETTY WEDDING AT TRINITY – Trinity Episcopal Church here was the scene of a very pretty marriage on Saturday last at 7 o'clock, when Miss Jeanie Shields Herrell, daughter of Captain and Mrs. James

Edward Herrell, became the bride of Mr. Walter Fullerton Bowen of Brookland, D.C. The Rev. John McGill performed the ceremony.

The beautiful decorations were in goldenrod and candles, with yellow shades. Miss Julia Lewis had charge of the music and played with good expression the wedding marches and Mendelssohn's "Spring Song."

The maid of honor, Miss Elizabeth Herrell, and the bridesmaids, Misses Anna Taylor, Carrie Makely, Selina Taylor and Estelle Holden, wore white mull with golden girdles and yellow pon-pons in the hair. The maid of honor carried yellow chrysanthemums, and the brides maids goldenrod.

The groom was attended by Mr. Michael Stephan as best man, and the following gentlemen were ushers, Messrs. George Purcell, Robert Herrell, Clarence Faithfull and H. Kinzel Laws.

The groom is a son of the late Dr. P. B. Bowen and a grandson of Dr. Walter Hore, at one time a surgeon in the United States navy.

Among the out-of-town guests at the wedding were Mr. and Mrs. C. M. Eddington of Richmond, Miss May W. Hundley of Mount Laurel, Va.; Mr. C. M. Faithfull of Liberty, Mo.; Miss Anna Louise Forbes Taylor of Kinsale, Va.; Mr. H. C. Hammond of Wellsville, Ohio; Mr. M. Stephan of Baltimore; Mr. and Mrs. David Oertley of Brookland; Mrs. M. H. Bowen and Mr. W. W. Hore of Washington; Mrs. V. W.Duval of Hyattsville, Mrs. Horner Malone of Brookland, Misses Makeley of Alexandria; Mr. and Mrs. C. E. Jordan of Haymarket, Va.; Mr. and Mrs. Arthur Lee Henry of Stone House, Va.

**HERRING, Edward** - Jan. 11, 1907 M. J. – NOKESVILLE, VA., Jan. 8, 1907.- The home of Mr. and Mrs. Simeon Long, near this place, was the scene of a very pretty wedding at high noon today, when their eldest daughter, Mattie, became the bride of Mr. Edward Herring.

The marriage ceremony was performed by Rev. Abram Conner of Manassas in the presence of a large circle of friends and acquaintances. Mr. Ray Hedrick was best man and his sister, Miss Sallie Hedrick, maid of honor. The bride was becomingly attired in white and the groom in the conventional black.

Immediately after the marriage ceremony a beautiful dinner, consisting of everything calculated to satisfy the inner man, was served.

Mr. Herring is the eldest son of Mr. Hastings W. Herring of near this place, and his genial disposition has made him one of the most popular young men of our neighborhood. The writer wishes the newly wedded pair a journey through life of unalloyed happiness and expresses the wish that henceforth they may be as "two lives with but a single thought; two hearts that beat as one."

**HEYL, William McLean** – Jul. 2, 1909 M. J. – FAUQUIER – Wm. McLean Heyl, and Miss Minnie C. Downs, both of Marshall, were married in Washington Thursday.—Fredericksburg Free Lance, June 26.

**HEYMOND, Ella M.** – Oct. 15, 1909 M. J. – A beautiful wedding was solemnized Oct. 6, at St. Margaret's church, St. Margaret's, Md., when Miss Ella M. Heymond, daughter of Mrs. Jane Heymond, of that place, became the bride of Mr. Claude E. Arnold, of Annapolis Junction. The church was lavishly decorated with wild heather and honeysuckle vines, the windows being banked and the chancel and chandeliers hung with the soft white blooms. As the last chord of the wedding march from Lohengrin sounded the bridesmaids, assembled in the vestibule, began singing sweetly together, "O, Perfect Love," and the whole party advanced slowly up the aisle, the bride leaning on the arm of her brother, Mr. Arthur P. Heymond, who gave her away, and attended by her maid of honor, Miss Nancy Byrd Turner, of King George, Va. They were met at the chancel by the groom and his best man, Mr. Maurice H. Arnold, and were made man and wife in the beautiful words of the Episcopal marriage service, read by the Rev. Alexander Galt, rector of the church. Then to the strains of Mendellsohn's march the party went out, making a lovely picture. The bride was gowned in white silk batiste with tulle veil and lilies of the valley and carried brides' roses. The maid of honor wore blue and carried pink roses. The bridesmaids were: Miss Alverta Arnold, of Baltimore, and Miss Clara Bell Kent, of Davidsonville, in white over green; Miss Jeannette MacMillan, of Baltimore, and Miss Bessie Turner, of King George, Va., in white over pink; Miss Laura Hanson, of Washington, and Miss Ada Moss, of Annapolis, in white over yellow, and Miss Marion Lewis, of Manassas, niece of the bride, as flower girl, in white. The ushers were: Mr. Paul Hines, of Annapolis Junction; Mr. Thornton Turner, of King George, Va., and Messrs. Thomas Arnold, Alex. Proskey, Corner Ridout and Thomas Corner, of Anne Arundel county. A reception for the bridal party was held at Mrs. Heymond's residence, immediately after which Mr. and Mrs. Arnold left for Washington, Richmond and other points. The gifts were many and handsome, and the two take with them the very loving wishes of a host of friends.

**HIBBS, E. Humphrey** – Nov. 22, 1901 M. J. - On Thursday morning last another beautiful wedding took place in our town. On this occasion Mr. E. Humphrey Hibbs and Miss Madie W. Davies were the contracting parties.

Trinity church was beautifully decorated with palms, ferns, chrysanthemums and other rare plants, and quite a crowd was in attendance, as Mrs. Dr. Wolfe took her place at the organ. Promptly at 10 o'clock the bridal party entered the church, the four ushers, Messrs. E. B. Giddings, J. Jenkyn, Will W., and Hawes Thornton Davies, preceding the bridal couple, and were met at the alter by Rev.W. H. K. Pendleton, the rector of Trinity church, who, in the beautiful and impressive ceremony of the Episcopal church, the twain were made one, the meanwhile Mrs. Wolfe playing softly at the organ.

The bride is a handsome blonde and was beautifully attired in navy blue broadcloth with hat to match. She was given away by her uncle, Mr. J. B. T. Thornton.

The groom is a prominent business man of the town and a member of the firm of Hibbs. & Giddings.

Mr. and Mrs. Hibbs were the recipients of many congratulations and beautiful presents. Among the latter was a deed for a valuable town lot from her uncle, Mr. J. B. T. Thornton.

The bridal party left on train No. 14 for a Northern tour and will probably attend the New York horse show.

Congratulations and best wishes are tendered them by THE JOURNAL.

**HIGGINS, Ambrose F.** – Jun. 15, 1906 M. J. - Mr. Ambrose F. Higgins and Miss Mary E. Brooks, both of Washington, D. C., were united in holy matrimony on Monday last, June 11, by Rev. J. K. Efird at the Lutheran Parsonage.

**HILL, Orrin K.** – Sept. 24, 1909 M. J. – Mrs. J. A. Carter and Miss Ada Carter have returned home after a pleasant visit to Maryland and Washington where they attended the marriage of their cousin, Miss Janie Owen to Orrin K. Hill, a prominent electrician of Brooklyn, N.Y. The bride was attended by her sister, Miss Carrie Owen.

**HILLEARY, Richard** – Jun. 11, 1909 M. J. – FAUQUIER – The marriage of Miss Susan Fitzhugh Hamilton, daughter of Mr. Hugh Hamilton, county treasurer of Fauquier county, and Richard Hilleary, of Warrenton, took place Tuesday afternoon at the home of the bride. Rev. Edwin S. Hinks, rector of St. James' Episcopal church, officiated.

**HILLEARY, Richard Washington** – Jun. 11, 1909 M. J. – FAUQUIER – Miss Susan Hamilton, daughter of Mr. Hugh Hamilton, and Mr. Richard Washington Hilleary, were married at "Scotis," the home of the bride, near Warrenton, on Tuesday evening at eight o'clock.

**HITT, Rosa** – Feb. 4, 1910 M. J. – CULPEPER – Mr. Oswold Cannon and Miss Rosa Hitt were married at the home of the bride Wednesday 26.—Exponent.

**HIXSON, Claudius** – Feb. 8, 1907 M. J. – A very quite but impressive wedding ceremony was performed by Elder J. N. Badger Wednesday at his home here when Miss Elizabeth Thomas and Mr. Claudius Hixson of Loudoun were married.

The bride was dressed in a handsome traveling suit of gray, with hat to match. The groom wore conventional black.

Miss Blanch Carruthers, niece of the bride, Miss Sallie Lewis and Mrs. Badger were present. Shortly after the ceremony a very delightful lunch was served.

The couple left on the afternoon train for their future home near Levi.

**HIXSON. Lydia** – Jun. 18, 1909 M. J.- LOUDOUN – Miss Lydia Hixson and Mr. Elmo Bondurant, of Hampden-Sidney, Va., were married at the home of the bride's father, Mr. Nelson Hixson, Wednesday June 2.

**HOBART, Harrison C.** – Jun. 10, 1910 M. J. – FAUQUIER - Prof. Harrison C. Hobart and Miss Annie L. Breeden were quietly married at the home of the bride's father Mr. John S. Breeden of Remington, at 11:30 Wednesday. The bridal couple left almost immediately after the ceremony for a month's stay at the seashore, after which they will make their home at Manassas.

**HOFFMAN, Lettie May** – Mar. 18, 1910 M. J. – On Tuesday at the Methodist Parsonage Rev. W. T. Gover officiated at the marriage of Miss Lettie May Hoffman, of Warren county, a sister of Mrs. T. F. Coleman, of Manassas, to Mr. Luther Lee Painter, of Shenandoah county.

**HOFFMAN, Lillian C.** – Jan. 7, 1910 M. J. – On Jan. 5, 1910, at the Baptist parsonage, Mr. Robert H. Florance and Miss Lillian C. Hoffman, of Prince William county, were united in marriage by Rev. T. D. D. Clark. The bride and groom left Manassas at 12:50 for a brief visit to Richmond after which they will return to their home near Gainesville. The kind wishes of a host of friends will attend them as they take up the duties of the new life upon which they have entered. Mr. Florance is a brother of the popular young pharmacist, Mr. J. A. Florance, until recently identified with the drug business of Mr. Walter Shannon. Mrs. Florance is the worthy and charming daughter of Mr. Wm. H. Hoffman, of the Catharpin neighborhood.

**HOLBROOK, S. S.** – Sept. 23, 1910 M. J. – FAIRFAX – Mr. S. S. Holbrook and Miss Minnie B. Thompson were married here Wednesday morning by Rev. E. L. Goodwin, and left on an early train for a bridal tour to points in Maryland and West Virginia.

**HOLLAND, Walter** – Aug. 10, 1906 M. J. - Miss Bessie Clark and Mr. Walter Holland were married here on Wednesday last.

**HOLLY, Lawrence E.** - Dec. 3, 1909 M. J – CULPEPER – Mr. George G. Thompson, jr., formerly of Culpeper, now district freight agent of the Southern railroad, with headquarters at Greensboro, N.C., and Miss Lawrence E. Holly, were married in Washington on Wednesday.—Exponent, Nov. 26

**HOLMES, Bessie E.** – Dec. 20, 1907 M. J. – On Thursday, Dec. 19, 1907, at Manassas, Va., Mr. Albert L. Bridwell and Miss Bessie E. Holmes of Prince William county, were united in marriage by Rev. T. D. D. Clark.

**HOPEWELL, Harry W.** – Jan. 28, 1910 M. J. – CULPEPER – Miss Gertrude Martin, of Stevensburg, Va., and Mr. Harry W. Hopewell, of Mount Solon, Augusta county, Va. were married Jan. 13 at Mount Solon. The bride is the principal of a school at Mossy Creek Augusta county.—Exponent, Jan. 21.

**HOPKINS, C. Maurice** - May 27, 1910 M. J. – Cards are out announcing the approaching marriage of Mr. C. Maurice Hopkins of this place, and Miss Eva Webster. Miss Webster is a native of Boston but has been residing with her mother, Mrs. Julius Daniel Webster, at their new Washington home. The happy nuptial event is to take place at Epiphany Episcopal church Wednesday afternoon, June the first.

**HORTON, Clarence** – Feb. 25, 1910 M. J. – Mr. Clarence Horton, of Washington, and Miss Katie Lesier, of Texas, were married in Washington, on Tuesday last. They spent several days this week with his parents, Mr. and Mrs. J. M. Horton. The young couple will make their future home in the capital.

**HORTON, Lizzie** – Aug. 17, 1906 M. J. - Miss Lizzie Horton, daughter of Mrs. Dora Horton of Potomac and Mr. Vanberg of Clifton were married in Washington last Tuesday.

**HOTTELL, Restry** – Aug. 24, 1906 M. J. - Married at the Southern Methodist Parsonage this town, Sunday, Aug. 19$^{th}$ by Rev. Selwyn K. Cockrell, Miss Janette Pitkins and Mr. Restry Hottell.

**HOTTLE, Cora** – Jan. 25, 1907 M. J. – Miss Cora Hottle, daughter of Mr. J. S. Hottle of Limstrong and William Griffin of Hardware, W. Va., were married in Alexandria county, Thursday, Jan. 17, 1907.

**HOTTLE, Milton** - Feb. 8, 1907 M. J. – Miss Elizabeth K. Conner, daughter of Rev. Abraham Conner and Mrs. Conner, was married January 29$^{th}$ to Mr. Milton Hottle of Ohio. The ceremony was performed by Rev. William Conner of Newport News, brother of the bride. The bride was beautifully attired in a gown of white mull.

Immediately following the ceremony a wedding supper was given at the parents' home for the relatives of both bride and bridegroom.

Mr. and Mrs. Hottle left for a Northern trip. They will make their future home in Ohio.

**HOUSE, John Nathaniel** – Aug. 20, 1909 M. J. – Miss Mae McMichael and Mr. John Nathaniel House were married on Thursday last.

**HOWER, Fannie** – Nov. 4, 1910 M. J. – A marriage license was issued in Washington Monday to Mr. Wm. C. Bridwell and Mrs. Fannie Hower, of Manassas.

**HUME, Mamie Lee** – Oct. 29, 1909 M. J. – ALEXANDRIA – Mr. Ralph Elwood Remington and Miss Mamie Lee Hume were quietly married at 6:30 o'clock last evening at the parsonage of the First Baptist church by the Rev. W. F. Watson. After the ceremony Mr. and Mrs. Remington left for an extended Southern tour. Upon their return they will reside at No. 117 south St. Asaph street.—Gazette, Oct. 23.

**HUNT, Eva** – Oct. 5, 1906 M. J. – Miss Eva Hunt, daughter of Mr. S. W. Hunt of Woolsey, and Mr. Cross of Fairfax were married at the Little River Baptist church on Wednesday last, Rev. T. D. D. Clark officiating.

**HUNT, Eva** - Oct. 19, 1906 M. J. – The wedding of Mr. Wilmer B. Cross of Fairfax county and Miss Eva Hunt, daughter of Mr. Silas Hunt of "The Oaks," Prince William county, was one of the prettiest seen for some time in Prince William. The wedding was at high noon, Wednesday, Oct. 3, at Little River Church, Rev. T. D. D. Clark of Manassas performing the ceremony.

The church was most tastefully decorated with flowers and palms and as the bride and groom, with their attendants, marched up the aisle to Hymen's favorite melody, magnificently rendered by Miss Robena Hay of Ashburn, Va., the scene resembled enchantment rather than reality.

After the ceremony the bride, groom and guests repaired to "The Oaks," where a sumptuous repast was served.

Miss Miller of Washington, who was maid of honor, Miss Day, and Miss Harris attended the bride, Mr. Eppa Hunt was best man and Messrs. John Lefevre, C. S. Hutchison and I. A. House were ushers.

Mr. and Mrs. Cross expect to leave shortly for Washington state where they will reside.

**HUNTER, Mabel Isabelle** – Jul. 22, 1910 M. J. – FAIRFAX – Miss Mabel Isabelle Hunter, daughter of Mr. and Mrs. John C. Hunter, of Accotink, and Thomas Mark Cragg, of Alexandria, were married at the Washington street Methodist Episcopal Church South Thursday night, July 7th, by the Rev. Harry M. Canter, pastor.

**HUTCHINSON, Annie M.** – Jul. 23, 1909 M. J.- A marriage license was issued in Washington Tuesday to Alfred Devers, of Alexandria, and Annie M. Hutchison, of Prince William county.

**HUTCHINSON, Benjamin B.** – Nov. 18, 1910 M. J. – LOUDOUN – A marriage license was issued in Leesburg on Tuesday of last week to Mr. Benjamin B. Hutchison and Miss Eva May Matthews, both of Loudoun. They were married by Rev. Stuart A. Gibson, Tuesday.

**HUTCHISON, G. A.** – Nov. 5, 1909 M. J. – We are publishing this week an interesting account of the Hutchison-Callaway nuptials which was received last week from Tennessee too late to appear in Friday's paper.

At the New Providence Presbyterian church in Maryville Thursday night, Oct. 21, was solemnized a wedding of much interest to Knoxville friends and relatives when Miss Elizabeth Sue Callaway became the bride of Mr. G. A. Hutchison, of Hickory Grove, Va. A special car took the Knoxville party over to Maryville for the wedding, and a large and brilliant assemblage witnessed the church ceremony. Rev. Joseph Calhoun, D. D., said the impressive ring service to an accompaniment of organ music, charmingly rendered by Mrs. Bartlett. In the personnel of the wedding party were Miss Annie Belle Callaway, maid of honor; Misses Isabelle and Susan Hutchison, Mary Belle Harrison and Beatrice Rutherford, bridesmaids; Mr. James B. Carson, best man; Messrs. Jos. and Thos. Callaway, A. M. Hill and Thos. C. Carson, ushers.

A color scheme of white and yellow characterized the details of the wedding arrangements, the several maids appearing in either white or yellow costumes and carrying arm bouquets of chrysanthemums of like shades. The bride's gown was a lovely creation of white satin, fashioned princess, and she carried a shower bouquet of bride's roses.

The church was decorated with a bank of palms and lighted by candles.

Following the ceremony a reception was tendered at the home of the bride's father, Mr. James Callaway, for members of the bridal party, relatives, out of town guests and intimate friends. The cutting of the wedding cake and its many favors were features of the occasion.

The bride is a niece of Mr. and Mrs. J. L. Callaway, Mrs. J. S. Callaway and Mr. Mrs. J. B. Carson, of Knoxville. Mr. Hutchison is a son of Mr. and Mrs. Westwood Hutchison, of Manassas, and a nephew of Mr. H. G. Hutchison, of Vonore, Tenn.

The many handsome gifts of linen, silver and cutglass attest the popularity of the contracting parties.

Among the out of town guests were Mr. and Mrs. Jno. Callaway, Mrs. J. B. Carson, Mrs. J. S. Callaway, Mr. and Mrs. Thos. Callaway, Misses Sue, Carrie, Elizabeth, and Julia Callaway and Mr. and Mrs. Boyton, of Knoxville; Mrs. H. G. Hutchison and Mr. and Mrs. W. S. Harrison, of Vonore; Miss Lavinia Ish, of Chattanooga; Mr. and Mrs. R. A. Hutchison, of Manassas, Va.

**HUTCHISON, Gustavus A.** – Oct. 22, 1909 M. J. – Among those who attended the marriage of Miss Elizabeth Sue Callaway and Mr. Gustavus A. Hutchison on Thursday of this week, at Maryville, Tenn., were Mr. Robert A. Hutchison and little daughter, Ruth, Miss Isabella Holden and Miss Susan Hutchison.

**HUTCHISON, Quinton** - Mar. 1, 1907 M. J.- Mr. Quinton Hutchison and Miss Clymedia Amidon of Dumfries were married on Sunday.

**HUTCHISON, Warren** – Jun. 24, 1910 M. J. – Miss Pearl Garner, daughter of Mr. Newton Garner, of this place, and Mr. Warren Hutchinson, were married in Alexandria on Saturday last. The young couple have the best wishes of the community for their future happiness.

**HUTTON, Margaret** – Oct. 28, 1910 M. J. – FAUQUIER – The wedding of Miss Margaret Hutton, the daughter of Mr. and Mrs. Henry I. Hutton, to Dr. Robert E. Ferneyhough which was celebrated Wednesday afternoon in the Baptist church in Warrenton, was one of wide interest in Virginia, as both the bride and groom are prominently related throughout the state. It was perhaps the most brilliant affair of the fall season in Warrenton. –Democrat.

**IDEN, Pauline Elizabeth** – Dec. 31, 1909 M. J. – On Wednesday evening at six o'clock, the home of Dr. and Mrs. B. F. Iden was the scene of a very pretty wedding, when Miss Pauline Elizabeth Iden became the bride of Mr. Sargent I. Ballard, of West Point, Mississippi. Miss Pauline Nicol, of Alexandria, and little Miss Jessie Adams, of Rectortown, who have been guests of the family this week, were the only ones to witness the ceremony outside of the immediate family.

The bride was attired in a handsome traveling suit of blue cloth, with hat to match, and carried bride roses. Rev. Leslie F. Robinson, rector of Trinity Episcopal church, performed the ceremony and the bride was given away by her father.

The bridal party left on the evening train for Washington, passing through Manassas yesterday for an extended tour through the Southern states. After February $1^{st}$ they will be in their future home in West Point.

**IRVING, Virginia** – Jun. 25, 1909 M. J. – ORANGE – Cards are out announcing the approaching marriage of Miss Virginia Irving, daughter of Mrs. Katherine M. Walker, to Mr. Frank W. McIntosh on Tuesday evening, June 29, at the bride's home in Farmville. Mr.

McIntosh, who is one of Orange's young men, has for sometime been chief clerk at White's drug store at Farmville.—Review.

**ISH, Mabel R.** - Mar. 29, 1907 M. J. – The Alexandria Gazette of Wednesday says the marriage of Miss Mabel R. Ish to Mr. Lewis E. Strother, both of Prince William county, took place yesterday afternoon, at Christ Church rectory. The ceremony was performed by the Rev. W. J. Morgan. Mrs. Strother is the daughter of the late Dr. M. A. and Sallie E. Atkinson Ish.

**ISH, Mollie** – Aug. 10, 1906 M. J. - Cards are out announcing the approaching marriage of Mr. Earnest Leonard and Miss Mollie Ish on the 26th of September. Both of this county.

**JACKSON, Paul** – Jul. 8, 1910 M. J. – A marriage license was issued in Washington Saturday to Mr. Paul Jackson and Miss Edith Laws, both of Front Royal. Miss Laws is a sister to Mr. H. Kinzel Laws, formerly of this place.

**JACOBS, Joseph M.** – Dec. 31, 1909 M. J. – FAUQUIER – Marriage licenses were issued in Washington this week to Frederick M. Day and Mary L. Beach, both of Fauquier county. Also to Jos. M. Jacobs of Calverton and Miss Carrie B. Green of Midland, Va.

**JANNEY, Cornelia Hamilton** – Mar. 1, 1907 M. J. – Dr. and Mrs. Chas. H. Janney have announced the engagement of their daughter, Miss Cornelia Hamilton Janney, to Mr. Philip M. Knot, son of Capt. and Mrs. Robert F. Knot. Mr. Knot is well known in Occoquan. We wish the happy fiancées much joy.

**JEFFRIES, Joseph A.** – Sept. 23, 1910 M. J. – FAUQUIER – Marriage licenses were issued in Washington on Thursday to the following Fauquier couples: Joseph B. Pulliam and Carolyn Spicer, both of Remington; Benjamin Gordon, of Markham, and India Chadwell, of Hume; Joseph A. Jeffries, of Warrenton, and Sallie Thompson, of Washington.

**JEFFRIES, Nannie** – Jan. 14, 1910 M. J. – FAUQUIER – Monday, at high noon, Jan. 3, Miss Nannie Jeffries, the pretty and accomplished daughter of Mrs. M. H. and J. P. Jefferies, late commonwealth's attorney of Fauquier, plighted her love to Louis Antonsanti, of Ponce, Porto Rico. The marriage was quietly solemnized at the rectory of the Trinity Episcopal church, Washington, by Rev. Richard P. Williams.

**JOHNSON, Jennie Page** – Oct. 17, 1885 M. G. - At the brides residence of Bellifair Mills on Thursday 3 P.M. Miss Jennie Page Johnson to Mr. Herbert Tolson, of Stafford County, Va.

**JOHNSON, William G.** - Nov. 9, 1906 M. J. - Miss Clara Eckhart, daughter of Mrs. A. Davis, was married in Washington on Tuesday last to Mr. Wm. G. Johnson of that city.

**JOLIFFE, Mary C.** – Oct. 22, 1909 M. J. – The marriage of Miss Mary C. Joliffe, daughter of the late Mr. and Mrs. William H. Joliffe, of Baltimore, to Mr. Hugh Thompson Clarkson, of Haymarket, Va., took place at noon yesterday at the home of the bride's aunt, Mrs. Nathaniel Bacon Crenshaw, on Lake avenue.

Rev. Chas. A. Hensel, rector of the Protestant Episcopal church of the Redeemer, performed the ceremony, which was followed by the reception for the members of the two families and intimate friends.

The bride was given in marriage by her cousin, Mr. Benjamin T. Moore. Her gown of heavy corded white silk, with a trimming of old lace, and tulle veil, caught with orange blossoms, was the same her mother had worn at her wedding. The bride of yesterday also wore ornaments of old family pearls. Her bouquet was of bride roses and maidenhair ferns.

The maid of honor was Miss Marion B. Wyatt, who wore a gown of embroidered white crepe de china a white picture hat trimmed with plumes and carried a shower bouquet of pink chrysanthemums. Two little cousins of the bride, Elizabeth Joliffe McElroy, were flower girl and ribbon bearer. Little Miss McElroy wore white and carried a basket of white flowers tied with blue ribbons.

The groom was attended by his brother, Mr. Walter Clarkson, of Philadelphia, as best man.

Later in the afternoon Mr. and Mrs. Clarkson left for an extended trip South. On their return they will live in Laurel, Maryland.

Among the guest at the wedding were: Dr. and Mrs. H. M. Clarkson, of Haymarket, Va., parents of the groom; Gen. and Mrs. W. Robinson, of Raleigh, N.C.; Mr. and Miss Gilless, of Washington; Mr. Charles Keyser, of Haymarket, Va.; Mr. Thomas Clarkson, of Laurel, Md.; Miss Katherine Crenshaw, of Philadelphia.—Baltimore Sun.

**JOLLEY, Ada Berry** – Sept. 24, 1909 M. J. – FAUQUIER – Mr. and Mrs. J. D. Jolley announce the engagement of their daughter, Ada Berry to H. W. Templeman of Washington, D. C. The wedding will take place at the home of the bride, Tuesday, September 28, 1909, at 11 a. m.

**JOLLIFFE, Blanche** – Jan. 28, 1910 M. J. – CULPEPER –W. W. Newman, of Viewtown, was married to Miss Blanche Jolliffe, of Culpeper, on Jan. 13, by Rev. E. W. Winfrey. The happy couple were the recipients of many pretty and useful presents.

**JOLLIFFE, Mary C.** – Sept. 17, 1909 M. J. – The marriage of Miss Mary C. Jolliffe to Mr. Hugh T. Clarkson is announced to take place in October at the home of the bride's aunt, Mrs. Elizabeth Crenshaw, Baltimore. One of the most pleasant social events of the past few weeks was a linen shower, given Miss Jolliffe by Miss DePauw. About twenty-five guests were present and the young bride-elect received quite a number of pretty gifts. Mr. Clarkson is the son of Dr. H. M. Clarkson, and is with the C. P. Telephone Co., of Washington. The young couple have many warm and interested friends here.

**JONES, Bessie** – Mar. 11, 1910 M. J. –Dr. and Mrs. Jones, of Alexandria, have announced the engagement of their daughter, Miss Bessie Jones to Mrs. Harry Beverley, of Thoroughfare. The wedding will take place the eighth of June.

**JONES, Elizabeth Winter** – May 13, 1910 M. J. – FAUQUIER – Dr. and Mrs. T. Marshall Jones of Alexandria, have issued invitations to the marriage of their daughter, Miss Elizabeth Winter to Mr. R. H. C. Beverley, of Fauquier county. The marriage is to take place on May 25th.

**JONES, Hilton** – Dec. 30, 1910 M. J.- Among the marriage licenses issued in Washington, on Saturday was one to Mr. Hilton Jones and Miss Bertha F. Williams, both of Prince William county.

**JONES, John Marshall** – Nov. 19, 1909 M. J. – LOUDOUN - The 24th of November is the date set for the marriage of Miss M. Jeannette Shriver to Mr. John Marshall Jones, of Alexandria, the wedding to be solemnized by Cardinal Gibbons, and the nuptial mass celebrated by the Rev. William Gaston Payne, uncle of the groom, in St. Mary's chapel, Union Mills, Md. and Mr. Jones is the second son of

Dr. and Mrs. T. Marshall Jones of this city. After their marriage Mr. and Mrs. Jones will reside on Cameron street, opposite Christ church.—Gazette

**JORDAN, Charlotte J.** – Apr. 8, 1910 M. J. - Mr. Christian A. Heineken and Mrs. Charlotte J. Jordan, both of Haymarket, were quietly married in Washington Wednesday of this week.

**JORDAN, Lucile** – Jan. 7, 1910 M. J. – The engagement of Miss Lucile Jordan, youngest daughter of Mr. and Mrs. C. E. Jordan to Mr. Carson, of Chicago, is announced, and the marriage is to take place in February, in Panama, where the family have spent several winters.

**JORDAN, Viola Lucile** – Mar. 18, 1910 M. J. –Cards have been received here from Mr. and Mrs. Charles E. Jordan, announcing the marriage of their daughter, Viola Lucile, to Mr. Albert Korson, on Saturday the twenty-sixth of February, at Culibra, Canal Zone. The young bride is a native of Haymarket, and resided here until a year or two ago, when her father, who is the senior member of the popular and well known firm of Jordan & Jordan accepted for a time, a position in Panama, where he was later joined by his family.

**KELLER, Carl Baxter** – May 3, 1907 M. J. – A charming wedding took place Wednesday evening April 24 at 8 o'clock in the church of Our Saviour, 13th and Irving streets, Brookland, D.C., where Miss Virgie Eudora Lambert daughter of the late Dr. Colin H. Lambert and Mrs. L. G. Lambert was married to Mr. Carl Baxter Keller, son of Mr. Chas. Keller, one of Brookland's oldest citizens.

The church was beautifully decorated with palms and spring flowers.

The bride, who was given in marriage by her brother, Mr. George Hunter Lambert, wore a handsome gown of white net, over taffeta. She wore a long tulle veil fastened with lilies of the valley, and the bridal bouquet was a shower of white sweep peas, lilies of the valley and maidenhair ferns.

Miss Hattie Lambert, sister of the bride, who was maid of honor, wore an attractive gown of pink batiste and lace and carried a large bunch of bride's roses.

The bridesmaids who were the Misses Jannette Lambert Harrell, Nellie L. Carr and Anna Bell Davidson, also wore gowns of pink with large white picture hats and carried bridesmaid roses.

Little Birdie May Ledman, niece of the bride, in a fairy-like frock of white batiste and lace, acted as ring bearer, the ring being carried on a large calla lily.

The groom was accompanied by his brother, Mr. Wm. P. Keller, who was best man.

The ushers were Messrs. Wesley Tayloe, Hunter Eddins and Walter Unddlekauf.

"Faithful and True" from Lohengrin's wedding march, was sung by the vested choir of the church of Our Saviour, assisted by member of the Epiphany choir.

Little Arthur Williams, carrying the cross, led the choir which preceded the bridal party. The ceremony was performed by the Rev. J. D. La Motthe of the church of the Epiphany. The white prayer book used for the ceremony was a gift to the bride from the rector of the church of Our Saviour, who was unable to be present.

The bride's going away gown was of Alice blue broadcloth with hat to match.

After the reception the happy couple left for a trip to Richmond, the Jamestown exposition and Norfolk. Upon their return they will reside with Mr. Keller's parents, 8th and Lawrence streets, Brooksland, D.C.

The bride received many costly and beautiful presents.

**KELLEY, Pearl L.** – Dec. 24, 1909 M. J. – The following marriage licenses were issued this week at the clerk's office: Monday, Lewis M. Swartz, Culpeper county, and Miss Pearl L. Kelley, Fauquier county; Chas. N. Davis and Miss Virgie Wolfe, both of Prince William; Tuesday, John F. Donovan, Rockingham county and Miss Florida V. Allison, Loudoun county; Wednesday, Aubrey Flynn, Fauquier county, and Miss Annie L. Thomas, Prince William county; Thursday, Wm. E. Beahm, Rappahannock county, and Miss Edith G. Priest, Fauquier county; Geo. Spinks, Fauquier county, and Miss Bessie Baggott, Prince William county.

**KELLY, Nanny G.** – Oct. 21, 1910 M. J.- FAUQUIER – At 9 o'clock Wednesday morning, the 12th inst., in the home of the father, Mr. A. D. Kelly, the marriage of Miss Nanny G. Kelly to Dr. J. A. Tyree, of Blackstone, Va., was impressively solemnized by Rev. Fleet James, the uncle of the bride.

**KERR, Harry Hyland** – Jan. 21, 1910 M. J. – FAUQUIER – On Saturday, Jan. 1, one of the prettiest weddings ever seen in Toronto took place at the residence of Mr. and Mrs. Chester Glass, New York, in Spadina Road (rented temporarily), when their only daughter, Dorothy Beatrice, and Dr. Harry Hyland Kerr, Washington, D. C., son of Dr. and Mrs. James Kerr, of Warrenton, Va., were married. The Venerable Archdeacon Cody, St. Paul's church, officiated. Dr. and Mrs. Kerr will reside at 1742 N. street N. W., Washington, D. C., where a house has been presented as a wedding gift.—Virginian, Jan. 13.

**KEY, John Baltzell** – Jun. 8, 1906 M. J. - Mr. and Mrs. W. B. Smitten announce the approaching marriage of their daughter, Ina Mary, to Mr. John Baltzell Key of Leonardtown, Md., on Wednesday, June 27, at Trinity Episcopal church at high noon.

**KEYS, Grover C.** – Aug. 19, 1910 M. J. – Mr. Grover C. Keys, of lower Prince William, and Miss Murphy, of Minnieville were married yesterday.

**KEYS, John W.** - Dec. 7, 1906 M. J. – Miss Emma A. Loveless and Mr. John W. Keys, both of this county, were married on Wednesday last at the residence of the officiating minister, Rev. Robert Smith of this place.

**KEYS, Owen** – Dec. 28, 1906 M. J. – Mr. Owen Keys, son of Mr. E. G. W. Keys, and Miss Sallie Kincheloe, daughter of Mr. Andrew Kincheloe, were married on Christmas day.

**KIBLER, Mary Elizabeth** – May 3, 1907 M. J. – Miss Mary Elizabeth Kibler, daughter of Mr. James Kibler, who formerly lived here, was married to Roy C. Truitt of Lincoln City, Del., on April 23. Mr. Truitt is a well to do young business man of that place. Mr. Kibler moved to Lincoln City from Manassas about two years ago.

**KINCHELOE, Lillie** – Jul. 10, 1896 M. G. – There appeared in a communication from Nokesville to the Warrenton Virginian, this week, the following concerning the marriage of Miss Kincheloe and Mr. Hedrick:

Mr. W. P. Hedrick and Miss Lillie, daughter of Mr. and Mrs. W. W. Kincheloe, of Brentsville, were married in Washington on last Wednesday. It was one of the old fashioned runaways. Her parents opposed the bands so strongly that they thought best to runway. So on Tuesday evening at about 11 o'clock accompanied by his cousins, Mr. John Hedrick and Miss Lillie Laws, they drove within a mile of

Brentsville, there taking a buggy—the brave knight drove to her house and at a given signal with hat and shoes in hand, she quickly responded and then the drive for Washington began which was made in about six hours. The groom is a prosperous young man of our town and we heartily congratulate him and wish him much happiness.

**KINCHELOE, Mable M.** - Nov. 22, 1901 M. J. – Mr. Willard Green, one of Maj. Sylvester's bluecoats, who was appointed on the Metropolitan police force less than a year ago, and who is attached to the Eighth precinct station, has been the recipient of many congratulations from his brother officers and other friends during the past two or three days.

Miss Mable M. Kincheloe was the name of his bride. She is a Virginia belle, nineteen years of age, the daughter of Mr. W. W. Kincheloe, a wealthy merchant of Prince William county, who resides near Manassas. Mr. Green had known Miss Kincheloe for three years or more prior to coming to Washington, but his attentions to the young lady were not appreciated by her parents, who objected on the ground that she was too young to make a matrimonial venture. The young lady came to Washington about two months ago to pursue her studies, and here she found it possible to frequently see the man of her choice.

On Saturday Mr. Green secured a day's leave of absence. There was no session at the business college where Miss Kincheloe was a pupil that day, and they decided to take a trip to Baltimore. On the way the romance was agreed to. In Baltimore they met a friend, and in short order a marriage certificate was procured. It took but a few minutes to have the ceremony performed by Rev. D. Guthree, a Presbyterian minister and after a short honeymoon spent in the Monumental City Mr. and Mrs. Green returned to Washington, and are living happily at 624 Rhode Island avenue northwest.—Washington Post of Tuesday.

**KINCHELOE, Pearl** – Aug. 3, 1906 M. J. - Miss Pearl Kincheloe, daughter of Mr. D. E. Kincheloe of Buckhall was married on Monday last to Mr. E. K. Evans of the same neighborhood. The ceremony took place in Washington, Rev. D. L. Blakemore officiating.

**KINCHELOE, Sallie** – Dec. 28, 1906 M. J. – Mr. Owen Keys, son of Mr. E. G. W. Keys, and Miss Sallie Kincheloe, daughter of Mr. Andrew Kincheloe, were married on Christmas day.

**KING, Gardner** - Jan. 18, 1907 M. J. – Mr. Gardner King of Nokesville and Miss Cassie Boley of Greenwich were married at the home of the bride's parents, Wednesday evening, Jan. 9, Rev. S. V. Hildebrand of Gainesville officiating.

**KING, Gardner** – Jan. 18, 1907 M. J. – GREENWICH -The home of William Boley, near this place, was the scene of a very pretty wedding at 8 p.m., Jan. 9, when her daughter Cassie, became the bride of Mr. King of Nokesville. The marriage ceremony was performed by Rev. S. V. Hilderbrand of Gainesville in the presence of a few friends. The bride was becomingly attired in blue silk. The writer wishes them a happy journey through life.

**KING, Henry Nicholas** – Dec. 30, 1910 M. J. – Mr. Henry Nicholas King, son of Mr. and Mrs. A. N. King, of Nokesville, and Miss Ruth Williams, of near Luray, Page county, were married at the home of the bride's parents, Mr. and Mrs. R. L. Williams, on Wednesday, Dec. 12, Elder Pitman of the Baptist church, officiating.

The bride was attired in a becoming gown of white messalline and carried a bouquet of bride's roses. The bride is a most attractive young lady and her departure from the home of her childhood is the source of much regret to her numerous friends and relatives.

Mr. King, the groom, who holds the position on lumber inspector for the Pennsylvania Railway Company has his head quarters in Florida.

On Monday a reception was tendered the wedding couple at the home of the groom's parents, in their new home near Nokesville.

A sumptuous dinner was served and congratulations extended to the happy pair. Mr. and Mrs. King will leave for Florida, their future home, within a few days with the good wishes of all.

Among those present at the reception, from a distance, were; Mr. H. W. Herring and family; Mr. A. J. Bradley; Mr. and Mrs. E. T. Garber; Mr. and Mrs. Jno. Hedrick; Mr. and Mrs. Benjamin King, of Washington; Mr. and Mrs. Thos. F. King, of Manassas; Mr. Samuel Flickinger, of Nokesville; Mr. M. T. King; Miss S. Yates; Mr. and Mrs. W. T. Allen and Mr. Clay Wood.

**KNOT, Philip M.** – Mar. 1, 1907 M. J. – Dr. and Mrs. Chas. H. Janney have announced the engagement of their daughter, Miss Cornelia Hamilton Janney, to Mr. Philip M. Knot, son of Capt. and Mrs. Robert F. Knot. Mr. Knot is well known in Occoquan. We wish the happy fiancées much joy.

**KOLBACH, Marie** – Sept. 24, 1909 M. J. – CULPEPER –Mr. Charles Crawford Wager, formerly of Culpeper, now a prominent real estate man in Pittsburg, and Miss Marie Kolback were married at Eric, Pa., on Saturday last, September 11th. Mr. Wager's many Culpeper friends extend their congratulations.— Exponent, Sept. 17

**KORSON, Albert** – Mar. 18, 1910 M. J. – Cards have been received here from Mr. and Mrs. Charles E. Jordan, announcing the marriage of their daughter, Viola Lucile, to Mr. Albert Korson, on Saturday the twenty-sixth of February, at Culibra, Canal Zone. The young bride is a native of Haymarket, and resided here until a year or two ago, when her father, who is the senior member of the popular and well known firm of Jordan & Jordan accepted for a time, a position in Panama, where he was later joined by his family.

**LAKE, James Ludwell** – Jul. 1, 1910 M. J. – LOUDOUN – Mr. James Ludwell Lake, son of Rev. I. B. Lake, was married to Miss Virginia Prudence Caldwell on Wednesday, June 15th, at Upperville, Va.

**LAMBERT, George E.** – Oct. 21, 1910 M. J. – FAIRFAX – A marriage license was issued in Washington, Wednesday, to Geo. E. Lambert and Phoebe E. Tucker, both of this town. –Herald.

**LAMBERT, Virgie Eudora** – May 3, 1907 M. J. – A charming wedding took place Wednesday evening April 24 at 8 o'clock in the church of Our Saviour, 13th and Irving streets, Brookland, D.C., where Miss Virgie Eudora Lambert daughter of the late Dr. Colin H. Lambert and Mrs. L. G. Lambert was married to Mr. Carl Baxter Keller, son of Mr. Chas. Keller, one of Brookland's oldest citizens.

The church was beautifully decorated with palms and spring flowers.

The bride, who was given in marriage by her brother, Mr. George Hunter Lambert, wore a handsome gown of white net, over taffeta. She wore a long tulle veil fastened with lilies of the valley, and the bridal bouquet was a shower of white sweet peas, lilies of the valley and maidenhair ferns.

Miss Hattie Lambert, sister of the bride, who was maid of honor, wore an attractive gown of pink batiste and lace and carried a large bunch of bride's roses.

The bridesmaids who were the Misses Jannette Lambert Harrell, Nellie L. Carr and Anna Bell Davidson, also wore gowns of pink with large white picture hats and carried bridesmaid roses.

Little Birdie May Ledman, niece of the bride, in a fairy-like frock of white batiste and lace, acted as ring bearer, the ring being carried on a large calla lily.

The groom was accompanied by his brother, Mr. Wm. P. Keller, who was best man.

The ushers were Messrs. Wesley Tayloe, Hunter Eddins and Walter Unddlekauf.

"Faithful and True" from Lohengrin's wedding march, was sung by the vested choir of the church of Our Saviour, assisted by member of the Epiphany choir.

Little Arthur Williams, carrying the cross, led the choir which preceded the bridal party. The ceremony was performed by the Rev. J. D. La Motthe of the church of the Epiphany. The white prayer book used for the ceremony was a gift to the bride from the rector of the church of Our Saviour, who was unable to be present.

The bride's going away gown was of Alice blue broadcloth with hat to match.

After the reception the happy couple left for a trip to Richmond, the Jamestown exposition and Norfolk. Upon their return they will reside with Mr. Keller's parents, $8^{th}$ and Lawrence streets, Brooksland, D.C.

The bride received many costly and beautiful presents.

**LANE, James M.** – Oct. 7, 1910 M. J. – LOUDOUN – Mr. Jas. M. Lane and Miss Alice J. Daymude, both of Lower Loudoun, were married in the parlors of the Leesburg Inn Wednesday morning, Rev. J. H. Wiltshire, of the Baptist church, officiating. –The Mirror

**LANN, Walter** – Oct. 12, 1906 M. J. – Miss Averick Parker Heineken, daughter of Mr. C. A. Heineken of Haymarket, was married on Tuesday last to Mr. Walter Lann of Aberdeen, Miss.

**LANN, Walter** – Oct. 12, 1906 M. J. – We are please to record the marriage of Mr. Walter Lann and Miss Averick Parker Heineken, second daughter of our prominent and highly esteemed fellow-citizen, Mr. C. A. Heineken, at "Mill Park" on Tuesday evening, October ninth, Rev. Cary Gamble, rector of St. Paul's Church, Haymarket, officiating.

On account of the recent bereavement in the family, the wedding took place quietly at home in the conservatory amidst a mass of palms and flowering plants, the effects of many candles making the whole scene a very impressive one. Only immediate members of the family and a few friends were present. We were pleased to greet the Right Rev. Dr. Robert A. Gibson, bishop of the diocese, on the occasion. The bride wore a very becoming dress of white crepe de chine, the veil being held in place by orange blossoms and carried brides roses and lilies of the valley and was given away by her father.

Miss Emma Heineken, the youngest sister of the bride, wearing white silk mull and carrying white carnations, was maid of honor, and Herman Heineken, brother of the bride, best man.

The couple left for a trip North followed by the best wishes for their future happiness by those present. Their home will be in Aberdeen, Miss., where Mr. Lann is one of the leading business men.

**LARKIN, C. M.** – Apr. 12, 1907 M. J. – Miss Lizzie J. Larkin, one of the teachers at Ruffner school, and Mr. C. M. Larkin were married at Trinity Church on Wednesday evening last, Rev. Mr. Gamble of Haymarket performing the ceremony. Mrs. W. A. Newman presided at the organ and the bride was attended by Miss Mason.

**LARKIN, Lizzie J.** – Apr. 12, 1907 M. J. – Miss Lizzie J. Larkin, one of the teachers at Ruffner school, and Mr. C. M. Larkin were married at Trinity Church on Wednesday evening last, Rev. Mr. Gamble of Haymarket performing the ceremony. Mrs. W. A. Newman presided at the organ and the bride was attended by Miss Mason.

**LAWS, Edith** – Jul. 8, 1910 M. J. – A marriage license was issued in Washington Saturday to Mr. Paul Jackson and Miss Edith Laws, both of Front Royal. Miss Laws is a sister to Mr. H. Kinzel Laws, formerly of this place.

**LAWS, Sallie** – Jan. 28, 1910 M. J. – FAUQUIER –Mr. John Ruffner and Miss Sallie Laws, both of Bristersburg, were quietly married in Washington on Thursday last. Mr. and Mrs. Ruffner have returned home near here. We wish them a long and happy life.

**LAYMAN, John E.** – Feb. 25, 1910 M. J. – CULPEPER – Mr. J. F. Carpenter, of Brandy, Va., announces the marriage of his daughter, on Feb. 12th, Grace, to Mr. John E. Layman, of Roanoke. They will be at home to their many friends after the 18th of February at 905 Patterson avenue, Roanoke, Va.—Exponent, Feb. 18.

**LEAHY, Catherine T.** – Aug. 20, 1909 M. J. – Mr. Thos. L. Spaight, of Washington, and Miss Catherine T. Leahy, of Prince William, were united in marriage August 19$^{th}$ by Rev. J. K. Efird, at the Lutheran parsonage, Manassas.

**LEDMAN, Eva** – Oct. 22, 1909 M. J.- An attractive wedding took place at Hotel Alton, the contracting parties being Miss Eva Ledman and Mr. Walter Neil, of Freestone, the postmaster at that place. The bride looked beautiful, being gowned in Persian taffeta. She carried a bouquet of white roses. The ceremony was performed by the pastor of the M. E. church South, Rev. C. L. Sydenstricker. Mr. and Mrs. Neil left on the 11 o'clock train for Washington and Baltimore. They will be at home to their friends the latter part of October. Their presents were numerous and handsome, both of the contracting parties being very popular in church circles.

**LEE, Fannie Stuart** – Sept. 7, 1906 M. J. – [Reprinted from the Washington Star of June 21, 1906, by request] The marriage of Miss Fannie Stuart Lee, daughter of Mr. William F. Lee of Manassas, Va., and Mr. William Alexander Henry of Ontario, Canada, took place at Mount Vernon Place Church last evening 8 o'clock, the Rev. William French Locke performing the ceremony. The bride wore a very becoming gown of Paris muslin, elaborately trimmed with lace and insertion, and carried a shower bouquet of bride roses and lilies of the valley. After the ceremony a luncheon was served at the home of the bride's cousin, Mrs. Clinton R. Tucker, 645 C street, northwest. At a late hour the couple left for a tour through Canada, stopping by way of Niagara.

Mr. Henry was not met during the encampment here as published at the time, but has been a friend of the family for several years.

**LEE, Nannie M.** – Feb. 25, 1910 M. J. – Mr. Thomas A. Metz, of Manassas, and Miss Nannie M. Lee, of Herndon, were married in Washington Wednesday of this week, Rev. A. H. Thompson performing the ceremony.

**LEE, Sadie** – Jun. 17, 1910 M. J. – Mr. Archie L. Lowe and Miss Sadie Lee, both of this county, were married on Wednesday last , at the residence of the officiating minister, Rev. T. D. D. Clark, of this place.

**LEE, William T.** – Sept. 17, 1909 M. J. – LOUDOUN – Mr. William T. Lee, of Bluemont, Loudoun county, and Miss Virginia

Fleming, of Landmark, Fauquier county, were married at the residence of Mrs. Lutie Carruthers, Round Hill, on Thursday last, by Rev. I. B. Lake, D. D., pastor of the Baptist Church of Upperville. They will reside near Bluemont.—Mirror, Sept. 10.

**LEFEVER, William** – Sept. 3, 1909 M. J.- LOUDOUN – Mr. William Lefever, of Ashburn and Miss Lelia V. Ankers, daughter of Mr. William Ankers, of Waxpool, were married at Mt. Hope Baptist church on Thursday of last week, Rev. G. W. Popkins officiating.

**LEFEVRE, William** – Aug. 27, 1909 M. J. – LOUDOUN – Marriage licenses were issued in Leesburg this week to Mr. Robert Elmer Connon and Miss Goldie Kalb Brooks, of Clarke's Gap, and to William Lefevre and Lelia V. Ankers, of Lower Loudoun.

**LEITH, Clarence M.** – May 6, 1910 M.J. – FAIRFAX – Mr. Clarence M. Leith, son of Dr. R. D. Leith, of Vienna, and Miss Mary W. White, daughter of Mr. Wm. G. White, of Baltimore, were married at the New Jerusalem Swedenborgain church in the latter city on the 19th inst., Rev. Arthur Mercer, of Brooklyn, N. Y., officiating. After an extensive wedding tour, they will reside in Detroit, Mich., where Mr. Leith holds a responsible position with the U. S. Fidelity and Guarantee Company.—Herald, April 29.

**LEMMON, Janet Southgate** – Sept. 24, 1909 M. J.- FAUQUIER – Invitations are out for the marriage of Miss Janet Southgate Lemmon, daughter of Mr. and Mrs. J. Southgate Lemmon, of Baltimore, and granddaughter of the late Colonel Dulaney, of "Welbourne," Upperville, to Mr. Richard Julian Roszel, of that town. The wedding is set for October 2, to take place at "Welbourne," near the home of the Dulaneys.

**LEONARD, Earnest** – Aug. 10, 1906 M. J. - Cards are out announcing the approaching marriage of Mr. Earnest Leonard and Miss Mollie Ish on the 26th of September. Both of this county.

**LESIER, Katie** – Feb. 25, 1910 M. J. – Mr. Clarence Horton, of Washington, and Miss Katie Lesier, of Texas, were married in Washington, on Tuesday last. They spent several days this week with his parents, Mr. and Mrs. J. M. Horton. The young couple will make their future home in the capital.

**LICKEY, Clara** – Jan. 21, 1910 M. J. – FAUQUIER – Mr. Dulany F. Carter, of Marshall, Fauquier county, and Miss Clara Lickey, of Round Hill, this county, were married recently in Washington.

**LINAWEAVER, Otto** – Nov. 4, 1910 M. J. – Rockville, Md., Nov. 2. Being unable to furnish $2,000 bail, Otto Linaweaver, who was married here Saturday afternoon under the name of Owen La Monta to Miss Lephia Buchanan, daughter of A. C. Buchanan, of Craigsville, Va., was committed to jail to await the action of the grand jury.

The offense with which Linaweaver is charged is that he swore falsely in giving his name as La Monta in making application for marriage license and in stating that he had not been divorced. The man's divorced wife, who was Miss Nellie Neville, of Washington, testified that she and Linaweaver were married in Rockville in July, 1907, by Rev. Thomas H. Campbell, pastor of the Baptist church, and that he was married under the name of Linaweaver. The court records were produced to corroborate the statement. Mrs. Linaweaver said she was granted a divorce from him in June of this year. Deputy Clerk of the Circuit Court Bowman testified that Linaweaver swore, in making application for the license last Saturday, that his name was La Monta and that he had never been divorced.

Linaweaver is a son of J. L. Linaweaver, of Manassas, Va. He lived in Washington several years and several weeks ago he represented himself as a palmist. Mr. Buchanan said the young man conducted himself in an exemplary manner in Craigsville, praying and participating in a revival in progress there. He was allowed to visit the Buchanan home.

When Linaweaver was arrested he had only about $2, but his bride had about $20. Linaweaver had with him a ticket showing that he had pawned two of the girl's rings in Alexandria, one of which, her father said, was valuable. Mr. Buchanan took the tickets with the intention of redeeming the rings on his way back home. He said he and his daughter would leave for their home tonight.—Baltimore Sun.

**LINDAMOOD, Bertie F.** - Dec.10, 1909 M. J. – FAIRFAX – A license was issued by the county clerk on Wednesday to E. D. Evans, of Shenandoah county, and Bertie F. Lindamood, of Clifton, after which they repaired to the parsonage of the M. E. church, South, where they were united in marriage by Rev. F. A. Strother.—Herald, Dec. 3.

**LITTLEJOHN, Horace T.** – Oct. 8, 1909 M. J.- LOUDOUN – Mr. Horace T. Littlejohn, a member of the drug firm of Purcell &

Littlejohn, of Leesburg, and Miss Ethel Thompson, daughter of Mr. H. A. Thompson, of the same town, were united in marriage at the residence of the bride at 5:15 o'clock on Wednesday afternoon, Rev. D. L. Blakemore officiating. The wedding was very quiet one, the ceremony being witnessed only by the immediate member of the families of the contracting parties. Mr. and Mrs. Littlejohn left on the east bound train for New York for a two weeks' tour in the north. They will reside in Leesburg.—Observer, Oct. 1.

**LITTLETON, Richard Conway** – Jul. 23, 1909 M. J. – LOUDOUN – At the home of the bride, at Covington, Va., on Thursday, July 8, 1909, by Rev. F. P. Berkley, pastor of the Baptist church, were married Mr. Richard Conway Littleton, of Leesburg, and Miss Mary Pattison Berkley, daughter of the officiating minister. They left by the late train over the C. & O. for a short trip North, and upon their return will reside at Covington.—Mirror, July 16.

**LLOYD, Lee Cockrell** – Nov. 18, 1910 M. J. – Miss Charley Waugh Brawner, daughter of Mr. and Mrs. Charles E. Brawner, of Manassas, and Mr. Lee Cockrell Lloyd, of Kentucky and New York, were married at 4:30 o'clock, Wednesday, in Washington, D.C.

The ceremony, which was attended only by the immediate family, was performed at the church of the Good Shepherd, by the assistant rector, Rev. Ginon.

Mr. and Mrs. Lloyd left immediately after the ceremony for their future home in Jamestown, N.Y.

**LLOYD, Mary Robertson** – Oct. 15, 1909 M. J.– Miss Mary Robertson Lloyd, eldest daughter of the bishop coadjutoe-elect of Virginia and Mrs. A. S. Lloyd, and Rev. Edmund Pendleton Dandridge, of Lewisburg, W. Va., were married last Friday at Christ Episcopal Church, Alexandria. The ceremony was performed by the bride's father, assisted by Bishop Peterkin, of West Virginia.

**LONG, Mattie** - Jan. 11, 1907 M. J. – NOKESVILLE, VA., Jan. 8, 1907.- The home of Mr. and Mrs. Simeon Long, near this place, was the scene of a very pretty wedding at high noon today, when their eldest daughter, Mattie, became the bride of Mr. Edward Herring.

The marriage ceremony was performed by Rev. Abram Conner of Manassas in the presence of a large circle of friends and acquaintances. Mr. Ray Hedrick was best man and his sister, Miss Sallie Hedrick, maid of honor. The bride was becomingly attired in white and the groom in the conventional black.

Immediately after the marriage ceremony a beautiful dinner, consisting of everything calculated to satisfy the inner man, was served.

Mr. Herring is the eldest son of Mr. Hastings W. Herring of near this place, and his genial disposition has made him one of the most popular young men of our neighborhood. The writer wishes the newly wedded pair a journey through life of unalloyed happiness and expresses the wish that henceforth they may be as "two lives with but a single thought; two hearts that beat as one.

**LOVE, George** – Oct. 15, 1909 M. J. – A marriage license was issued at the clerk's office yesterday to Mr. Geo. Love, of Prince William county, and Miss Maggie A. Morris, of Lousia county. The bride-elect gave her age as 14.

**LOVELESS, Blanche** – Jul. 23, 1909 M. J.– A marriage license was issued in Washington Monday to William Patterson and Blanche Loveless, both of Prince William.

**LOVELESS, Emma A.** - Dec. 7, 1906 M. J. – Miss Emma A. Loveless and Mr. John W. Keys, both of this county, were married on Wednesday last at the residence of the officiating minister, Rev. Robert Smith of this place.

**LOWE, Archie L.** – Jun. 17, 1910 M. J. – Mr. Archie L. Lowe and Miss Sadie Lee, both of this county, were married on Wednesday last, at the residence of the officiating minister, Rev. T. D. D. Clark, of this place.

**LOWE, Lillie** – Jul. 1, 1910 M. J. –Miss Lillie Lowe, daughter of Mr. M. C. Lowe, of Fayman, and Mr. Alvin English, of Stafford county, were married on Thursday last.

**LOWNDES, Ada Linton** – Oct. 1, 1909 M. J. – Cards have been received here, to the marriage of Miss Ada Linton Lowndes to Mr. Charles H. H. Thomas on the fourteenth of October, at St. Pauls Church, Washington, D.C.

**LUNSFORD, Annie M.** – Jan. 28, 1910 M. J. – Mr. Guilford Money, of Quantico, and Miss Annie M. Lunsford, of Stafford Court House, were married Wednesday in Washington.

**LUTTRELL, David Harris** – Nov. 18, 1910 M. J. – LOUDOUN - Cards have been issued announcing the approaching married of Miss Katharine Braden Milton to Mr. David Harris Luttrell. This interesting event will take place in Epiphany Church, Washington, D.C., on Wednesday, Nov. 16, at 12 o'clock.—Blue Ridge News.

**LUTZ, Cora** – Oct. 28, 1910 M. J.- LOUDOUN – Cards have been issued for the marriage of Miss Cora Lutz, daughter of Mr. and Mrs. S. S. Lutz, of Springwood, near Leesburg, to Mr. J. R. H. Alexander, attorney and mayor of Leesburg. The ceremony will be performed at Springwood November 2.—Alex. Gazette.

**LYNCH, Leo A.** – Nov. 26, 1909 M. J. – Yesterday morning, at 10 o'clock, Miss Leo A. Lynch became the bride of Mr. George Chisolm, of Washington, at the home of the bride on Centre street. Father Patrick performed the ceremony. The bridal party left on the twelve o'clock train for an extensive tour through the Southern states.

**LYNCH, Margaret Ellen** - Feb. 15, 1907 M. J. – Miss Margaret Ellen Lynch, daughter of Mrs. Martin Lynch of this place, and Mr. Peyton Neylon of Washington, formerly of Wellington, were married on Tuesday last.

**LYNCH, W. E.** - Mar. 15, 1907 M. J. –Mrs. May Noonan announces the approaching marriage of her daughter, Mary Gertrude to Mr. W. E. Lynch of Manassas, Va. The wedding will take place Wednesday, April 3 at St. Mary Catholic Church, Patton, Pa.

**LYNN, Eunice L.** – Oct. 1, 1909 M. J. – Marriage licenses were issued at the Clerk's office this week to Henry B. Wingfield, of Hanover county, and Miss Eunice L. Lynn, of Prince William county, and to Jacob C. Vogle, of Pennsylvania, and Miss Mary E. Rollins, of Prince William county.

**LYNN, Eunice Lucille** – Oct. 8, 1909 M. J. –Mr. W. S. Lynn's home was the scene of a very pretty wedding on Wednesday of last week when his daughter, Miss Eunice Lucille and Mr. H. B. Wingfield, of Richmond, were united in marriage by Rev. Mr. Leighton, pastor of Broad Street church, Richmond, of which the groom was a member.

The bride was becomingly attired in cream Lansdowne, made princess. She carried a shower bouquet of bride's roses and lilies of the valley and was attended by her sister, Miss Lois Lynn, who acted as flower girl during the ring ceremony. Among the out of town guests were Mrs. L. A. Clarke, Mrs. Aubrey Clarke, Mr. J. W. Gregg and wife, Mr. Wallace Gregg and wife, of Washington; Mrs. H. Clay Lynn and Mr. James Wingfield and mother, of Richmond.

Mr. and Mrs. Wingfield have gone on an extended bridal trip to New York, Niagara Falls and Canada, and will be at home to their friends after November 1, at their future residence on Broad street, Richmond. The presents were handsome and numerous.

**LYNN, Mary Elizabeth** – Jul. 2, 1909 M. J. – LOUDOUN – Major B. W. Lynn has announced the engagement of his youngest daughter, Miss Mary Elizabeth Lynn, to Mr. Ballard Preston Boulware, of Richmond, Va. The Richmond Times Dispatch of Sunday contained a portrait of Miss Lynn, and in referring to the announcement says: "Miss Lynn is a charming type of a Virginia girl, and the announcement of her engagement to Mr. Boulware will be of wide interest."—Enterprise

**LYNN, Pearl** – Jun. 11, 1909 M. J. – Miss Pearl Lynn, of Prince William, Va., and Ernest A. Thompson, of Maryland, were married at Rockville, Md., Thursday, June 3, by Rev. W. D. Keene.

**LYNN, Sallie** - Jan.18, 1907 M. J.- Mr. Landy Suthard, living near Limstrong and Miss Sallie Lynn of Independent Hill were married last week.

**MACON, J. Conway** – Jun. 17, 1910 M. J. – CULPEPER – Hon. and Mrs. C. C. Taliaferro, of Orange, have issued cards for the marriage of their daughter, Miss Francis Armistead Taliaferro, to Mr. J. Conway Macon, formerly of Orange, now of Pittsburg. The ceremony will take place at St. Thomas Episcopal church, at Orange, on the evening of Wednesday, June 22nd, at 8:30 o'clock.

**MACONNAUGHEY, Samuel S.** – Feb. 28, 1896 M. G. - On Wednesday Mr. Samuel S. Maconnaughey and Miss Susan E Skinner, of Hoadley neighborhood, came to this place and were married by Rev. Robert Smith at his residence. The bridal couple was accompanied by the bride's mother and the groom's brother.

**MADDOX, Charles H.** – Feb. 18, 1910 M. J. – Mr. Charles H. Maddox and Miss Edna M. Morgan, of lower Prince William, were married in Washington City on Wednesday of this week by Rev. J. B. McLaughlin.

**MADDOX, Julia M. D.** – Feb. 15, 1907 M.J. – From the Alexandria Gazette of Saturday. On Wednesday afternoon Pemmie Tim Cross of Manassas and Miss Julia M. D. Maddox of Washington, went to Rockville, Md., after obtaining a marriage license went to the Catholic church rectory, where they met Rev. Father Rosensteel of Forest Glen. Father Rosensteel told the young couple that he could not marry them because they did not have any letter of identification from the home parish of either.

The couple left, stating that they would get such letters and return as soon as possible.

**MADDOX, Nellie Rae** - Oct. 26, 1906 M. J. – Married at Leonardtown, Md., Tuesday, Oct. 23, Miss Nellie Rae Maddox of this place to Mr. Robert M. Bailey.

**MADDOX, Nellie Rae** – Nov. 9, 1906 M. J. – From the St. Mary's (MD.) Gazette. A quiet marriage took place Tuesday evening last at the rectory of the M. E. Church, near Leonardtown, the contracting parties being Miss Nellie Rae Maddox of Manassas and Mr. Robt. M Bailey of Kinsale, Va., the Rev. H. R. Miller officiating.

The groom is a prominent and successful business man of Kinsale, and the bride is one of Prince William's most charming and popular belles.

After the marriage, a reception was held at Moore's Hotel, where many of Mr. Bailey's St. Mary's friends had the pleasure of meeting his charming bride.

The happy couple left here Wednesday morning for Kinsale, their future home.

Our best wishes for a long and happy married life.

From the Northern Neck News.

Mr. Robert Bailey's large circle of friends here most cordially congratulate him on his marriage and wish for him and his fair bride all that is best in this life and the next. Mrs. Bailey is a sister of Mrs. Dr. Hammond and from Manassas, Prince William county.

**MAGILL, John Randolph** – Oct. 22, 1909 M. J. – FAUQUIER – "Denton," the home of Miss Rosa Roszel, at The Plains, was the scene of her marriage to Mr. John Randolph Magill. The ceremony was followed by a reception and dance.

**MARCHER, John E.** – Feb. 28, 1896 M.G. - A marriage license was issued in Washington during the first of the week to John E. Marcher, of Alexandria, and Grace F. Sanbourn, of Occoquan.

**MARLOW, Frances Edwards** – Jun. 11, 1909 M. J. – LOUDOUN – Miss Frances Edwards Marlow, daughter of Mrs. Marlow and the late Edward Grandison Marlow, and Edward Franklin Conklin, of Washington, were married Tuesday in St. James' Episcopal Church, Leesburg, by Rev. William H. Burkhardt.—Alex. Gazette.

**MARSTELLER, Monnie Elizabeth** – Jul. 30, 1909 – Mr. Coleman Cockerille, of Washington, and Miss Monnie Elizabeth Marsteller, daughter of Mr. S. A. Marsteller, of this county, were married Monday afternoon of last week at Rockville, Md., by Rev. Dr. Packard in the presence of an aunt of the bride and a few friends. After the ceremony they left for a wedding trip, which will include visits to Niagara, Toronto, New York and Atlantic City. On their return they will reside at 1364 Kenyon street, N. W., Washington.

**MARSTON, Letitia Marshall** – Sept. 17, 1909 M. J. – Mr. D. S. White and Mrs. Letitia Marshall Marston, both of Washington, were quietly married last Saturday evening at the home of Mrs. Marston's mother, Mrs. Marshall, on West street. Rev. W. T. Gover performed the ceremony. Only a few friends of the family were present.

**MARTIN, Gertrude** – Jan. 28, 1910 M. J. – CULPEPER – Miss Gertrude Martin, of Stevensburg, Va., and Mr. Harry W. Hopewell, of Mount Solon, Augusta county, Va. were married Jan. 13 at Mount Solon. The bride is the principal of a school at Mossy Creek Augusta county.—Exponent, Jan. 21.

**MARTIN, William M.** – Nov. 18, 1910 M. J. – One of the most interesting weddings in the history of Fairfax county occurred on Tuesday last at the home of Mr. Pickton Thomas, near Fairfax Courthouse, when his sister, Mrs. Bettie Ferguson, became the bride of Mr. William M. Martin, of Fauquier.

The groom, who owned up to the advanced age of eighty, and who gave his bride's as the same, is the only surviving member of the jury which served on the famous John Brown trial previous to the Civil War.

Promptly at 2 o'clock the aged couple, preceded by two charming little flower girls, entered the beautifully decorated room, where the impressive ceremony was performed by Eld. J. N. Badger, of Manassas. The bride, who looked almost girlish and shy, wore a dress of black cloth and carried a bunch of white chrysanthemums.

Following the ceremony a sumptuous wedding dinner was served, shortly after which the happy couple left for their future home a few yards distant where the bride had lived all alone for a number of years. Their many friends wish them much happiness in the remaining years of their life. Quite a number of relations and friends were present, among whom were Elder J. N. Badger and wife and Mrs. B. J. Holden, of Manassas, Va.

**MARTINS, C. J.** – Jan. 25, 1907 M. J. – HONEYMOON IN JAIL – A special from Fredericksburg to the Washington Post, last Monday, says C. J. Martins of this city, who says he was married in Washington Saturday to Miss Mattie Lee Abel of Quantico arrived here Saturday night with his bride. Today he was arrested, charged with larceny of clothing from the Virginia Clothing House, where until recently he was employed.

Mayor Wallace fined him $25 and cost. Lacking funds, Martins went to jail for ninety days. Subsequently the bride paid the fine.

**MASON, Mary** – Dec. 9, 1910 M. J. – On Thursday night, of last week, as the guests were gathering at The Prince William Hotel to take part in the dance to be given under the auspices of The Manassas Orchestra, a telegram was received by Mr. Lucas, proprietor to the hotelry, requested that he have a minister on hand upon the arrival of train No. 44 due at Manassas 6:35 o'clock.

There were no further details, but Mr. Lucas, inferring that a marriage was on hand rang up Dr. Hervin U. Roop, of Eastern College, and asked him to officiate in the prospective wedding.

Upon the arrival of the train Dr. William J. Crittenden, of Orange, accompanied by Miss Mary Mason, repaired at once to the hotel parlor where they were quietly married. After taking supper, and receiving the congratulations of the host and others, the happy couple boarded the 8:10 o'clock train for Washington and Baltimore.

**MATEER, C. R.** – Dec. 3, 1909 M. J. – FAIRFAX – Miss Daisie Wood, daughter of Mrs. H. V. Wood, of Fort Myer Heights, and Mr. C. R. Mateer, of Colvin Run, were married in Brown's Chapel Wednesday, Nov. 17, by The Rev. C. H. Wagner, of Herndon.

**MATTHEW, Laura.** – Jun. 8, 1906 M. J. - (Received last week too late for publication). A simple but very pretty wedding was solemnized yesterday morning, May 31, at the Matthew farm, near Stone house P. O., when Laura, youngest daughter of Mrs. Matthew, was joined in marriage to Mr. L. J. Moncrief of the U. S. A.

The attractive and happy young couple left for their future home in Georgia last night, where Mr. Moncrief expects soon to serve the government in a civil capacity.

It is worthy of mention that this wedding dated its beginning from the military invasion of our peaceful county during the maneuvers of 1904. Mr. Moncrief was stationed as a guard over the home of this then unknown bride. His guard soon changed to regard and now he is guardian for good, Better the arrow of cupid than the sword of Mars.

May length of day and joy of heart attend them.

**MATTHEWS, Arabella D.** – May 20, 1910 M. J. – Miss Arabella D. Matthews, daughter of Charles B. Matthews, of Aldie, and Mr. Fenton L. Piggott, of Lincoln, were married Saturday at the home of the bride by Rev. J. N. Badger, of Manassas.

**MATTHEWS, Benjamin F.** – Apr. 22, 1910 M. J. – Mr. Benjamin F. Matthews and Miss Irva Anderson, both of upper Prince William, were married Wednesday in the Baptist parsonage by Rev. T. D. D. Clark.

**MATTHEWS, Eva May** – Nov. 18, 1910 M. J. – LOUDOUN – A marriage license was issued in Leesburg on Tuesday of last week to Mr. Benjamin B. Hutchison and Miss Eva May Matthews, both of Loudoun. They were married by Rev. Stuart A. Gibson, Tuesday.

**MATTHEWS, Mary Sydnie** – Oct. 1, 1909 M. J.- The marriage of Mr. John Goldsborough White, formerly of Haymarket, now of El Paso, Texas, to Miss Mary Sydnie Matthews, of Van Buren, Arkansas, is announced to take place at the home of the bride, on the sixth of October. Mr. White has the sincere congratulations of many friends here.

**MAYHUGH, Garnett T.** – Oct. 21, 1910 M. J. –FAIRFAX – Miss Elizabeth Virginia Bayliss and Mr. Garnett T. Mayhugh, of Fairfax county, were married in Rockville Saturday.

**MAYHUGH, Mamie** – Jun. 8, 1906 M. J. - On the afternoon of Tuesday, June 5, 1906, there was a tastefully conducted marriage service celebrated at the beautiful home of the officiating minister, Rev. A. B. Carrington of Greenwich, Va.

The contracting parties were Miss Mamie Mayhugh, daughter of Mr. L. Mayhugh of Greenwich and Mr. Edward Bell of Washington, D. C.

Immediately after the ceremony the company was invited into the handsomely arranged dining room by Mrs. Carrington where light refreshments were served.

Beautiful flowers everywhere and a very handsomely attired bride and groom with a numerous following of pretty girls and admiring beaux helped to make the occasion very impressive.

The happy couple left on the evening train for Washington City, there future home.

**MAYHUGH, Noah** – Dec. 30, 1910 M. J. – Mr. Noah Mayhugh and Miss Maude D. Ellis, daughter of Mr. and Mrs. Jas. B. Ellis, of Gainesville, were married at the home of the bride's parents, on $21^{st}$ instant, the Rev. Homer Welsh, pastor of the Gainesville M. E. church, officiating. Miss Grace Ellis was maid of honor and Mr. James V. Ellis, of Washington, was best man. Miss Mandy Ellis and Mr. Bruce Sinclair were waiters. The ceremony was performed in the presence of a large company of relatives and friends.

The parlor was decorated beautifully with evergreens. The bride was gowned in a princess of white silk. After the wedding ceremony a sumptuous supper was served. Mr. and Mrs. Mayhugh are well known residents of Gainesville, and their numerous friends wish them much happiness and success in life.

**MCCLAREN, Nellie Gerrald** – Sept. 23, 1910 M. J. – FAUQUIER – A quiet, but pretty wedding took place Wednesday evening, September $7^{th}$, at the home of Mr. Le Blond Burdett, In Tacoma Park, D.C., when Miss Nellie Gerrald McClaren and Mr. Cleighton Addison Triplett, of Rectortown, Va., were married.

**MCCLOSKY, William C.** – Dec. 9, 1910 M. J. – Mr. William C. McClosky and Miss Lucy Margaret Muddiman, of Washington, were married at the home of the bride's sister, Mrs. Walter S. Hixson, 1106 New York avenue, on Wednesday. Mrs. McClosky is a daughter of the late Henry Muddiman, of Manassas, and a niece of Messrs. Dave and Geo. Muddiman, of this place.

**MCCOY, W. E.** - Oct. 5, 1906 M. J. – Mr. W. E. McCoy and Miss Luna E. Crosby – both of this county were married last Wednesday at the residence of the bride's parents, near Bristow. Rev. J. K. Efird, officiating.

**MCDANIEL, Laura** – Oct. 15, 1909 M. J. – Cards are out announcing the engagement of Miss Laura McDaniel, of Haymarket, and Mr. Frank Kellog Raymond, of Washington.

**MCDONALD, Bessie** – Dec. 10, 1909 M. J. – FAUQUIER – Miss Bessie McDonald and Mr. Lavigious Payne, both of Fauquier, were married at the bride's home, near Lakota, on Nov. 1, Rev. Mr. Cleming, of Jeffersonton, officiating. They will make Fauquier county their future home.

**MCDONALD, William** – Jul. 9, 1909 M. J. – CULPEPER – Mr. William McDonald and Miss Ida Shepherd were married Tuesday afternoon at 7:30 o'clock by the Rev. C. E. Pleasants, at the Methodist parsonage on Belmont. The bride is a resident of Albermarle, her home being at Boyd's Tavern. Mr. McDonald is a painter from Philadelphia, but his home is now at Brandy Station, Va. The happy pair left this morning for a trip over the C. & O.—Exponent, July 2.

**MCGILL, John** – Aug. 13, 1909 M. J. – FAUQUIER – The engagement of Mr. John McGill to Miss Rosalie Roszel, both of this neighborhood, has lately been announced. The date of the marriage is not yet known. This is the season's fifth engagement, of which at least one of the interested parties lives in this community. The other four are: Miss Francis Fleming to Mr. Henley Carter, of Mt. Jackson, Miss Delia Slaughter to Dr. Selby, of Warrenton, Mr. J. W. Slaughter to Mr. Spencer, of Philadelphia, and Dr. Richard Mason to Miss Heath, of Washington, D. C.

**MCGLONE, Rosa** – Oct. 29, 1909 M. J. – The marriage is announced of Miss Rose McGlone, formerly of Baltimore, and Mr. Thos. S. Meredith, the well known citizen of Gainesville, at the Catholic church of St. Joan Baptiste in East eighty-sixth street, last Saturday afternoon. The ceremony was performed by Rev. A. Litellier in the presence of a few witnesses, including the bride's bothers, Messrs. John J. McGlone, secretary of the Atlantic Transport Line; I.V. McGlone, secretary to Mr. Thomas F. Ryan and George A. McGlone.

The bride is a daughter of Mrs. Elizabeth McGlone, now of Jefferson county, W. Va. Mr. Meredith is a brother of the late Congressman Meredith, of the eighth district, and of Dr. J. C. Meredith, of Manassas. The couple will make their home in Gainesville.

**MCINTOSH, Charles Brower** – Oct. 26, 1906 M. J.- Married, Wednesday, Oct. 17, at Ewell Chapel, Rev. Cary Gamble officiating,

Mr. Chas. Brower McIntosh to Miss Minerva Gray, eldest daughter of Mr. Turner Gray, of Fauquier. A beautiful wedding supper was served them at Mr. Peter Polen's.

**MCINTOSH, Frank W.** – Jun. 25, 1909 M. J. – ORANGE – Cards are out announcing the approaching marriage of Miss Virginia Irving, daughter of Mrs. Katherine M. Walker, to Mr. Frank W. McIntosh on Tuesday evening, June 29, at the bride's home in Farmville. Mr. McIntosh, who is one of Orange's young men, has for sometime been chief clerk at White's drug store at Farmville.— Review.

**MCINTYRE, Louise M.** – Jun. 22, 1906 M. J. - Failing to overcome the objection of her parents, who, she said, had selected another man to be her husband, Miss Louisa M. McIntyre of Warrenton eloped to Washington Tuesday with William Armstrong, jr., of Norfolk, and the couple were married in the forenoon by Rev. J. B. McLaughlin, in the latter's office in the Columbian building, on Fifth street northwest. The bridegroom is a student in the Bethel Military Academy, near Warrenton, and it was there he made the acquaintance of the young lady who yesterday became his bride.

To the marriage license clerk at the city hall both of the parties gave their age as 22 years. The young lady is a daughter of Major McIntyre, a well-known resident of Warrenton. When the ceremony was over she told the clergyman that her parents objected to the marriage because they had decided upon another man for her husband, but that she had made up her mind not to marry a man she did not love. Mr. and Mrs. Armstrong left Washington yesterday afternoon for Norfolk.

**MCLEAN, Lousie** – Aug. 10, 1906 M. J. - Simon Asburn Smith of Philadelphia and Miss Louise McLean of Washington were married on the 5$^{th}$ day of May last, at Baltimore, the Rev. Dr. David T. Neely officiating.

The bride is a daughter of J. W. McLean of Neverlet, Va., and a grand-daughter of the late Maj. Wilmer McLean at whose house the surrender of Lee to Grant took place and the papers were drawn up and signed which terminated the civil war.

Mr. Smith is a son of the late Capt. Ad. E. Smith, Sixty-second Regiment, Pennsylvania volunteers, who served with distinction under Col. Sam Black; also is a brother of Mrs. G. W. Lynch of Petworth, D. C. Mr. And Mrs. Smith are in Erie, Pa., at present where they expect to pass the summer.

**MCLEAREN, Owen** – Nov. 4, 1910 M. J. – FAUQUIER – Mr. Owen McLearen and Miss Lera Bodine were married in Washington on the 15th, landing in Catlett Sunday to be greeted by a shower of rice and many good wishes. We wish the young couple good luck and many happy years and we expect to hear more bells of the same kind in the near future.—Virginian.

**MCLINN, Ina** – Mar. 22, 1907 M. J. – Mr. D. D. Baker, son of Mr. C. W. Baker of Orlando and Miss Ina McLinn of Loudoun were married in Washington on Thursday of last week.

**MCMICHAEL, Mae** – Aug. 20, 1909 M. J. – Miss Mae McMichael and Mr. John Nathaniel House were married on Thursday last.

**MCQUINN, George** – Nov. 12, 1909 M. J. – Mr. and Mrs. Wilson Decatur, of Stafford county, announce the approaching marriage of their daughter, Miss Annie E. Decatur, to Geo. McQuinn, of Washington. The ceremony will take place on Wednesday, Nov. 10, at Salem M. E. church, 3:30 p. m.

**MEADE, Elizabeth** – Sept. 16, 1910 M. J. – Dr. and Mrs. Starkweather entertained on Friday last in honor of Miss Elizabeth Meade, who was married to Rev. Chas. W. Sydnor, of the Southern Diocese, on September 1st at Pohick church.

**MEETZE, Manton** – Aug. 6, 1909 M. J.– Mr. Manton Meetze, of Bristow, and Miss Fannie Taylor, of Zulla, Fauquier county, were married yesterday in Washington.

**MERCHANT, Lula McLain** –Dec. 20, 1907 M. J. – Miss Lula McLain Merchant of this place, was married on Friday last to Mr. R. L. Groff of Washington.

**MEREDITH, Thomas S.** – Oct. 29, 1909 M. J. – The marriage is announced of Miss Rose McGlone, formerly of Baltimore, and Mr. Thos. S. Meredith, the well known citizen of Gainesville, at the Catholic church of St. Joan Baptiste in East eighty-sixth street, last Saturday afternoon. The ceremony was performed by Rev. A. Litellier in the presence of a few witnesses, including the bride's bothers, Messrs. John J. McGlone, secretary of the Atlantic Transport Line;I.V. McGlone, secretary to Mr. Thomas F. Ryan and George A. McGlone.

The bride is a daughter of Mrs. Elizabeth McGlone, now of Jefferson county, W. Va. Mr. Meredith is a brother of the late Congressman Meredith, of the eighth district, and of Dr. J. C. Meredith, of Manassas. The couple will make their home in Gainesville.

**MERTZ, Amelia** – Nov. 5, 1909 M. J. – Miss Amelia Mertz, daughter of Mr. and Mrs. J. A. Mertz, of Nokesville, became the bride of Mr. Frederick Montague, of Jefferson, South Dakota, in Seattle, Washington, on October 23. The couple left on their wedding trip to Vancouver, British Columbia. They expect to visit Virginia in a short while.

**METZ, Thomas A.** – Feb. 25, 1910 M. J. – Mr. Thomas A. Metz, of Manassas, and Miss Nannie M. Lee, of Herndon, were married in Washington Wednesday of this week, Rev. A. H. Thompson performing the ceremony.

**MILLS, Monk** - Jan. 4, 1907 M. J. – Mr. Monk Mills and Miss Fannie Davis, daughter of Mr. Richard Davis, both of lower Prince William, were married on Wednesday last.

**MILLS, Myrtle** - Dec. 28, 1906 M. J. – Mr. Lucien Davis and Miss Myrtle Mills, both of lower Prince William, were married on Monday last, Elder Smoot officiating.

**CORRECTION** – Jan. 4, 1907 - The announcements of two weddings were given us last Friday morning , just before going to press, and in some way the names were gotten wrong.

Mr. Lucien Fairfax (not Davis) and Miss Myrtle Mills, daughter of Mr. Richard Mills, were married on the 24$^{th}$, Elder Smoot officiating.

**MILTON, Katharine Braden** – Nov. 18, 1910 M. J. – LOUDOUN - Cards have been issued announcing the approaching married of Miss Katharine Braden Milton to Mr. David Harris Luttrell. This interesting event will take place in Epiphany Church, Washington, D.C., on Wednesday, Nov. 16, at 12 o'clock.—Blue Ridge News.

**MOFFETT, Irma M.** – Jul. 29, 1910 M. J. – LOUDOUN – A marriage license was issued in Washington on Thursday of last week to Mr. George H. Shryock, of Ashburn, and Miss Irma M. Moffett, of Arcola.

**MONCRIEF, L. J.** – Jun. 8, 1906 M. J. - (Received last week too late for publication). A simple but very pretty wedding was solemnized yesterday morning, May 31, at the Matthew farm, near Stone house P. O., when Laura, youngest daughter of Mrs. Matthew, was joined in marriage to Mr. L. J. Moncrief of the U. S. A.

The attractive and happy young couple left for their future home in Georgia last night, where Mr. Moncrief expects soon to serve the government in a civil capacity.

It is worthy of mention that this wedding dated its beginning from the military invasion of our peaceful county during the maneuvers of 1904. Mr. Moncrief was stationed as a guard over the home of this then unknown bride. His guard soon changed to regard and now he is guardian for good, Better the arrow of cupid than the sword of Mars.

May length of day and joy of heart attend them.

**MONEY, Guilford** – Jan. 28, 1910 M. J. – Mr. Guilford Money, of Quantico, and Miss Annie M. Lunsford, of Stafford Court House, were married Wednesday in Washington.

**MONTAGUE, Frederick** – Nov. 5, 1909 M. J. – Miss Amelia Mertz, daughter of Mr. and Mrs. J. A. Mertz, of Nokesville, became the bride of Mr. Frederick Montague, of Jefferson, South Dakota, in Seattle, Washington, on October 23. The couple left on their wedding trip to Vancouver, British Columbia. They expect to visit Virginia in a short while.

**MOORE, Dr. Alexandria B.** – Jun. 25, 1909 M. J. – FAUQUIER – Dr. Alexandria B. Moore, of The Plains, Fauquier county, Va., a recent graduate of the University of Virginia, and Miss Carolyn Bell Watson, of Falls Church, Va., who graduated last year from the University Training School for Nurses, were quietly married at Christ Episcopal Church, Charlottesville, Sunday afternoon, June $20^{th}$, Rev. Harry B. Lee officiating. Only a few intimate friends were present.

**MORGAN, Edna M.** – Feb. 18, 1910 M. J. – Mr. Charles H. Maddox and Miss Edna M. Morgan, of lower Prince William, were married in Washington City on Wednesday of this week by Rev. J. B. McLaughlin.

**MORRIS, Maggie A.** – Oct. 15, 1909 M. J. – A marriage license was issued at the clerk's office yesterday to Mr. Geo. Love, of Prince William county, and Miss Maggie A. Morris, of Lousia county. The bride-elect gave her age as 14.

**MORRISON, Annie** – Dec. 3, 1909 M. J. – FAIRFAX – A marriage license was granted in Washington last week to Harvey J. Peabody and Annie Morrison, both of Fairfax county.—Herald, Nov. 26

**MOSES, Vera McFarland** – Dec. 3, 1909 M. J. – LOUDOUN – Mr. and Mrs. James Moses, of New York, have issued cards for the marriage of their daughter, Vera McFarland, to Mr. Edward Matthews Chamberlain, of Paeonian Springs, this county. The ceremony will take place in St. Thomas' church in New York, on Dec. 1. Miss Helen Meeks, of Paeonian, will be maid of honor.

**MUDDIMAN, Lucy Margaret** – Dec. 9, 1910 M. J. – Mr. William C. McClosky and Miss Lucy Margaret Muddiman, of Washington, were married at the home of the bride's sister, Mrs. Walter S. Hixson, 1106 New York avenue, on Wednesday. Mrs. McClosky is a daughter of the late Henry Muddiman, of Manassas, and a niece of Messrs. Dave and Geo. Muddiman, of this place.

**MUNDAY, Ernest L.** – Dec. 31, 1909 M. J. – LOUDOUN – The announcement is made of the marriage of Mr. Ernest L. Munday, of Waxpool, and Miss Lulu A. Wynkoop, of Round Hill, Va., which took place at the residence of Mr. and Mrs. Lucius H. Thadew, 2213 M. St., N. W. Washington, D.C., at noon on Saturday. The ceremony was performed by the Rev. G. W. Popkins, of Waxpool, Va., in the presence of a few intimate friends of the contracting parties, after which the happy couple left for their future home, Ashburn Loudoun county, where they will be pleased to receive their many friends.—Mirror, Dec. 17.

**MURPHY, Miss** – Aug. 19, 1910 M. J. – Mr. Grover C. Keys, of lower Prince William, and Miss Murphy, of Minnieville were married yesterday.

**MYERS, Genevieve** – Jul. 30, 1909 M.J. – LOUDOUN – Miss Genevieve Myers and Mr. Elmer L. Beales, of Hamilton, this county, were married at the residence of the bride in that town, on Wednesday evening, Rev. S. V. Hildebrand officiating.—News, July 22.

**MYERS, Howard** – Jun. 4, 1909 M. J. – FAIRFAX – Elder and Mrs. I. M. Neff announce the marriage of their daughter, Miss Mary

Elizabeth, to Mr. Howard Myers, at Fairfax, Monday April 26$^{th}$, 1909 – Herald.

**NALLS, Maud** – Dec. 21, 1906 M. J. – A marriage license was granted on Saturday last to Mr. Norman Brady and Miss Maud Nalls, both of this county.

**NASH, Emily** – Jul. 10, 1896 M. G. – A marriage license was recently issued in Washington to Daniel Newman and Emily Nash, both of Accotink.

**NEFF, Mary Elizabeth** – Jun. 4, 1909 M. J. – FAIRFAX – Elder and Mrs. I. M. Neff announce the marriage of their daughter, Miss Mary Elizabeth, to Mr. Howard Myers, at Fairfax, Monday April 26$^{th}$, 1909 –Herald.

**NEIL, Walter** – Oct. 22, 1909 M. J.– An attractive wedding took place at Hotel Alton, the contracting parties being Miss Eva Ledman and Mr. Walter Neil, of Freestone, the postmaster at that place. The bride looked beautiful, being gowned in Persian taffeta. She carried a bouquet of white roses. The ceremony was performed by the pastor of the M. E. church South, Rev. C. L. Sydenstricker. Mr. and Mrs. Neil left on the 11 o'clock train for Washington and Baltimore. They will be at home to their friends the latter part of October. Their presents were numerous and handsome, both of the contracting parties being very popular in church circles.

**NELSON, Birdie M.** – May 27, 1910 M. J. – A marriage license was issued on Saturday to Mr. Roy R. Pote and Miss Birdie M. Nelson, both of this county. Rev. A.Conner was the officiating minister.

**NELSON, Caroline Peyton** – Jan. 28, 1910 M. J. – FAUQUIER – The engagement of Miss Caroline Peyton Nelson, daughter of Mrs. Geo. W. Nelson, to Mr. John Britton, on Trenton, N. J., has been announced; the wedding to take place in the early summer.

**NELSON, Charles Emory** – Jul. 1, 1910 M. J. – LOUDOUN – The marriage of Miss Bertha Alice Bridges, daughter, of Mr. and Mrs. Benjamin Bridges, to Mr. Charles Emory Nelson, was beautifully solemnized at the residence of the bride's parents, in Washington, at 7:30 o'clock Wednesday evening.

**NELSON, Joseph** – Mar. 18, 1910 M. J. – It may be of interest to note that the Mrs. Delia F. Fair, who yesterday became the bride of Mr. Joseph Nelson, is the widow of the late Charles Fair, an account of whose tragic death is given on the first page of this issue. Mr. Nelson, her present husband, lost his last wife about five weeks ago.

**NELSON, Joseph** – Mar. 18, 1910 M. J. – Mr. Joseph Nelson and Mrs. Delia F. Fair, both of lower Prince William, were married yesterday at the Lutheran Parsonage by Rev. J. K. Efird.

**NELSON, Silas** – Dec. 3, 1909 M. J. – Marriage licenses were issued in Washington this week to Silas Nelson and Miss Grace Patterson both of Prince William and Willie C. Randall, of Merrifield, Va., and Miss Bertie I. Pearson, of Manassas.

**NESBIT, Edith** – Jun. 10, 1910 M. J. – FAUQUIER – On Wednesday, June 1st, at "Alwington," the palatial home of Mr. and Mrs. Scott Nesbit, Miss Edith Nesbit and Mr. Laz Noble, formerly of Indianapolis, but now a prominent business man of Chicago, were united in the holy bonds of matrimony.

**NEUFER, Anna J.** – Nov. 11, 1910 M. J. – A current issue of a Wilmington, De., paper contains the following interesting announcement; Rev. George L. Wolfe, pastor of the First Methodist Protestant Church, received a letter requesting him to announce the marriage he performed on August 17, last, when he united in wedlock at his residence, Abram M. C. Bubb, of Woodbridge, Va., and Miss Anna J. Neufer, of Prince William county, Virginia.

**NEWMAN, Daniel** – Jul. 10, 1896 M. G. - A marriage license was recently issued in Washington to Daniel Newman and Emily Nash, both of Accotink.

**NEWMAN, W. W.** – Jan. 28, 1910 M. J. – CULPEPER –W. W. Newman, of Viewtown, was married to Miss Blanche Jolliffe, of Culpeper, on Jan. 13, by Rev. E. W. Winfrey. The happy couple were the recipients of many pretty and useful presents.

**NEYLON, Peyton** - Feb. 15, 1907 M. J. – Miss Margaret Ellen Lynch, daughter of Mrs. Martin Lynch of this place, and Mr. Peyton Neylon of Washington, formerly of Wellington, were married on Tuesday last.

**NOBLE, Laz** – Jun. 10, 1910 M. J. – FAUQUIER – On Wednesday, June 1st, at "Alwington," the palatial home of Mr. and Mrs. Scott Nesbit, Miss Edith Nesbit and Mr. Laz Noble, formerly of Indianapolis, but now a prominent business man of Chicago, were united in the holy bonds of matrimony.

**NOLAN, Nicholas** – Jan. 14, 1910 M. J. – FAUQUIER –Miss Hazel Gray, youngest daughter of Mr. and Mrs. Tom Gray, and Mr. Nicholas Nolan, both of Meetze, Va., were married at the Methodist parsonage in Warrenton, Wednesday, Dec. 29, Rev. J. L. Kibler, offciating. The bride wore a London smoke-colored suit, lace waist and a large white picture hat and veil and made a most charming bride. Mr. Nolan is a popular and industrious young man of this county. Their many friends wish them both a happy married life.—Democrat, Jan. 8

**NOONAN, Mary Gertrude** - Mar. 15, 1907 M. J. – Mrs. May Noonan announces the approaching marriage of her daughter, Mary Gertrude to Mr. W. E. Lynch of Manassas, Va. The wedding will take place Wednesday, April 3 at St. Mary Catholic Church, Patton, Pa.

**O'NEIL, John K.** – Oct. 8, 1909 M. J.- Mr. John K. O'Neil, son of Mr. and Mrs. Dennis O'Neil, and Miss Ora Dickerson, of Burnleys, Va., were married last week at the home of the bride.

**ORRISON, Agnes Elizabeth** – Oct. 29, 1909 M. J. – LOUDOUN – Mr. and Mrs. W. W. Orrison, of Ashburn, have issued cards for the marriage of their daughter, Agnes Elizabeth, to Dr. Sandford Williams French, of New York. The wedding will take place in the Presbyterian church, at Ashburn, on Wednesday, Oct. 27, at 2 o'clock.

**ORRISON, Agnes** – Nov. 5, 1909 M. J. – LOUDOUN – Miss Agnes Elizabeth Orrison, daughter of Mr. and Mrs. W. W. Orrison, of Ashburn, Loudoun county, and Dr. Sanford William French, of New York city, were married Wednesday afternoon in the Presbyterian church at Ashburn, by Rev. Dr. Nelms, of the church of the Ascension. The bride wore a handsome gown of messaline satin, draped princess style, trimmed with lace and pearls, and a tulle veil fastened with orange blossoms. She was given away by her brother, Mr. Foster Orrison, and her matron of honor was Mrs. Harry Rider Sanford and the bridesmaid Miss Ruby Orrison. The ushers were Messrs. William A. Woodruff, of New York, and Lieut. Charles A. Fair, U. S. N., of

Washington. After a reception at the bride's home Doctor and Mrs. French left for an extended tour North. Returning they will reside in Washington.—Mirror, Oct. 29.

**OWEN, Janie** – Sept. 24, 1909 M. J. – Mrs. J. A. Carter and Miss Ada Carter have returned home after a pleasant visit to Maryland and Washington where they attended the marriage of their cousin, Miss Janie Owen to Orrin K. Hill, a prominent electrician of Brooklyn, N.Y. the bride was attended by her sister, Miss Carrie Owen.

**PAINTER, Luther Lee** – Mar. 18, 1910 M. J. – On Tuesday at the Methodist Parsonage Rev. W. T. Gover officiated at the marriage of Miss Lettie May Hoffman, of Warren county, a sister of Mrs. T. F. Coleman, of Manassas, to Mr. Luther Lee Painter, of Shenandoah county.

**PANCOAST, Lousie E.**– Jun. 11, 1909 – M. J. – LOUDOUN – Mr. Henry B. Taylor, of Lincoln, and Miss Lousie E. Pancoast, second daughter of Mr. and Mrs. Joseph H. Pancoast, were united in marriage at the home of the bride, near Silcott Springs, at 2:30 o'clock on Wednesday of last week, according to the impressive rites of the Society of Friends.

**PARTLOW, Wallace E.** – May 13, 1910 M. J. – Mr. Wallace E. Partlow and Miss Alidion Herndon, both of Prince William county, were married yesterday at the Lutheran parsonage by Rev. J. K. Efird, the pastor.

**PATTERSON, Anna** – Oct. 22, 1909 M. J. – A marriage license was issued in Washington on Oct. 13 to John T. Hale, of Dumfries, and Anna Patterson, of Prince William.

**PATTERSON, Anne** – Apr. 29, 1910 M. J. –Miss Anne Patterson, one of the most popular young ladies to visit this vicinity, is now the guest of Miss Jane DePauw. Her engagement to Mr. Rogers Woodhull, of Dayton, Ohio, is announced, the marriage to take place in the early autumn.

**PATTERSON, Bettie** – Feb. 4, 1910 M. J. – Mr. Jas. R. Chesher and Miss Bettie Patterson, both of Prince William county, were married in Washington Wednesday.

**PATTERSON, Grace** – Dec. 3, 1909 M. J. – Marriage licenses were issued in Washington this week to Silas Nelson and Miss Grace Patterson both of Prince William and Willie C. Randall, of Merrifield, Va., and Miss Bertie I. Pearson, of Manassas.

**PATTERSON, William** – Jul. 23, 1909 M. J.- A marriage license was issued in Washington Monday to William Patterson and Blanche Loveless, both of Prince William.

**PATTIE, Luther J.** – Dec. 21, 1906 M. J. – A marriage license was issued in Washington Wednesday to Mr. Luther J. Pattie and Miss Bertha J. Polen both of Catharpin, this county.

**PAYNE, Eliza F.** – Dec. 31, 1909 M. J. – LOUDOUN – A very pleasant marriage occurred at the parsonage, Saturday, Dec. 18, 1909, when Miss Eliza F. Payne became the bride of Mr. H. Gordon Tribby, Rev. D. L. Blakemore pronouncing the solemn words that made them man and wife. After the bridal trip to Washington and other points, the young couple will make their home in Hillsboro, this county.

**PAYNE, James** – Jul. 23, 1909 M. J. – Miss Edith Simpson and Mr. James Payne, both of Prince William, were married yesterday in Washington.

**PAYNE, Lavigious** – Dec. 10, 1909 M. J. – FAUQUIER – Miss Bessie McDonald and Mr. Lavigious Payne, both of Fauquier, were married at the bride's home, near Lakota, on Nov. 1, Rev. Mr. Cleming, of Jeffersonton, officiating. They will make Fauquier county their future home.

**PAYNE, Miss** – May 6, 1910 M. J. – The home of Mr. and Mrs. C. B. Holtzclaw was the scene of a very pretty wedding when Miss Payne, of Orlean, and Mr. Goode were married, Rev. Mr. Brad officiating.

**PAYNE, Robert A.** – Jan. 21, 1910 M. J. – Mr. Robt. A. Payne and Miss Virgie R. Whitmer were married yesterday afternoon at the home of Mr. Arthur Raymond, at Buckhall. Rev. H. S. Willey performing the ceremony.

**PAYNE, Roxie** – Apr. 8, 1910 M. J. – A marriage license was issued in the clerk's office Wednesday to Mr. Lucien Randall, of Stafford county, and Miss Roxie Payne, of Prince William.

**PAYNE, Sanford J.** – Jan. 14, 1910 M. J. – FAUQUIER – Miss Mary E. Bradford, of Warrenton, and Mr. Sanford J. Payne, of Flint Hill, Va., were married Dec. 29, 1909, at the home of Rev. V. H. Council, pastor of Orlean Baptist church. The bride wore a navy blue broadcloth gown. There were no attendants.

**PAYNE, W. W.** - Oct. 12, 1906 M. J. – Mr. W. W. Payne of Alexandria, formerly of this county, was married last week to Mrs. Price of Stafford county.

**PEABODY, Harvey J.** – Dec. 3, 1909 M. J. – FAIRFAX – A marriage license was granted in Washington last week to Harvey J. Peabody and Annie Morrison, both of Fairfax county.—Herald, Nov. 26

**PEACOCK, Florence** – Jan. 7, 1910 M. J. – LOUDOUN – Miss Florence Peacock, daughter of Mr. H. B. Peacock, of Wheatland, this county, and Mr. Millard Birdsall, son of Mr. Eli Birdsall, of Purcellville, were married at the bride's home by Rev. W. B. Dorsey, of the Methodist church last week. After a short bridal tour South they will reside near Purcellville.—Mirror, Dec. 31.

**PEARSON, Bertie I.** – Dec. 3, 1909 M. J. – Marriage licenses were issued in Washington this week to Silas Nelson and Miss Grace Patterson both of Prince William and Willie C. Randall, of Merrifield, Va., and Miss Bertie I. Pearson, of Manassas.

**PEARSON, Emma L.** – Oct. 8, 1909 M. J. – FAUQUIER – The wedding of Miss Emma L. Pearson to Mr. Robert Scott Wilson, both of this county, is announced to take place in the Baptist church at Marshall, Va., October $9^{th}$ at 6:15 p. m. No cards will be issued.— Democrat. Oct. 2.

**PEARSON, James H.** – Apr. 29, 1910 M. J. – Mr. James H. Pearson, of Belvoir, Fauquier county, and Miss Claude Ennis, daughter of Mr. Thos. E. Ennis, of near Buckhall were united in marriage Wednesday at the home of the bride's parents. Rev. J. F. Britton performed the ceremony, immediately after which the bride and groom, accompanied by the bride's sister, Miss Maud Ennis, left for Belvoir.

**PEARSON, Lelia** - Sept. 7, 1906 M. J. – Miss Lelia Pearson was married recently to Mr. John Riley both of this county. Rev. W. T. Wine officiating.

**PERRY, Elsie L.** – Dec. 17, 1909 M. J. – A marriage license was issued in Washington Tuesday to Alton A. Davis and Miss Elsie L. Perry, both of Prince William, and the young people were united in marriage by Rev. C. W. Whitmore.

**PERRY, Martha W.** – Oct. 12, 1906 M. J. – Mr. P. T. Weedon of Washington, formerly of this county, and Miss Martha W. Perry of Philadelphia were married on Tuesday last.

**PEYTON, Nanette** – Oct. 28, 1910 M. J. – FAUQUIER – Miss Nanette Peyton, daughter of Mr. and Mrs. Robt. Peyton, of "Edenburne," near The Plains, and Mr. W. Grafton, of Washington, were married on Wednesday, at the home of the bride.

**PIGGOTT, Fenton L.** – May 20, 1910 M. J. – Miss Arabella D. Matthews, daughter of Charles B. Matthews, of Aldie, and Mr. Fenton L. Piggott, of Lincoln, were married Saturday at the home of the bride by Rev. J. N. Badger, of Manassas.

**PITKINS, Janette** – Aug. 24, 1906 M. J. - Married at the Southern Methodist Parsonage this town, Sunday, Aug. 19th by Rev. Selwyn K. Cockrell, Miss Janette Pitkins and Mr. Restry Hottell.

**POLEN, Bertha J.** – Dec. 21, 1906 M. J. – A marriage license was issued in Washington Wednesday to Mr. Luther J. Pattie and Miss Bertha J. Polen both of Catharpin, this county.

**POLLEY, Jas. P. R.** – Dec. 21, 1906 M. J. – On Tuesday last a marriage license was granted Mr. Jas. P. R. Polley and Mrs. Martha Brandt, both of this county. The ceremony was performed by Rev. Dr. Hamner.

**POTE, Roy R.** – May 27, 1910 M. J. – A marriage license was issued on Saturday to Mr. Roy R. Pote and Miss Birdie M. Nelson, both of this county. Rev. A.Conner was the officiating minister.

**POWELL, Llewellyn** – Jun. 18, 1909 M. J. – ALEXANDRIA - The marriage of Miss Ruth Ashton, daughter of Mr. Horace Ashton, and Dr. Llewellyn Powell, both of this city, was solemnized at 11 o'clock Tuesday morning at Christ Episcopal Church, in the presence of a large gathering of friends and relatives. The ceremony was performed by Rev. William J. Morton, rector. The bride was unattended, and was attired in a dark gray traveling gown and green hat. The groom had for his best man, Dr. William Syme, of Washington. Those serving as ushers were William G. Chapman, William G. Leadbeater, D. Edgar Snowden, of Washington; John Thornton Ashton, brother of the groom.

**POWERS, Wadsworth T.** – Apr. 29, 1910 M. J. – A marriage license was issued in the clerk's office yesterday to Mr. Wadsworth T. Powers, of Bellfair Mills, Va., and Miss Mary E. Tulloss, daughter of Dr. W. R. Tulloss, of Haymarket. The marriage will take place on Saturday, May 7$^{th}$.

**POWERS, Wadsworth T.** – May 13, 1910 M. J. – A beautiful wedding was solemnized Saturday at noon at the home of Mrs. Annie Tulloss, in Fauquier county, when her granddaughter, Miss Mary E. Tulloss, daughter of Dr. W. R. Tulloss, of Haymarket, became the bride of Mr. Wadsworth T. Powers, of Stafford county.

The ceremony was performed by Rev. Dr. Shopoff in the presence of a number of friends and relatives. The parlor was beautifully decorated with cut flowers and potted plants. The bride entered on the arm of Mrs. R. W. Powers, as matron of honor, and was met at the altar by the groom and his best man, Mr. Ellis Perry, of Stafford county. The bride, who is one of Fauquier's most charming women, was becomingly attired in gray silk and carried brides-roses. Her matron of honor wore blue silk and carried pink roses.

After the ceremony a wedding dinner was enjoyed by the guests. The happy couple left immediately for Stafford where an elegant supper was given at the home of Mrs. Mary Powers, after which they left for their new home, carrying the best of wishes with them.

**PRICE, Fannie** – Nov. 25, 1910 M. J. – FAUQUIER – Rev. Stockton W. Cole, of Remington, and Miss Fannie Price were married Monday afternoon at 5 o'clock, at the residence of the bride's father, Hon. J. M. Price, of Bealeton. There were only the family and a few intimate friends present when Rev. T.P. Brown, pastor of the Bealeton Baptist church, united them in marriage. The bridal couple took the evening train for a short trip north, after which they will attend the

General Baptist Association at Roanoke and be back to their future home in Remington by the 1st of December or perhaps sooner. This is a marriage that will meet with the hearty approval of all that know the contracting parties. Miss Price is a young woman, who besides having her full share of womanly charms and graces, is such a splendid church worker, so talented as an organist and in all that will make her an ideal helpmate for a pastor, that Rev. Cole is to be congratulated. And Mr. Cole, who has charge of seven churches in Fauquier, Culpeper and Rappahannock is a Christian worker that deserves just such a wife. We can pay him no higher nor more deserved compliment.

**PRICE, Mrs.** - Oct. 12, 1906 M. J. – Mr. W. W. Payne of Alexandria, formerly of this county, was married last week to Mrs. Price of Stafford county.

**PRIEST, Edith G.** – Dec. 24, 1909 M. J. – The following marriage licenses were issued this week at the clerk's office: Monday, Lewis M. Swartz, Culpeper county, and Miss Pearl L. Kelley, Fauquier county, Chas. N. Davis and Miss Virgie Wolfe, both of Prince William; Tuesday, John F. Donovan, Rockingham county and Miss Florida V. Allison, Loudoun county; Wednesday, Aubrey Flynn, Fauquier county, and Miss Annie L. Thomas, Prince William county; Thursday, Wm. E. Beahm, Rappahannock county, and Miss Edith G. Priest, Fauquier county; Geo. Spinks, Fauquier county, and Miss Bessie Baggott, Prince William county.

**PRIEST, Edith G.** – Jan. 7, 1910 M. J. – At his resident on Christmas morning Rev. Dr. Hamner married Wm. E. Beahm of Washington, D.C., to Miss Edith G. Priest, of Prince William county. The young couple will reside in Washington, D. C.

**PULLIAM, Joseph A.** – Sept. 23, 1910 M. J. – FAUQUIER – Marriage licenses were issued in Washington on Thursday to the following Fauquier couples: Joseph B. Pulliam and Carolyn Spicer, both of Remington; Benjamin Gordon, of Markham, and India Chadwell, of Hume; Joseph A. Jeffries, of Warrenton, and Sallie Thompson, of Washington.

**PURCELL, Mamie** – Sept. 9, 1910 M. J. – The engagement of Miss Mamie Purcell, daughter of Capt. and Mrs. J. R. Purcell, to Mr. Wilmer Stradley, of Wilmington, De., has been announced. The wedding will take place early in October.

**PUTNAM, Ida B.** – Mar. 11, 1910 M. J. – A marriage license was issued in Washington yesterday to Mr. Jos. E. Gheen, of Prince William, and Miss Ida B. Putnam, of Culpeper county.

**RAINER, Lena** – May 10, 1907 M. J. – Mr. W. V. Brown and Mrs. Lena Rainer, both of Manassas, were married yesterday.

**RANDALL, J. I.** - Nov. 16, 1906 M. J. – Miss Essie Bell, daughter of Mr. G. W. Bell, was married on Wednesday last, at her father's home at Sinclair's Mill, to Mr. J. I. Randall of this place, Rev. S. K. Cockrell officiating.

**RANDALL, Lucien** – Apr. 8, 1910 M. J. – A marriage license was issued in the clerk's office Wednesday to Mr. Lucien Randall, of Stafford county, and Miss Roxie Payne, of Prince William.

**RANDALL, William J.** – Oct. 29, 1909 M. J.- Mr. Wm. J. Randall, of Wellington, and Miss Mamie Wenzer, of Fairfax county, were married last week in Washington.

**RANDALL, Willie C.** – Dec. 3, 1909 M. J. – Marriage licenses were issued in Washington this week to Silas Nelson and Miss Grace Patterson both of Prince William and Willie C. Randall, of Merrifield, Va., and Miss Bertie I. Pearson, of Manassas.

**RANDOLPH, Archibald Cary** – Jul. 16, 1909 M. J. – LOUDOUN – Mr. and Mrs. Richard Hunter Dulany, of Grafton Hall, have announced the engagement of their daughter, Miss Eva Randolph Dulany, to Dr. Archibald Cary Randolph, of Willwood.

**RANDOLPH, Archibald Cary** – Apr. 29, 1910 M. J. – At Grafton Hall, Fauquier county, at noon Tuesday, Miss Eva Randolph Dulany, daughter of Mr. and Mrs. Richard Hunter Dulany, of Grafton Hall, was married to Dr. Archibald Cary Randolph, of Baltimore, formerly of Clarke county. The bride is a very attractive girl, and has been for several seasons a favorite at Greenbrier White Sulphur Spring. These springs were formerly owned by her father and were sold a few months ago. She is a niece of Mrs. Robert Neville, of Washington. The pair will live in Baltimore.

**RATRIE, Alice Sophenia** – Feb. 18, 1910 M. J. – CULPEPER – Cards are out announcing the marriage of Miss Alice Sophenia Ratrie to Mr. Robert Caleb Stark, both of Culpeper county. The marriage took place on Monday, February the seventh, at "Liberty Hall," the home of the bride. Mrs. Stark is the youngest daughter of the late. H. H. Ratrie.

**RAYMOND, Frank Kellog** – Oct. 15, 1909 M. J. – Cards are out announcing the engagement of Miss Laura McDaniel, of Haymarket, and Mr. Frank Kellog Raymond, of Washington.

**REDMON, Sadie** - Apr. 5, 1907 M. J. – Married at the residence of the officiating minister, Rev. Robert Smith, on Friday last, Miss Sadie Redmon to Mr. William Warring—both of Prince William.

**REDMOND, Virginia** – Nov. 11, 1910 M. J. – LOUDOUN – Mr. Wm. Cornell, of Fairfax, and Miss Virginia Redmond, of Loudoun, were married in the parlors of the Leesburg Inn on Thursday, by Rev. J. H. Wiltshire.

**REEVES, Correne J.** – Dec. 24, 1909 M. J. – Miss Correne J. Reeves, daughter of Mr. Henry W. Reeves, of Prince William county, Va., and Dr. H. W. Acheson, one of the leading veterinaries of Washington, D.C. were married Wednesday, Dec. 22, at 7:30 p.m., at St. Andrew's church, Washington, Rev. George Calvert Carter officiating.

The bride was escorted by her brother, Mr. Courtney Reeves, and was tastefully gowned in white messaline silk and carried a bouquet of violets and lilies of the valley.

**REEVES, Eliza** – Dec. 3, 1909 M. J. – Mr. Joseph Gough and Miss Eliza Reeves, both of this county, were married in Manassas last week.

**REID, Anna Elise** – Feb. 4, 1910 M. J. – The marriage of Mr. Walter Beaumont Clarkson, of Philadelphia, son of Dr. H. M. Clarkson, of this town, to Miss Anna Elise Reid, took place on January the thirty-first in Washington, D. C., of which city the bride was a resident. The ceremony was performed by Rev. Robert Talbot.

**REID, Hezekiah** – Nov. 18, 1910 M. J. –A marriage license was issued Wednesday to Mr. Hezekiah Reid and Mrs. Media F. Bryant, of Hoadley.

**REID, Maggie** – Jul. 29, 1910 M. J. – The officiating minister, Rev. J. K. Efird, advises us that Mr. Harvey Thorpe and Miss Maggie

Reid were not married until July 26, four days after our announcement of the marriage. Just a little mistake in the date that was all. Shall we announce two others ahead of time?

**REMINGTON, Ralph Elwood** – Oct. 29, 1909 M. J. – ALEXANDRIA – Mr. Ralph Elwood Remington and Miss Mamie Lee Hume were quietly married at 6:30 o'clock last evening at the parsonage of the First Baptist church by the Rev. W. F. Watson. After the ceremony Mr. and Mrs. Remington left for an extended Southern tour. Upon their return they will reside at No. 117 south St. Asaph street.—Gazette, Oct. 23.

**RENNER, Mollie** – Nov. 22, 1901 M. J. - Married, at the Southern Methodist parsonage, in Manassas, Nov. 14, 1901, By Rev. W. G. Hammond, Mr. Nelson L. Ennis and Miss Mollie Renner, all of Prince William county, Va.

**RENO, James N.** – Feb. 4, 1910 M. J. – FAUQUIER – James N. Reno and Miss Maggie Cordelia Wines were married at the home of the bride's sister near Auburn on Thursday, Jan. 20th, 1910. Rev. David Campbell Mayers officiated. About twenty guests were present and an elaborate supper was served after the ceremony.

**REYNOLDS, Lelia** – Nov. 4, 1910 M. J. – FAIRFAX – Miss Lelia Reynolds, daughter of Mr. and Mrs. Francis H. Reynolds, of Fairfax county, and the Rev. Frederick Albert Ernest Warren, of Chase City, Va., were married in Christ Protestant Episcopal church, Alexandria, Wednesday afternoon, the rector, Rev. W. J. Morton, officiating. Rev. Mr. Warren is a native of England, and was ordained at the Episcopal Theological Seminary last June.

**RICE, Robert H.** – Nov. 4, 1910 M. J. – FAIRFAX – A marriage license was issued by the County Clerk on the 18th inst., to Robert H. Rice and Florance G. Heistand.—Herald.

**RIFFE, Elinor Sohnson** – Nov. 4, 1910 M. J.- The approaching marriage of Mr. Robert Raymond Woolfe, formerly of this place, to Miss Elinor Sohnson Riffe, of Hinton, W. Va., has been announced. The ceremony will take place November sixteenth. Mr. Woolfe's friends here wish him much happiness.

**RILEY, John** - Sept. 7, 1906 M. J. – Miss Lelia Pearson was married recently to Mr. John Riley both of this county. Rev. W. T. Wine officiating.

**RILEY, Laura** - Dec. 28, 1906 M. J.- Married, Dec. 23, at the home of the bride by Rev. J. K. Efird, Mr. Willie Cornwell and Miss Laura Riley, both of this county.

**RISON, Frances S.** – Apr. 22, 1910 M. J. – Mr. Quenton A. Carney and Miss Frances S. Rison, both of Dumfries, were married Tuesday in Washington.

**RITENOUR, Nettie E.** – Nov. 5, 1909 M. J. – A marriage license was issued at the clerk's office on Thursday, October 28, to Mr. Chas. E. Workman, of Rockingham county, and Miss Nettie E. Ritenour, of Fauquier county.

**RIXEY, Adalena Bettus** – Oct. 22, 1909 M. J.- CULPEPER –An approaching marriage that will prove very interesting to Culpeper is that of Miss Adalena Bettus Rixey to Mr. Gordon Livingston Todd. The cards are out and the marriage will take place in the chapel of the university at 6 o'clock on Tuesday, Oct. 26. Miss Rixey is well known in Culpeper as Miss Lena Rixey, eldest daughter of Mr. and Mrs. Rixey, formerly of Culpeper.

**RIXEY, Mary Barbour** – Jul. 8, 1910 M. J. – The engagement of Miss Mary Barbour Rixey, daughter of the late Hon. John F. Rixey, who represented the Eighth District in congress, to Dr. Robert F. Compton, is announced. The wedding will be celebrated at the home of the bride's mother near Charlottesville. Dr. Compton is a member of the medical faculty of the University of Virginia.

**RIXEY, Mary Barbour** – Oct. 28, 1910 M. J.- The marriage of Miss Mary Barbour Rixey, daughter of the late Congressman John F. Rixey and niece of Rear Admiral Rixey, to Dr. Robert F. Compton will take place on Tuesday, November $8^{th}$, at the home of Miss Rixey's mother, near Charlottesville. Dr. Compton is a member of the faculty of the University of Virginia.

**RIXEY,Mary Barbour** – Nov. 11, 1910 M. J. –Mrs. John F. Rixey, widow of the late Congressman Rixey, of the Eighth district, has issued cards for the wedding of her daughter, Miss Mary Barbour Rixey, to Dr. Robert French Compton, which is to take place on the afternoon of November 8, at "Gowan Lee," the home of Rixey, near Charlottesville.

**RIXEY, Sallie** - Jan. 11, 1907 M. J. – From the Alexandria Gazette. The marriage Tuesday of William A. Dearmont, the well known turf-man and steeplechase rider of White Post, Clarke county, and Miss Sallie Rixey, daughter of Hon. John F. Rixey, member of Congress from the Eight Virginia district, of Culpeper, was solemnized at 4:30 o'clock Tuesday at the Presbyterian manse at Strasburg, Rev. A. C. Link, officiating. The bride and groom took the 5 o'clock train on the Southern Railway for Washington, on their wedding trip. They are to make their home at "Dearmont Hall," in Clarke county.

The bride is well known in society in Virginia and Washington.

**CORRECTION-** Jan. 18, 1907 – The announcement of the marriage of Miss Sallie Rixey, in last week's JOURNAL from the Alexandria Gazette, stated that she was the daughter of Hon. John F. Rixey, member of Congress from the Eighth district. Miss Rixey is the daughter of Mr. Thomas P. Rixey a brother of the Congressman.

**ROBERTS, A. M.** – Sept. 16, 1910 M. J. – FAUQUIER – A pleasant surprise to all their friends was to learn on Friday that Mr. A. M. Roberts and Miss Eva Heflin, both of The Plains, had been married in Washington Thursday. They returned to Warrenton Saturday and drive to The Plains, which will hereafter be their home.—Virginian.

**ROBERTSON, Elizabeth M.** – Feb. 25, 1910 M. J. – Mr. John S. Strother, of Fauquier, and Miss Elizabeth M. Robertson, of this county, were married Wednesday in the Baptist parsonage by Rev. T. D. D. Clark. The young couple will reside in Washington.

**ROBERTSON, Everett P.** – Sept. 17, 1909 M. J. – Mr. Everett P. Robertson, of Bristow and Miss Hattie M. Herndon, of Nokesville, were married last week in Washington.

**ROBERTSON, G. W.** – Jul. 10, 1896 M. G. - Marriage licenses were granted this week to Mr. Geo. E. Hayth and Miss Maria A. Sayers, and Mr. G. W. Robinson and Miss Leonora Crouch, daughter of Mr. Elias Crouch—all of this county.

**ROBERTSON, Quilla** – Dec. 30 , 1910 M. J. – Mr. Quilla Robertson and Miss Stella Vetter, daughter of Mr. Jacob Vetter, of Wellington, were married at the Lutheran church, in this place, on Wednesday morning, Rev. J. K. Efird, pastor of the church, officiating.

The bride, who is a pretty brunette, was gowned in a princess white silk, trimmed in white satin, and carried a bouquette of flowers.

Mr. Frank Bell was best man and Miss Nina Vetter, sister of the bride, was maid of honor.

The bride's travelling suit was of Navy blue cloth with hat and gloves to match.

After a sumptuous luncheon the happy pair left on the midday train for a trip to Baltimore and Philadelphia.

**ROBERTSON, Thomas Ross** – Jul. 27, 1906 M. J. - Dr. and Mrs. H. M. Clarkson announce the marriage of their daughter, Jean, to Gen. Thomas Ross Robertson of North Carolina at St. Paul's Church, Haymarket, Tuesday, August 7, at 6 o'clock. No cards except to friends at a distance.

**ROBERTSON, Thomas Ross** – Jul. 27, 1906 M. J. - A special dispatch from Wilmington, N.C., to the Richmond Times Dispatch says:

Friends in this city have received invitations to a marriage that is of much importance to society and the military of the State. They are to the wedding of Adjutant-General Thomas Ross Robertson of the North Carolina National Guard, and Miss Jean Clarkson, daughter of Dr. and Mrs. Henry Mazyck Clarkson of Haymarket, Va., the event to be celebrated Thursday, August 7th, in St. Paul's Church, Haymarket.

General Robertson is of Charlotte, N.C., and is delightfully remembered in Wilmington, as he has been in attendance upon a number of encampments at Wrightsville, near here, and was always prominent in the social functions attendant upon the encampments.

The Raleigh (N.C._ Observer of a recent date says:

Wedding invitations have been received by friends which will be read with interest and pleasure in North Carolina, where the groom-to-be is a prominent lawyer and a leading figure in the North Carolina National Guard.

The invitation reads as follows:

Dr. and Mrs. Henry Mazyck Clarkson request the honor of your presence at the marriage of their daughter,
> Jean,
> to
> General Thomas Ross Robertson,
> Tuesday, August the seventh,
> nineteen hundred and six;
> > at six o'clock,
> Saint Paul's Church,

Haymarket, Virginia

General Robertson is now a citizen of Charlotte, where he is a prominent attorney. He has long been a member of the military force of the State, captain of his home company, colonel of the First Regiment, and serving during the Spanish-American War when his company went to Cuba, now Adjutant-General of the North Carolina National Guard, appointed by Governor Glenn. He is a clever and popular gentleman and his bride-elect is a charming lady of Virginia, a member of one of the most prominent and influential families in the State. It will be of special interest to the people of Raleigh to know that after the first of October General and Mrs. Robertson will make Raleigh their home.

There will go to the happy event some of the most prominent people in North Carolina, among these Governor Glenn and a large number of officers of the North Carolina National Guard.

**ROBERTSON, Thomas Ross** – Aug. 10, 1906 M. J. - The marriage of Miss Jean Clarkson and General Thomas Ross Robertson took place in St. Paul's church, Haymarket, Tuesday, Aug.7, at 6 p.m. The ceremony was impressively performed by the rector, Rev. Cary Gamble. The bride is the youngest daughter of Dr. and Mrs. H. M. Clarkson and is one of the most attractive and popular young women in the neighborhood. Gen. Robertson is a distinguished lawyer of Charlotte, N. C., as well as Adjutant-General of the state troops.

The church was beautifully decorated by the bride's friends, the color scheme being white and green ablaze with the mellow radiance of white lights. The wedding marches as well as other music, were finely rendered by Miss Norton Tyler. The matron of honor, Mrs. Thomas B. Clarkson, wore a gown of white crepe de chene and carried white roses. The bride's maids, Misses Fanny White, Hallie Meade, May Beverly, Belle Price, Florence Gillis and Mary Price were gowned in white organdie trimmed net lace and carried large bouquets of pink roses. The order of entering the church was unique and pretty, the matron of honor and bride's maids came from the vestry room and walking down the aisle with the bride at the church door, there, preceded by the ushers, Mr. Alexander B. Andrews, Jr., Col. Westcott Robertson, Mr. Hugh Clarkson, Major Joseph T. Cannon, Capt. Wm. R. Robertson and Mr. Lee M. Clarkson, they came up the circle followed by the bride on the arm of her father by whom she was given away.

The bride's gown was an exquisite white fabric, imported from China by a relative in the Navy. It was made princess with train and elbow sleeves, the yoke made of thread lace. The Tulle veil was beautifully arranged with orange blossoms, her flowers were a shower bouquet of bride roses and she looked a typical and lovely bride.

The bridegroom with his best man, Gen. Francis A. Macon, came from the vestry room and met the bride at the chancel. Gen. Robinson, the best man and ushers were in full evening dress with boutonnieres of white gardenias. The bridal party was very imposing as it passed up the aisle and the beautiful tableau and the chancel steps of " fair women and brave men" is one that will long be remembered by all present. Mrs. Clarkson, the bride's mother wore black "feau de soie"with duchess lace, Mrs. Robert Lee Reading of California, sister of the bride, wore her own wedding dress of white crepe de chene and looked very handsome.

An elaborate luncheon was given before the wedding at the bride's home to the bridal party, relatives and a few friends.

The presents were numerous and handsome. Among those from a distance present were Mrs. Hugh Thompson of New York the bride's aunt, Mrs. Reading, Miss Love and Mr. Breckinridge of Washington, Mrs. Charles Phelps of Baltimore, Mrs. Samuel Claggett of Frederick county, M. D. and Mr. Hugh Thompson of New York.

Gen. and Mrs. Robertson left on the evening train for an extended tour South.

**ROBERTSON, William V.** – Apr. 29, 1910 M. J. – Mr. Wm. V. Robertson, of Rockville, Md., and Miss Josephine Forsyth were quietly married at the bride's parents near Haymarket, on Thursday, April 21$^{st}$, at 5:30 p.m., Rev. Homer Welsh officiating.

**ROBINSON, Robert** – Dec. 3, 1909 M J - Mr. Robert Robinson and Miss Bertha Stevens, of the Greenwich neighborhood, were married Wednesday noon at the home of the bride, Rev. W. S. Willey performing the ceremony.

**ROBINSON, Robert** – Dec. 10, 1909 M. J. – At the home of the bride, Mr. and Mrs. P. J. Stevens' youngest daughter, Miss Bertha, was married to Mr. Robt. Robinson on Wednesday, Dec. 1$^{st}$, at high noon by Rev W. S. Willey.

**ROBINSON, Rosa** – Jun. 4, 1909 – M. J. – Mr. Frank Colbert and Miss Rosa Robinson, both of Manassas, were married Wednesday, May 26, at the Methodist Parsonage by Mr. W. T. Gover.

**ROBINSON, Walter** - Dec. 10, 1909 M. J. – That the marriage of Miss Nellie Spinks to Mr. Walter Robinson, an announcement of which appears in the local columns of this issue, is fraught with more than the ordinary touch of romance as indicated by the following items which appeared in the Alexandria Gazette of Dec. 6 and 7 respectively:

Charles H. Spinks, a farmer, who lives at Haymarket, last night called at the First precinct station in Washington to see the man who eloped with his fourteen year old sister, Nellie Spinks. The irate brother was armed with a revolver, and the police took the weapon from him and locked him up. Miss Spinks and Walter Robinson, nineteen years old, left Haymarket on Thursday night last for Washington intending to be married in that city. Detectives met the couple at Union station, sent the girl to the House of Detention, and placed Robinson in a cell at the First precinct station, awaiting word from the girl's parents in Haymarket.

Mr. and Mrs. Walter Robinson, of Haymarket, the young couple who were married in Rockville, Md. Saturday afternoon after having been pursued by the little bride's brother and after having spent a night in the hands of the police of Washington, Saturday afternoon went back to Haymarket to ask the forgiveness of the girl's parents. They were accompanied by Charles Spinks and Roy Spinks, the bride's brothers, who had become reconciled to the match and who attended the ceremony in Rockville.

**ROBINSON, Walter H.** – Dec. 10, 1909 M. J. – Miss Nellie Spinks, of Haymarket and Mr. Walter H. Robinson, of Wellington, were married last Saturday afternoon at Rockville, Md., by Rev. S. R. White, a retired Baptist minister, at whose home the ceremony took place.

**ROGERS, Annie Isabelle** – Apr. 15, 1910 M. J. – FAUQUIER – Miss Annie Isabelle Rogers, daughter of Mr. Jessie Rogers, and Mr. Luck Adair Tiffany, son of Mr. and Mrs. W. S. Tiffany, were quietly married at the parsonage at Upperville, Va., by Dr. I. B. Lake, Wednesday, March 30, at 3 p.m. They returned to the home of the groom, where a reception was given them.—Loudoun Mirror.

**ROGERS, WilliamThomas Clagget** – Jun.3, 1910 M. J. – The marriage of Mr. William Thomas Clagget Rogers of Leesburg, a present resident of Haymarket, to Miss Anna Louise Ferguson of Belmont, Loudoun county, is announced to take place on Tuesday evening of next week, at the Episcopal Chapel, Belmont. The ceremony will be performed by Rev. Mr. Burkhardt, Rector of St. James church, Leesburg.

**ROGERS, Wade Hampton** – Mar. 25, 1910 M. J. –Mr. Wade Hampton Rogers, one of the first boys of Manassas, who has been living in Washington state for twenty-one years, spent Saturday and Sunday with his niece, Mrs. R. S. Hynson, on his way to Washington, where he was united in marriage with Miss Mary Anna Crouch, Wednesday. When a boy Mr. Rogers was student at Ruffner Public School, under Mr. Wm. R. Will, the school's first male principal, who is now professor in Brand-Stratton Business College, Baltimore.

**ROGERS, W. T. C.** – Jun. 17, 1910 M. J. – LOUDOUN – One of the most beautiful weddings ever seen took place in the historic Belmont Chapel, near Leesburg, on Tuesday afternoon , when Miss Anna Louise Ferguson became the bride of Mr. W. T. C. Rogers, Rev. W. H. Burkhardt, of Leesburg, performed the ceremony.

**ROLLINS, Joseph** - Sept. 21, 1906 M. J. – Mr. Jos. Rollins and Miss Carrie Vogel, daughter of Mr. Phillip Vogel – all of this county – were married on Tuesday afternoon at St. Joseph Church at the Catholic Institute. The happy couple left on the evening train for Latrobe, Penn.

**ROLLINS, Mary E.** – Oct. 1, 1909 M. J. – Marriage licenses were issued at the Clerk's office this week to Henry B. Wingfield, of Hanover county, and Miss Eunice L. Lynn, of Prince William county, and to Jacob C. Vogle, of Pennsylvania, and Miss Mary E. Rollins, of Prince William county.

**ROSENBERGER, Nancy Elizabeth** – Sept. 23, 1910 M. J. – Mr. and Mrs. Geo. M. Rosenberger announce the marriage of their daughter Nancy Elizabeth to Mr. George William Wilson on Wednesday, September 21, 1910, at Bristow, Va. At home after October 1$^{st}$, The Nansemond, 22 and N street, N. W. Washington, D. C.

**ROSENBERGER, Nannie** – Sept. 2, 1910 M. J. – The engagement of Miss Nannie Rosenberger, daughter of Mr. G. R. Rosenberger, of this place, to Mr. George Wilson, of Alexandria, is reported.

**ROSS, Ali Elizabeth** – Dec. 24, 1909 M. J. – Mr. George Augustus Wood and Miss Ali Elizabeth Ross were married on Wednesday, Dec. 15, at the home of Mrs. Jessie Griffith, the Rev. W. S. Jackson, officiating.

**ROSZEL, Richard Julian** –Sept. 24, 1909 M. J.- FAUQUIER – Invitations are out for the marriage of Miss Janet Southgate Lemmon, daughter of Mr. and Mrs. J. Southgate Lemmon, of Baltimore, and granddaughter of the late Colonel Dulaney, of "Welbourne," Upperville, to Mr. Richard Julian Roszel, of that town. The wedding is set for October 2, to take place at "Welbourne," near the home of the Dulaneys.

**ROSZEL, Rosa** – Oct. 22, 1909 M. J. – FAUQUIER – "Denton," the home of Miss Rosa Roszel, at The Plains, was the scene of her marriage to Mr. John Randolph Magill. The ceremony was followed by a reception and dance.

**ROSZEL, Rosalie** – Aug. 13, 1909 M. J. – FAUQUIER – The engagement of Mr. John McGill to Miss Rosalie Roszel, both of this neighborhood, has lately been announced. The date of the marriage is not yet known. This is the season's fifth engagement, of which at least one of the interested parties lives in this community. The other four are: Miss Francis Fleming to Mr. Henley Carter, of Mt. Jackson, Miss Delia Slaughter to Dr. Selby, of Warrenton, Mr. J. W. Slaughter to Mr. Spencer, of Philadelphia, and Dr. Richard Mason to Miss Heath, of Washington, D. C.

**ROUND, Nora Vera** – Jun. 3, 1910 M. J. –Cards are out announcing the coming marriage of Mr. William Willis Davies and Miss Nora Vera Round, eldest daughter of Mr. Geo. C. Round of this place, at Trinity Episcopal church, Wednesday evening, June 15, at 6:30. Owing to the wide acquaintance of both families, no invitations have been issued in the county.

**ROUND, Nora Vera** – Jun. 17, 1910 M. J. – Because of the wide acquaintance of the contracting parties, and the prominence of the families connected, the marriage of Miss Norma Vera Round and Mr. William Willis Davies is of unusual interest to the society of Manassas and vicinity. The wedding took place Wednesday evening, June 15, at 6:30 o'clock at Trinity Episcopal church, of this place, the former rector, Rev. F. L. Robinson, officiating.

The church was beautifully decorated with palms, ferns and pink roses banked around the altar—the color scheme being green, pink, and white. "O Promise Me" well sung by Miss Florence Hall of Brookville, Pa., preceded the wedding march from Lohengrin, played by Miss Mabel Bennett, cousin of the bride, of Washington, assisted by Miss Charlotte Smith of Manassas. The ushers, Hon. R. Ewell Thornton of Fairfax; H. Thornton Davies, John J. Davies, of Culpeper; William Harold Lipscomb, L. Frank Pattie and George C. Round, Jr., preceded Miss Ruth Althea Round, sister of the bride. Miss Round, as maid of honor, was attired in a gown of pink satin messaline and a picture hat. She was followed by Miss Emily Maitland Round, youngest sister of the bride, who was dressed in white over pink, and carried a large basket of flowers which she spread in the path of the bride.

The bride, dressed in an elaborate gown of white crepe meteor with pearl and renaissance lace trimmings and a tulle veil caught with lilies of the valley, approached the altar on the arm of her father, Hon. George Carr Round. They were met at the chancel by the groom and his uncle, Judge J. B. T. Thornton, who served as best man.

After a beautiful and an impressive ceremony the bridal party passed out of the church to the strains of Mendelssohn's wedding march.

A reception to the relatives and out of town guests was held at the home of the bride's parents during the evening, the success of which was largely due to the efforts of Miss Althea E. Loose, cousin of the bride, and an instructor in the Harrisonburg Normal School.

After a short trip to various points in the East, Mr. and Mrs. Davies will return to Manassas for permanent residence, in a new dwelling which will be erected during the summer.

The bride is an Alumna of Goucher College and the Barnard Hospital of Baltimore, Md., and has held for several years the position of Sanitary Supervisor of the former institution. The bride's mother is a native of London, Canada. Through her, the bride is 13$^{th}$ in descent from the lawyer-poet of Scotland, Sir Richard Maitland, after whom the Maitland Club of Glasgow was named; and through her she is likewise descended from Colonel Richard Blood, one of Cromwell's fighters immortalized by Sir Walter Scott. Through her father she is 9$^{th}$ from Caleb Carr, the Quaker Governor of Rhode Island and traces descent from the Hopkins and Church families which furnished a Signer of the Declaration of Independence, Stephen Hopkins, and the hero of the King Phillips' War, Capt. Benjamin Church. The bride is a Daughter of the Revolution through Bartram Round, a lieutenant in the Scituate Hunters of Rhode Island and through his wife, Alce Wilkinson, she is

9th in descent from Lawrence Wilkinson, a lieutenant in the army of Charles I, who, in Browning's Americans of Royal Descent, Pedigree LXXII is given as 16th from King Edward I of England and as descended from the Royal Houses of France and Spain.

The groom received his education in William and Mary College and the University of Virginia. He is connected with the Health Office of the District of Columbia. His is of an old and prominent family of Virginia. His grandfather, Major W. W. Thornton, was the first superintendent of schools in the county, and served in the Prince William cavalry of the Confederate army. His father was of a well-known English family. Born in England and educated at Christ College, Oxford, he came to Virginia in his early manhood and at once took an active interest in our public questions. The groom's present family is identified with the affairs of the state and are prominent in business circles.

Many relatives and friends were in attendance at the wedding, among them—Mrs. R. Ewell Thornton and Miss Helen Moore of Fairfax; Mrs. Harriet I. Davies and her sister, Miss Lelia Green, from Aden; Miss Grace Abbott from Ilion, N.Y.; Dr. Jac Reichley of York, P.; Dr. Frank Hornbaker of Occoquan; Mrs. Dr. Noland of Loudoun, and Miss Martha P. Hall from Binghamton, N.Y. Among Washingtonians were—Dr. Maitland C. Bennett and wife, Dr. Harrison M. Bennett, Dr. Charles B. Chamberlin and wife, Mr. H. F. Tompkins and wife, Misses Alice and Catharine Boorman and Mrs. L. Adelia Pine, the sister of Mr. Round, The following were present from Baltimore—Mrs. Clara F. Hanneman, Miss Florence Hall, Dr. Wisner and wife, Miss Edith Rickert and Miss Bertha Austin.

With the happy couple now on their beautiful honeymoon go the best wishes of a large circle of friends who will welcome their return.

**RUFFNER, John** – Jan. 28, 1910 M. J. – FAUQUIER –Mr. John Ruffner and Miss Sallie Laws, both of Bristersburg, were quietly married in Washington on Thursday last. Mr. and Mrs. Ruffner have returned home near here. We wish them a long and happy life.

**RUSSELL, James** – Apr. 1, 1910 M. J. – Mr. Jas. Russell and Miss Daisy M. Cornwell, both of Canova, were married at high noon yesterday at the home of the bride, by Rev. T. D. D. Clark, pastor of the Manassas Baptist church. Mr. and Mrs. B. C. Cornwell, of Manassas, were present at the ceremony.

**RUST, Esther May** – May 25, 1906 M. J. – Cards are out announcing the marriage of Miss Esther May, daughter of Capt. and

Mrs. John R. Rust to Mr. Chas. James Gilliss June 12 at 5:30 p.m. at St. Paul's Church, Haymarket. Mr. Gilliss has charge of the bureau of silk industry, Agricultural Department.

**RUST, Esther May** – Jun. 22, 1906 M. J. - Miss Esther May Rust, daughter of Capt. John R. and Mrs. Nannie A. Rust of Wayside, near Haymarket, who a few years ago moved from the Valley of Virginia, where they numbered among their relatives the Marshalls, the Ashbys and others, was married on the afternoon of the 12th of June at 5:30 o'clock, to Mr. Charles James Gilliss of Washington D.C., son of the late Col. James Gilliss, U.S. Army and grandson of Commodore Gillis, U.S. navy. The ceremony was solemnized at St. Paul's church, Haymarket, which was tastefully decorated with evergreens, potted plants and cut flowers. The Rev. C. W. S. Hollis of the Presbyterian church, the bride's pastor, officiated, assisted by Rev. W. W. Gillis, brother of the groom, and Rev. Cary Gamble, rector of St. Paul's.

The bride was gowned in white crepe de chien en princesse, her veil being caught up by orange blossoms and she carried in her hand a bunch of bride roses. her maid of honor, Miss Florence S. Gillis, sister of the groom, was attired in white point d'es prit, and carried sweet peas. The groom's best man was Mr. Robert A. Rust, brother of the bride. Mr. Walter Gilliss of New York, Mr. Jno. D. Rust of Fairfax and Messrs. Walter B. and Hugh T. Clarkson of Washington city were the ushers.

Miss Hallie Meade presided at the organ and rendered the wedding marches from Mendelssohn and Lohengrin.

The newly-wedded pair drove to Manassas and there took the train for Philadelphia and Cape May, and on their return they will reside at Beaumont, the recently built country home of the groom.

The wedding presents were numerous and costly.

A very pleasant reception was tendered the bridal party at the hospitable home of the bride's parents, at which there were present among others from abroad, Mrs. Jas. Gilliss, Misses Julia and Helen Gillis, Mrs. Edward Stellwagen and Miss Stellwagen, Miss Dolly Loud and Mr Aleck N. Breckenridge of Washington, D.C.; Gen. T. R. Robertson, of Charlotte, N. C. ; Miss Kathryn McKay, Greenville, Va., Miss Virginia McKay, Cumberland, Md.; Miss Elizabeth Jones, Culpeper, Va.; Miss Elizabeth Rust, Front Royal, Va.; Mrs. Caldwell, New York; Messrs. Ashby Rust, Thomas McKay, Miss Lou Marshall, Miss LeHew, Mrs. Leach, Mrs. Johnston and Miss Johnston of Warren Co, Va.

**RYER, Henry C.** – Jan. 7, 1910 M. J. – FAIRFAX – Mrs. Grace S. Brown and Henry C. Ryer, of Falls Church, were married on Christmas day at the home of the bride in Washington, Rev. W. S. O. Thomas, of Falls Church, officiating.

**SABINE, Annie Leona** – Jun. 10, 1904 M. J. - Mr. Alfonso Calvert and Miss Annie Leona Sabine were married at the Greenwood Baptist church, this county, on Sunday, June 5.

**SAFFER, M. Lillian** – Sept. 16, 1910 M. J. – Miss M. Lillian Saffer, daughter of Mr. and Mrs. F. E. Saffer, of Manassas, Va., and Mr. Wm. W. Cullen, son of Mr. and Mrs. N. J. Cullen, of Paeonion Springs, Loudoun county, Va., were married Wednesday, Sept. 14, at 3 p.m. at the home of the bride's parents by Rev. W. T. Gover.

The couple were attended by Miss Beatrice Biebetheiser, of Baltimore, Md., and Mr. Harry A. Cullen, a brother of the groom.

The bride was attired in a blue traveling suit, hat and gloves to match.

The couple left for an extended trip north accompanied by their attendants. Upon their return the will reside at 2015 S st., n.w., Washington. Will be at home to their many friends after Oct. 1st.

**SALISBURG, George A.** – Apr. 1, 1910 M. J. – Miss Edith Charlton, whose articles on Domestic Science have been of so much interest to our readers, was married to Mr. George A. Salisburg, at Crawford, Nebraska, on March 26, 1910.

**SANBOURN, Grace F.** – Feb. 28, 1896 M. G. - A marriage license was issued in Washington during the first of the week to John E. Marcher, of Alexandria, and Grace F. Sanbourn, of Occoquan.

**SANDERS, Angie** – Oct. 1, 1909 M. J. – A pretty but quiet wedding took place in the quaint little town of Buckland, Prince William county, Tuesday morning, September 28th at 10 o'clock, when Miss Angie Sanders and Mr. T. Keller Grayson, of New Baltimore, were married at "The Willows," the home of the bride's father, Mr. W. W. Sanders. Rev. Mr. Council, of Warrenton performed the ceremony.

The bride was becomingly attired in a handsome suit of blue broadcloth with hat and gloves to match. She was unattended, and only relatives were present. The house was prettily decorated, the couple standing during the ceremony under a bower of autumn leaves and a bell of golden rod and ferns. A wedding breakfast was served, after which Mr. and Mrs. Greyson left for an extended tour North. They will reside in New Baltimore, where they will be "at home" to their friends after October fifteenth.

**SAYERS, Maria A.** – Jul. 10, 1896 M. G. - Marriage licenses were granted this week to Mr. Geo. E. Hayth and Miss Maria A. Sayers, and Mr. G. W. Robinson and Miss Leonora Crouch, daughter of Mr. Elias Crouch—all of this county.

**SAYRES, Rebecca** – Apr. 1, 1910 M. J. – Mr. Frank Crouch and Miss Rebecca Sayres, both of this county, were married Wednesday by Rev. Dr. Hamner at his residence on East Main street.

**SCHAFFER, Phoebe** – Mar. 18, 1910 M. J. – A marriage license was issued on Tuesday to Mr. Jack L. Switzer, of Illinois, and Miss Phoebe Schaffer, of Pennsylvania.

**SCHOOLFIELD, R. A.** –Dec. 31, 1909 M. J. – CULPEPER – A marriage of interest to the people of Culpeper is that of Mrs. Sadie Vass Van Wagener to Mr. R. A. Schoolfield, of Danville. The marriage took place on Tuesday evening, the twenty-first of this month, in New York, at the Waldolf-Astoria. Mr. Schoolfield first married Miss Belle Vass, who died several years ago. Miss Sadie Vass, is a daughter of Mr. James Vass, formerly of Culpeper, and is well remembered by many of her schoolmates as a sweet and lovely girl in every way.

**SCHUE, Joseph Milton** – Dec. 17, 1909 M. J. – LOUDOUN – Mr. and Mrs. Samuel H. Ball, of Leesburg, announce the engagement of their daughter, Bessie Robena, to Mr. Joseph Milton Schue, of Parksely, Va., the wedding to take place Wednesday, Dec. 29, at the home of the bride.—News, Dec. 10.

**SCHWAB, Lucille Rosamond** – Oct. 15, 1909 M. J. – FAUQUIER – Mr. and Mrs. William W. Schwab announce the engagement of their daughter, Lucille Rosamond, to Mr. Harry Brown Sullivan, of Elkwood, Va. The marriage will take place on Wednesday, Oct. 20, at 2:30 o'clock, at the Baptist church at New Baltimore.— Democrat, Oct. 9

**SCHWAB, Lucile R.** – Oct. 29, 1909 M. J. – FAUQUIER – On Wednesday afternoon at 2:30 Miss Lucile R. Schwab and Mr. Harry

Brown Sullivan were married at New Baltimore, Rev. V. H. Council performing the ceremony.

**SCOTT, Maggie** – Jan. 18, 1907 M. J. – Mr. William Warning and Miss Maggie Scott were married yesterday at the residence of the officiating minister, Rev. Robert Smith.

**SELBY, John Hunter** – Oct. 15, 1909 M. J.- FAUQUIER – At the Episcopal church in The Plains, Wednesday evening, Miss Delia Towles Slaughter, daughter of Mrs. John Philip Slaughter, and Dr. John Hunter Selby, of Warrenton, were married. The church was beautifully decorated.

The bridesmaids were Misses Catherine Peyton, Estelle Hable, Frances Fleming, Mabel Fletcher, of Fauquier; Alice Wilson, of Columbia, S.C., and Edna Saunders of Washington.

The matrons of honor were Mrs. Marion Speeden, of New Jersey, and Mrs. William Scott McLeod, of New York.

Dr. Selby was attended by Dr. Harry H. Howard, as best man. The ushers were Roderick McDonald and Dr. R. C. L. Adams of Columbia, S.C.; Webb Maddox, of Marshall; Dr. Rich Mason and Dr. E. W. Scott, of The Plains.—Democrat, Oct. 9.

**SELECMAN, Marguerite** – Nov. 22, 1901 M. J. - The marriage of Miss Marguerite Selecman to Rev. Hunter Davis was celebrated at the home of the bride's father, Mr. W. R. Selecman in Washington, D. C., on Thursday last. The bride was charmingly attired in pearl grey silk crepe de cline over pearl grey taffeta silk and carried white bride roses. The house was beautifully decorated with palms and chrysanthemums. A wedding breakfast followed the ceremony, which was performed by Rev. W. F. Locke of Front Royal, Va. The guests numbered 85 persons. The presents were beautiful and numerous. Among those who attended from Occoquan were: Dr. C. Lee Starkweather, Mr. Edwin Cockrell, Mr. and Mrs. Daniel W. Ritterbusch, Mr. and Mrs. R. C. Hammill and son Perry and Miss Rowena Selecman.

**SENIOR, Grace Edna** – Apr. 12, 1907 M. J. – The marriage of Miss Grace Edna Senior of Washington, a frequent visitor here, and Mr. Myron Tilden, has been announced.

**SHACKELFORD, Hattie** – Aug. 17, 1906 M. J. - The marriage of Mr. Oscar Demory and Miss Hattie Shackelford took place at the home of the bride near Broad Run, Va., Wednesday, Aug. 15th, at 4 p. m., Rev. Mr. Hollis officiating.

**SHACKLEFORD, R. B. S.** – Feb. 11, 1910 M. J. – The marriage of Dr. R. B. S. Shackelford, the popular young physician of this vicinity, to Miss Mary Field Bolling, of Charlesville, Va., took place in that town on Tuesday evening last, in Christ Church. The ceremony was performed by Rev. Harry Lee.

The bride wore a handsome gown of white messaline with silver and pearl trimmings. Her only attendant was her school girl sister, Miss Sallie Stuart Bolling, who wore an attractive gown of white organdie with green trimmings. The groom was attended by Dr. Archibald Cary Randolph, of Baltimore, as best man.

Following the ceremony a reception was given at the bride's home, which was attended by guests from a distance, relatives, and intimate friends of the bride and groom.

**SHACKELFORD, R. S. B.** – Jan. 21, 1910 M. J. – The engagement of Dr. R. S. B. Shackelford, of Maynadier Sanitarium, near town, to Miss Mary Bolling, of Charlottesville, is announced. The wedding is expected to take place on the eighth of February, at the Episcopal church in Charlottesville.

**SHELTON, William** – Jun 17, 1910 M. J. – FAUQUIER – On Saturday, June 4th, at "Brooklyn Farm," the home of Mr. and Mrs. Robert Smith, was witnessed the marriage of their daughter, Miss Lillian Smith to Mr. William Shelton, of Washington, D.C.

**SHELTON, William F.** – Apr. 29, 1910 M. J. – FAUQUIER – Mr. and Mrs. Robert L. Smith announce the engagement of their daughter, Lillie Erva, to Mr. Wm. F. Shelton, of Washington, D.C. The marriage will take place in early summer.

**SHEPHERD, Harriet V.** – Oct. 28, 1910 M. J. –Marriage license was issued in Washington yesterday to Mr. Harry C. Carter, of this county, and Miss Harriet V. Shepherd, of Fairfax.

**SHEPHERD, Harriet V.** – Nov. 4, 1910 M. J. –FAIRFAX – A marriage license was issued in Washington Wednesday to Henry C. Carter, of Prince William county, and Harriet V. Shepherd, of Fairfax county—Rev. Jno. W. Smith officiating.

**SHEPHERD, Ida** – Jul. 9,1909 M. J. – CULPEPER – Mr. William McDonald and Miss Ida Shepherd were married Tuesday afternoon at 7:30 o'clock by the Rev. C. E. Pleasants, at the Methodist parsonage on Belmont. The bride is a resident of Albermarle, her home being at Boyd's Tavern. Mr. McDonald is a painter from Philadelphia, but his home is now at Brandy Station, Va. The happy pair left this morning for a trip over the C. & O.—Exponent, July 2.

**SHEPPERD, Hattie** – Nov. 4, 1910 M. J. – Mr. Harry Carter, one of Occoquan's most popular young men, was married in Washington on Wednesday last to Miss Hattie Shepperd, of Fairfax. They returned from their bridal trip on Saturday evening where a large crowd awaited them with an old time serenade. The young couple have the best wishes of the entire community for their future happiness.

**SHIRLEY, Ethel** – Feb. 25, 1910 M. J. – FAUQUIER – Mr. Ford G. Anderson and Miss Ethel Shirley of Warrenton, were married in Wilmington, Del., on Wednesday, Feb. 15, by the Rev. W. H. Laird of the Episcopal church. Mr. Anderson is a member of the well known firm of Nusbaum & Anderson, clothiers of this place, and Miss Shirley is the beautiful daughter of Sergeant J. W. Shirley, of this place.

**SHRIVER, Jeannette** – Nov. 19, 1909 M. J. – LOUDOUN - The 24$^{th}$ of November is the date set for the marriage of Miss M. Jeannette Shriver to Mr. John Marshall Jones, of Alexandria, the wedding to be solemnized by Cardinal Gibbons, and the nuptial mass celebrated by the Rev. William Gaston Payne, uncle of the groom, in St. Mary's chapel, Union Mills, Md. and Mr. Jones is the second son of Dr. and Mrs. T. Marshall Jones of this city. After their marriage Mr. and Mrs. Jones will reside on Cameron street, opposite Christ church.—Gazette

**SHRYOCK, George H.** – Jul. 29, 1910 M. J. – LOUDOUN – A marriage license was issued in Washington on Thursday of last week to Mr. George H. Shryock, of Ashburn, and Miss Irma M. Moffett, of Arcola.

**SHUMATE, S. Sidney** – Dec. 31, 1909 M. J. – FAUQUIER – Miss Stuart Strother and Mr. S. Sidney Shumate were married Monday afternoon at Warrenton at the home of the bride. The wedding was quiet, only the immediate family and a few friends being present. The bride is a daughter of Mr. and Mrs. A. W. Strother. The ceremony was performed by Rev. J. L. Kibler, of the Methodist church. The wedding march was played by Miss Gertrude Kibbler.

**SHUMATE, Sydney** – Jan. 7, 1910 M. J. – FAUQUIER – The marriage of Miss Stuart Strother, daughter of Mr. A. W. Strother of this place, and Mr. Sydney Shumate, son of Judge W. G. B. Shumate of Calverton, Va., was solemnized on Monday, Dec. 27, at the home of the bride's father, on main street, in the presence of a few friends and relatives. The Rev. M. Kibler, pastor of the Methodist church, officiated, and the wedding march was beautifully rendered by Miss Gertrude Kibler. The bride was handsomely gowned in a dark green broadcloth suit with gold trimmings and hat to match. After receiving the blessings and congratulation of a host of friends and relatives the happy couple left on the evening train for the home of the groom at Calverton.

**SIMPSON, Charles Augustus** – Jun. 17, 1910 M. J. – The Herndon Observer, announces the engagement of Miss Elizabeth Darlington, daughter of Mr. J. J. Darlington, of Washington, to Dr. Charles Augustus Simpson, of the same city.

**SIMPSON, Edith** – Jul. 23, 1909 M. J. – Miss Edith Simpson and Mr. James Payne, both of Prince William, were married yesterday in Washington.

**SIMPSON, Lella Cannor** – Jun. 11, 1909 – M. J. – LOUDOUN – Mr. Thomas P. Simpson, the well known contractor and builder, of Bluemont, was married in West Virginia early in May to his daughter-in-law, Mrs. Lella Cannor Simpson.—Enterprise.

**SIMPSON, Thomas P.** – Jun. 11, 1909 – M. J. – LOUDOUN – Mr. Thomas P. Simpson, the well known contractor and builder, of Bluemont, was married in West Virginia early in May to his daughter-in-law, Mrs. Lella Cannor Simpson.—Enterprise.

**SINCLAIR, C. A. S.** – Apr. 22, 1910 M. J. – FAIRFAX – Mr. C. A. S. Sinclair and Miss Louise J. Swann, daughter of Mr. C. Orrick Swann, were married at the residence of the bride's aunt, Mrs. Frances Swann Williams, near Vienna, on Tuesday last, at 1 o'clock, Rev. Edward Callehder officiating. Mr Talbott Sinclair, brother of the groom, was best man, and Miss Pattie Washington, of Alexandria, was Maid of Honor. Later the bridal couple left in a special car for Alexandria, where they took the train for an extensive tour through the South.

**SISSON, Blanche** – Aug. 12, 1910 M. J. – FAIRFAX – Mr. Robt. T. Ballard, of Vienna, and Miss Blanche Sisson, of Legato (daughter of Mr. E. B. Sisson), were married in Atlantic City recently. They will reside in Vienna.

**SKINNER, Susan**– Feb. 28, 1896 M. G. - On Wednesday Mr. Samuel S. Maconnaughey and Miss Susan E Skinner, of Hoadley neighborhood, came to this place and were married by Rev. Robert Smith at his residence. The bridal couple was accompanied by the bride's mother and the groom's brother.

**SLAUGHTER, Delia Towles** – Oct. 15, 1909 M. J.- FAUQUIER – At the Episcopal church in The Plains, Wednesday evening, Miss Delia Towles Slaughter, daughter of Mrs. John Philip Slaughter, and Dr. John Hunter Selby, of Warrenton, were married. The church was beautifully decorated.

The bridesmaids were Misses Catherine Peyton, Estelle Hable, Frances Fleming, Mabel Fletcher, of Fauquier; Alice Wilson, of Columbia, S.C., and Edna Saunders of Washington.

The matrons of honor were Mrs. Marion Speeden, of New Jersey, and Mrs. William Scott McLeod, of New York.

Dr. Selby was attended by Dr. Harry H. Howard, as best man. The ushers were Roderick, McDonald and Dr. R. C. L. Adams of Columbia, S.C.; Webb Maddox, of Marshall; Dr. Rich Mason and Dr. E. W. Scott, of The Plains.—Democrat, Oct. 9.

**SMITH, Catherine Louise** – Jun. 25, 1909 M. J. – FAIRFAX - Mrs. Orion Triplett, of Fairfax county, has issued invitations to the marriage of her daughter, Miss Catherine Louise Smith, to Dr. Thomas Franklin Dodd, of Stuarts Draft, son of Mr. and Mrs. George Y. Dodd, of Braddock Heights. The wedding will take place Wednesday evening, June 30, at 8:30 o'clock, in Christ Church.—Alex. Gazette.

**SMITH, Cora E.** - Nov. 2, 1906 M. J. – Married on Tuesday last at the residence of the officiating minister, Rev. Robt. Smith, Mr. William E. Bailey and Miss Cora E. Smith, both of this county.

**SMITH, Elizabeth** – Aug. 20, 1909 M. J. – FAUQUIER – Miss Elizabeth Smith, daughter of Mr. A. J. Smith, and Prof. Carlisle H. Gilkeson, of French Camp, Miss., were married in the Presbyterian church, Bealeton, Va., on August $4^{th}$, at 8:30 a. m. The church was tastefully decorated in green with white flowers. Mrs. H. E. Guthrie sister of the groom, was matron of honor. The bride entered the church with the maid of honor, her sister, Miss Eleanor G. Smith. These were joined in front of the pulpit by the groom and the best man, Mr. Samuel F. Gilkeson, who entered the building by the rear door. The wedding march was played by Miss Marian Smith, of Fauquier Springs. The ceremony was performed by Rev. L. F. Harper, the pastor of the bride, using the ring ceremony. After the ceremony the bridal party drove to "Pleasant Hill," the home of Mr. and Mrs. Smith, where a delightful reception was held. The happy couple left amidst at shower of rice on the 10:20 train for Montreal, Canada. They will make their home in French Camp, Miss., where Prof. Gilkeson is teaching.

The guests from a distance were Mr. and Mrs. Guthrie, of Louisiana, Mr. Sam. F. Gilkeson, of Augusta county, Va., Mrs. Sampson and Miss Sampson of West Virginia, Miss Bettie Gilkeson, of Mississippi, Miss Emma Shannon, of Manassas, Va., Mr. and Mrs. Walter Smith, of Fairfax county, Mr. Philip Smith, of Tennessee, Miss Margaret Smith, of Manassas.—Democrat, Aug. 14.

**SMITH, Florence Lyon** – Nov. 5, 1909 M. J. – LOUDOUN – Cards are out announcing the marriage of Miss Florence Lyon Smith, daughter of Mr. and Mrs. Charles G. Smith, of Washington to Dr. William Richards Blair, of Mount Weather. The ceremony took place at Hohenheim, on the mountains above Bluemont, the bride's home, Dr. Frank Sewell, of Washington, officiating. They will reside at Mount Weather.

**SMITH, Frank** - Feb. 1, 1907 M. J. – Mr. Frank Smith and Miss Edith Wood, sister of Mrs. Jos. Herring of this place, were quietly married Tuesday morning at the residence of the officiating minister, Rev. S. H. Flory. Frank, in entering the matrimonial state, has sprung a surprise upon his many friends of the community. Being an old sailor he will doubtless know how to steer his matrimonial craft free of the reefs of domestic disaster.

**SMITH, John Ambler** – Sept. 3, 1909 M. J. – FAUQUIER – Miss Etta Duncan, of Fauquier county, and Mr. John Ambler Smith, of Washington, were married recently. The bride is a granddaughter of Colonel John Matthew Monroe. Mr. Smith is the youngest son of John Ambler Smith, who was in Congress for several years.

**SMITH, Lillian** – Jun 17, 1910 M. J. – FAUQUIER – On Saturday, June 4$^{th}$, at "Brooklyn Farm," the home of Mr. and Mrs.

Robert Smith, was witnessed the marriage of their daughter, Miss Lillian Smith to Mr. William Shelton, of Washington, D.C.

**SMITH, Lillie Erva** – Apr. 29, 1910 M. J. – FAUQUIER – Mr. and Mrs. Robert L. Smith announce the engagement of their daughter, Lillie Erva, to Mr. Wm. F. Shelton, of Washington, D.C. The marriage will take place in early summer.

**SMITH, Mildred Earle** – Oct. 1, 1909 M. J. – CULPEPER – Mr. and Mrs. Charles Edward Smith have issued cards for the marriage of their daughter, Miss Mildred Earle Smith, to Mr. Samuel Edward Booker, the event to take place in Saint Stephen's church on Thursday, October 15th, at half past twelve o'clock.—Exponent, Sept.24.

**SMITH, Simon Asburn** – Aug. 10, 1906 M. J. - Simon Asburn Smith of Philadelphia and Miss Louise McLean of Washington were married on the 5th day of May last, at Baltimore, the Rev. Dr. David T. Neely officiating.

The bride is a daughter of J. W. McLean of Neverlet, Va., and a grand-daughter of the late Maj. Wilmer McLean at whose house the surrender of Lee to Grant took place and the papers were drawn up and signed which terminated the civil war.

Mr. Smith is a son of the late Capt. Ad. E. Smith, Sixty-second Regiment, Pennsylvania volunteers, who served with distinction under Col. Sam Black; also is a brother of Mrs. G. W. Lynch of Petworth, D. C. Mr. And Mrs. Smith are in Erie, Pa., at present where they expect to pass the summer.

**SMITH, Thomas P.** – Feb. 28, 1896 M. G. - Mr. Thomas P Smith jr., of this county, was married at Campbells, N. Y., to Miss Anna Maline Williams, of that place on the 18th instant.

**SMITTEN, Ina Mary** – Jun. 8, 1906 M. J. - Mr. and Mrs. W. B. Smitten announce the approaching marriage of their daughter, Ina Mary, to Mr. John Baltzell Key of Leonardtown, Md., on Wednesday, June 27, at Trinity Episcopal church at high noon.

**SOURS, Henry** – Feb. 4, 1910 M. J. – CULPEPER – Laurel Mills, Jan. 24.—Mr. Henry Sours and Miss Lillie Cloud eloped to Hagerstown, Md. last Tuesday and were married. When they returned to Kimball a heavy snow had fallen and as they had several miles to walk before getting to the house of Mr. Fox a brother-in-law of the groom they started but found the snow too deep for the bride to walk. Mr. Sours left her at a farm house and went for a buggy and when he came back he could not find his bride for sometime as he could not tell the house at which he had left her.

**SPAIGHT, Thomas L.** – Aug. 20, 1909 M. J. – Mr. Thos. L. Spaight, of Washington, and Miss Catherine T. Leahy, of Prince William, were united in marriage August 19$^{th}$ by Rev. J. K. Efird, at the Lutheran parsonage, Manassas.

**SPICER, Carolyn** – Sept. 23, 1910 M. J. – FAUQUIER – Marriage licenses were issued in Washington on Thursday to the following Fauquier couples: Joseph B. Pulliam and Carolyn Spicer, both of Remington; Benjamin Gordon, of Markham, and India Chadwell, of Hume; Joseph A. Jeffries, of Warrenton, and Sallie Thompson, of Washington.

**SPIES, Edward Emerentia.** – Jun. 24, 1910 M. J. – Mrs. Anna E. Spies, of this place, attended the wedding of Mr. Edward Emerentia Spies and Miss Margaret Ada Creamer in Washington on Wednesday last.

**SPINDLE, Lillian W.** – Aug. 31, 1906 M. J. - Married on Tuesday last at the Church of the Holy Comforter, Washington, D.C. Miss Lillian W. Spindle of Bristow, to Mr. Edward A. Daley of Brooklyn, N.Y.

**SPINKS, George** – Dec. 24, 1909 M. J. – Mr. George Spinks, of Fauquier county, and Miss Bessie Baggott, of Prince William county, were married yesterday noon at the parsonage of the M. E. church, South, by the pastor, Rev. W. T. Gover.

**SPINKS, George** – Dec. 24, 1909 M. J. – The following marriage licenses were issued this week at the clerk's office: Monday, Lewis M. Swartz, Culpeper county, and Miss Pearl L. Kelley, Fauquier county, Chas. N. Davis and Miss Virgie Wolfe, both of Prince William; Tuesday, John F. Donovan, Rockingham county and Miss Florida V. Allison, Loudoun county; Wednesday, Aubrey Flynn, Fauquier county, and Miss Annie L. Thomas, Prince William county; Thursday, Wm. E. Beahm, Rappahannock county, and Miss Edith G. Priest, Fauquier county; Geo. Spinks, Fauquier county, and Miss Bessie Baggott, Prince William county.

**SPINKS, Nellie** – Dec. 10, 1909 M. J. – Miss Nellie Spinks, of Haymarket and Mr. Walter H. Robinson, of Wellington, were married last Saturday afternoon at Rockville, Md., by Rev. S. R. White, a retired Baptist minister, at whose home the ceremony took place.

**SPINKS, Nellie** - Dec. 10, 1909 M. J. – That the marriage of Miss Nellie Spinks to Mr. Walter Robinson, an announcement of which appears in the local columns of this issue, is fraught with more than the ordinary touch of romance as indicated by the following items which appeared in the Alexandria Gazette of Dec. 6 and 7 respectively:

Charles H. Spinks, a farmer, who lives at Haymarket, last night called at the First precinct station in Washington to see the man who eloped with his fourteen year old sister, Nellie Spinks. The irate brother was armed with a revolver, and the police took the weapon from him and locked him up. Miss Spinks and Walter Robinson, nineteen years old, left Haymarket on Thursday night last for Washington intending to be married in that city. Detectives met the couple at Union station, sent the girl to the House of Detention, and placed Robinson in a cell at the First precinct station, awaiting word from the girl's parents in Haymarket.

Mr. and Mrs. Walter Robinson, of Haymarket, the young couple who were married in Rockville, Md. Saturday afternoon after having been pursued by the little bride's brother and after having spent a night in the hands of the police of Washington, Saturday afternoon went back to Haymarket to ask the forgiveness of the girl's parents. They were accompanied by Charles Spinks and Roy Spinks, the bride's brothers, who had become reconciled to the match and who attended the ceremony in Rockville.

**STARK, Robert Caleb** – Feb. 18, 1910 M. J. – CULPEPER – Cards are out announcing the marriage of Miss Alice Sophenia Ratrie to Mr. Robert Caleb Stark, both of Culpeper county. The marriage took place on Monday, February the seventh, at "Liberty Hall," the home of the bride. Mrs. Stark is the youngest daughter of the late. H. H. Ratrie.

**STEPHENS, Lillie M.** – Jul. 29, 1910 M. J. – A marriage license was issued in Washington Monday to Mr. Earl Compton, of Fairfax county, and Miss Lillie M. Stephens, of Fauquier county.

**STEVENS, Bertha** – Dec. 3, 1909 M J - Mr. Robert Robinson and Miss Bertha Stevens, of the Greenwich neighborhood, were married Wednesday noon at the home of the bride, Rev. W. S. Willey performing the ceremony.

**STEVENS, Bertha** – Dec. 10, 1909 M. J. – At the home of the bride, Mr. and Mrs. P. J. Stevens' youngest daughter, Miss Bertha, was married to Mr. Robt. Robinson on Wednesday, Dec. 1$^{st}$, at high noon by Rev W. S. Willey.

**STONE, Belle** – Aug. 19, 1910 M. J– FAUQUIER – Mr. and Mrs. Geo. B. Stone, of Warrenton, have announced the engagement of their daughter, Belle, to George S. Winter. The wedding will take place on August 17$^{th}$. Miss Stone is one of the most attractive and popular girls of the younger set and has spent several winters in Washington. Mr. Winter is a native of Washington. For the past year he has been in the employ of the canal commission in Panama, where the young couple will reside.—Democrat.

**STONEBURNER, Bessie E.** – Jan. 14, 1910 M. J. – FAIRFAX – Mr. Owen M. Bancroft and Miss Bessie E. Stoneburner were married by Rev. F. A. Strother, at the parsonage of the M. E. church, South, on Wednesday last. Refreshments were served by the pastor and his good lady, after which the happy groom and his pretty bride went on their way rejoicing.

**STONNELL, S. B.** – Aug. 19, 1910 M. J. – Miss Pauline Catlett, nineteen years old, of Buckton, Va., and Mr. S. B. Stonnell, of Occoquan, were married Wednesday afternoon in Washington by Rev. D. C. McLeod. The wedding marked the culmination of a romance and elopement, in which the bride's love for her sweetheart overcame her parents' opposition to the match.

Although young Stonnell is the only son of Mr. S. B., a wealthy farmer, near Occoquan, who owns 2,000 acres of land in the Old Dominion, the parents of Miss Catlett are said to have selected another man for their son-in-law, and did not look with favor on the suit of the young farmer.

But Cupid, not to be outdone by parental objection, put into the head of young Stonnell the notion of visiting Washington, instead of Front Royal, and when the suggestion was made to Miss Catlett she concurred.

**STRADLEY, Wilmer** – Sept. 9, 1910 M. J. – The engagement of Miss Mamie Purcell, daughter of Capt. and Mrs. J. R. Purcell, to Mr. Wilmer Stradley, of Wilmington, De., has been announced. The wedding will take place early in October.

**STROTHER, John S.** – Feb. 25, 1910 M. J. – Mr. John S. Strother, of Fauquier, and Miss Elizabeth M. Robertson, of this county, were married Wednesday in the Baptist parsonage by Rev. T. D. D. Clark. The young couple will reside in Washington.

**STROTHER, Lewis E.** - Mar. 29, 1907 M. J. – The Alexandria Gazette of Wednesday says the marriage of Miss Mabel R. Ish to Mr. Lewis E. Strother, both of Prince William county, took place yesterday afternoon, at Christ Church rectory. The ceremony was performed by the Rev. W. J. Morgan. Mrs. Strother is the daughter of the late Dr. M. A. and Sallie E. Atkinson Ish.

**STROTHER, Stuart** – Dec. 31, 1909 M. J. – FAUQUIER – Miss Stuart Strother and Mr. S. Sidney Shumate were married Monday afternoon at Warrenton at the home of the bride. The wedding was quiet, only the immediate family and a few friends being present. The bride is a daughter of Mr. and Mrs. A. W. Strother. The ceremony was performed by Rev. J. L. Kibler, of the Methodist church. The wedding march was played by Miss Gertrude Kibbler.

**STROTHER, Stuart** – Jan. 7, 1910 M. J. – FAUQUIER – The marriage of Miss Stuart Strother, daughter of Mr. A. W. Strother of this place, and Mr. Sydney Shumate, son of Judge W. G. B. Shumate of Calverton, Va., was solemnized on Monday, Dec. 27, at the home of the bride's father, on main street, in the presence of a few friends and relatives. The Rev. M. Kibler, pastor of the Methodist church, officiated, and the wedding march was beautifully rendered by Miss Gertrude Kibler. The bride was handsomely gowned in a dark green broadcloth suit with gold trimmings and hat to match. After receiving the blessings and congratulation of a host of friends and relatives the happy couple left on the evening train for the home of the groom at Calverton.

**SUBLETT, Eliza Lawrason** – Jun. 11, 1909 M. J. – FAUQUIER – Mrs. G. H. Sublett, of Warrenton, announces the engagement of her daughter Eliza Lawrason, to Chas. Russe. Deane, formerly of Albermarle county. The wedding will take place in October.—Alex. Gazette

**SULLIVAN, Harry Brown** – Oct. 15, 1909 M. J. – FAUQUIER – Mr. and Mrs. William W. Schwab announce the engagement of their daughter, Lucille Rosamond, to Mr. Harry Brown Sullivan, of Elkwood, Va. The marriage will take place on Wednesday, Oct. 20, at 2:30 o'clock, at the Baptist church at New Baltimore.—Democrat, Oct. 9

**SULLIVAN, Harry Brown** – Oct. 29, 1909 M. J. – FAUQUIER - On Wednesday afternoon at 2:30 Miss Lucile R. Schwab and Mr. Harry Brown Sullivan were married at New Baltimore, Rev. V. H. Council performing the ceremony.

**SUTHARD, Landy** - Jan.18, 1907 M. J. - Mr. Landy Suthard, living near Limstrong and Miss Sallie Lynn of Independent Hill were married last week.

**SUTHERLAND, Nora** – Apr. 12, 1907 M. J. – Mr. D. J. Calvert of Dumfries and Miss Nora Sutherland were married in Washington on Wednesday last.

**SWANN, Louise J.** – Apr. 22, 1910 M. J. – FAIRFAX – Mr. C. A. S. Sinclair and Miss Louise J. Swann, daughter of Mr. C. Orrick Swann, were married at the residence of the bride's aunt, Mrs. Frances Swann Williams, near Vienna, on Tuesday last, at 1 o'clock, Rev. Edward Callehder officiating. Mr Talbott Sinclair, brother of the groom, was best man, and Miss Pattie Washington, of Alexandria, was Maid of Honor. Later the bridal couple left in a special car for Alexandria, where they took the train for an extensive tour through the South.

**SWART, Hamilton** – Dec. 30 , 1910 M. J. – Mr. Hamilton Swart and Miss Cordelia L. Cather were married in Washington yesterday. The bride is a sister of Mr. W. H. Cather, of Manassas, and the groom a well-to-do farmer of near Sudley, in this county.

**SWARTZ, Lewis M.** – Dec. 24, 1909 M. J. – The following marriage licenses were issued this week at the clerk's office: Monday, Lewis M. Swartz, Culpeper county, and Miss Pearl L. Kelley, Fauquier county, Chas. N. Davis and Miss Virgie Wolfe, both of Prince William; Tuesday, John F. Donovan, Rockingham county and Miss Florida V. Allison, Loudoun county; Wednesday, Aubrey Flynn, Fauquier county, and Miss Annie L. Thomas, Prince William county; Thursday, Wm. E.

Beahm, Rappahannock county, and Miss Edith G. Priest, Fauquier county; Geo. Spinks, Fauquier county, and Miss Bessie Baggott, Prince William county.

**SWEET, William Elisha** – Jun. 18, 1909 M. J. – Adjacent to the picturesque village of Occoquan, above the rushing mill-race that hurls its turbulent waters back into its mother steam, Occoquan River, yet hidden in a miniature amphitheater among the wooden hills, lies Rattlesnake Camp. A bubbling spring, a collection of gleaming tents, a long deal table and a roaring camp fire that throws its fitful gleam athwart the rippling surface of the stars and stripes stretched high up between two trees, and the picture is complete, except for the throng of young folk, moving in and out among the tents in noisy, care free confusion, which adds to the scene the one lacking touch of color and life.

In this charming spot occurred a wedding on last Tuesday at noon, which carried the mind of the spectator back to the fabled village of Arcadia. The contracting parties were Miss Zoa Langdon Clifton, of Baltimore, and Mr. Wm. Elisha Sweet, of Erie, Pa. Rev. F. L. Robinson, rector of Trinity Church, Manassas, performed the ceremony. Miss Bertha S. Austin, of Baltimore, was the only attendant, and Mr. G. Raymond Ratcliffe gave away the bride.

The ceremonies were ushered in with Lohengrin's Wedding March, sung by the assembled campers, and the bride and groom to be stood before the rustic altar, under the star spangled banner, to be united in the holy bonds of wedlock. The beautiful, solemn words of the marriage ceremony were unaccompanied by the customary strains of the pipe organ, but the murmur of the hidden waters floated upward, mingled with the gentle crooning of the wind among the tree-tops, while silvery bird notes wove threads of melody into the woof of the semi-silence—and Nature played an obbligato.

The bride was attired in an Empire gown of snowy linen, elaborately hand embroidered, and the bridesmaid, Miss Austin, wore a green gown cut Empire.

Those present to witness the ceremony were Mrs. G. Raymond Ratcliffe, of Manassas, who is chaperoning the party, Mrs. A. A. Hynson, of Occoquan, Misses Elizabeth Myer, of Washington, Norma V. Round, of Manassas, Margaret E. Newman, of Waynesboro, Pa., Martha P. Hall, of Binghampton, N.Y., and Bertha S. Austin, of Baltimore; Messrs. G. Raymond Ratcliffe, of Manassas, Wm. Edward Austin, of Baltimore, Joseph Parker, of Baltimore, Thomas Clarke, of Washington, W. Willis Davies, of Manassas, Reid Hynson, of

Occoquan, and Drs. J. C. Reichley, of York, Pa., Frank Hornbaker, of Occoquan and J. Marye Lewis, of Manassas. These, with the exception of the Occoquan guests, and Dr. Lewis and Mr. Davies, of Manassas, comprise the regular camping party at Rattlesnake Camp.

**SWETNAM, Bettie K.** – Sept. 23, 1910 M. J. – FAIRFAX – Mr. Ernest P. Harrison and Miss Bettie K. Swetnan were married Wednesday evening at the home of Mrs. Jennie Swetnan, the bride's mother, at Burke, Rev. Burnley Harrison, the groom's brother, performing the ceremony.

**SWETNAM, Roberta R.** – Nov. 4, 1910 M. J. – FAIRFAX – Mr. Dallas Berry, of Ashgrove, and Miss Roberta R. Swetnam, daughter of Mr. and Mrs. E. R. Swetnam, were married Wednesday evening, at the home of the bride's parents, at Fairfax Station, Rev. F. A. Strother officiating.

**SWETNAN, Roberta Randolph** – Nov. 11, 1910 M. J. – LOUDOUN – A quiet wedding occurred at the home of Mr. and Mrs. E. R. Swetnan, of Fairfax, on Wednesday evening, October 26, when their oldest daughter, Miss Roberta Randolph and Mr. Dalias Berry, son of the late Owens Berry, were united in marriage by the Rev. F. A. Strother.

**SWITZER, Jack L** – Mar. 18, 1910 M. J. – A marriage license was issued on Tuesday to Mr. Jack L. Switzer, of Illinois, and Miss Phoebe Schaffer, of Pennsylvania.

**SYDNOR, Charles W.** – Sept. 16, 1910 M. J. – Dr. and Mrs. Starkweather entertained on Friday last in honor of Miss Elizabeth Meade, who was married to Rev. Chas. W. Sydnor, of the Southern Diocese, on September 1st at Pohick church.

**TALBOTT, Francis Boswell** – Jan. 21, 1910 M. J. – FAUQUIER – A beautiful and interesting double wedding took place on the afternoon of Jan. 5 at Sunnyside, the home of Mr. and Mrs. Moore Carter Blackwell, when their daughter, Miss Eva Ashton Blackwell, was married to Mr. Warren W. Goodman of Montana, and their granddaughter, Miss Grayson McLean Blackwell, became the bride of Mr. Francis Boswell Talbott, of Maryland. The double ceremony was most impressively performed by Rev. Edwin S. Hinks. Mr. and Mrs. Goodman, after a trip through Mexico and California, will make their home in Montana. Mr. and Mrs. Talbott will reside in Calvert county, Maryland.

**TALIAFERRO, Agnes Marshall** – Feb. 25, 1910 M. J. – CULPEPER – Win.Taliaferro, of Rapidan, has issued invitation to the marriage of his daughter, Miss Agnes Marshall Taliaferro to Small A. Clement, Ensign, United States Navy. The ceremony is to take place on Wednesday, Feb. 23$^{rd}$, in St. Paul Episcopal church, Oakland, Cal., where his is stationed.

**TALIAFERRO, Francis Armistead** – Jun. 17, 1910 M. J. – CULPEPER – Hon. and Mrs. C. C. Taliaferro, of Orange, have issued cards for the marriage of their daughter, Miss Francis Armistead Taliaferro, to Mr. J. Conway Macon, formerly of Orange, now of Pittsburg. The ceremony will take place at St. Thomas Episcopal church, at Orange, on the evening of Wednesday, June 22$^{nd}$, at 8:30 o'clock.

**TAPSCOTT, Evelyn T.** – Jan. 21, 1910 M. J. – A marriage license was issued in Washington Wednesday to Mr. Eppa H. Williams and Miss Evelyn T. Tapscott, both of Prince William county.

**TATE, Allen Ernest** – Dec. 23, 1910 M. J. – Mr. Allen Ernest Tate and Miss Lillian Eckhart, of Washington, were married in that city last week. Miss Eckhart was formerly a resident of Manassas, her mother being the owner of the hotel Maine in this place which burned some years ago while she was the hostess.

**TAYLOR, Fannie** – Aug. 6, 1909 M. J.- Mr. Manton Meetze, of Bristow, and Miss Fannie Taylor, of Zulla, Fauquier county, were married yesterday in Washington.

**TAYLOR, Henry B.** – Jun. 11, 1909 – M. J. – LOUDOUN – Mr. Henry B. Taylor, of Lincoln, and Miss Lousie E. Pancoast, second daughter of Mr. and Mrs. Joseph H. Pancoast, were united in marriage at the home of the bride, near Silcott Springs, at 2:30 o'clock on Wednesday of last week, according to the impressive rites of the Society of Friends.

**TAYLOR, Oliver C.** – Dec. 10, 1909 M. J. – CULPEPER – On Wednesday, December 1$^{st}$, at the home of her parents, Mr. and Mrs. W. D. Clarke, Miss Sarah Gertrude Clarke was married to Mr. Oliver C. Taylor, of Pennsylvania. Mr. and Mrs. Taylor will spend their honeymoon in Pittsburg with his relatives, and in Newark N. J., with Mr. and Mrs. Jennings. Mrs. Jennings was Miss May Clarke. Miss Sallie Clarke is a beautiful girl, who is much beloved by those who know her for bright and amiable disposition.

**TEMPLEMAN, H. W.** – Sept. 24, 1909 M. J. – FAUQUIER – Mr. and Mrs. J. D. Jolley announce the engagement of their daughter, Ada Berry to H. W. Templeman of Washington, D. C. The wedding will take place at the home of the bride, Tuesday, September 28, 1909, at 11 a. m.

**THOMAS, Annie L.** – Dec. 24, 1909 M. J. – The following marriage licenses were issued this week at the clerk's office: Monday, Lewis M. Swartz, Culpeper county, and Miss Pearl L. Kelley, Fauquier county, Chas. N. Davis and Miss Virgie Wolfe, both of Prince William; Tuesday, John F. Donovan, Rockingham county and Miss Florida V. Allison, Loudoun county; Wednesday, Aubrey Flynn, Fauquier county, and Miss Annie L. Thomas, Prince William county; Thursday, Wm. E. Beahm, Rappahannock county, and Miss Edith G. Priest, Fauquier county; Geo. Spinks, Fauquier county, and Miss Bessie Baggott, Prince William county.

**THOMAS, Charles H. H.** – Oct. 1, 1909 M. J. – Cards have been received here, to the marriage of Miss Ada Linton Lowndes to Mr. Charles H. H. Thomas on the fourteenth of October, at St. Pauls Church, Washington, D.C.

**THOMAS, Elizabeth** – Feb. 8, 1907 M. J. – A very quite but impressive wedding ceremony was performed by Elder J. N. Badger Wednesday at his home here when Miss Elizabeth Thomas and Mr. Claudius Hixson of Loudoun were married.

The bride was dressed in a handsome traveling suit of gray, with hat to match. The groom wore conventional black.

Miss Blanch Carruthers, niece of the bride, Miss Sallie Lewis and Mrs. Badger were present. Shortly after the ceremony a very delightful lunch was served.

The couple left on the afternoon train for their future home near Levi.

**THOMASSON, Nannie** – Feb.18, 1910 M. J. – Mr. W. Magnese Bragg, was married at Roanoke, Va., on Tuesday last to Miss Nannie Thomasson, of that city. Mr. Bragg, who is now a route agent for the Southern Express Company at Roanoke and who was formerly stationed here as assistant to Messrs. W. B. Rogers and F. E. Morris, is a son of Mr. and Mrs. H. R. Bragg, of Haymarket, and became very popular while here. Mr. C. C. Wenrich, of this place acted as best man for Mr. Bragg.

**THOMPSON, Ernest A.** – Jun. 11, 1909 M. J. – Miss Pearl Lynn, of Prince William, Va., and Ernest A. Thompson, of Maryland, were married at Rockville, Md., Thursday, June 3, by Rev. W. D. Keene.

**THOMPSON, Ethel** – Oct. 8, 1909 M.J.- LOUDOUN – Mr. Horace T. Littlejohn, a member of the drug firm of Purcell & Littlejohn, of Leesburg, and Miss Ethel Thompson, daughter of Mr. H. A. Thompson, of the same town, were united in marriage at the residence of the bride at 5:15 o'clock on Wednesday afternoon, Rev. D. L. Blakemore officiating. The wedding was very quiet one, the ceremony being witnessed only by the immediate members of the families of the contracting parties. Mr. and Mrs. Littlejohn left on the east bound train for New York for a two weeks' tour in the north. They will reside in Leesburg.—Observer, Oct. 1.

**THOMPSON, George G.** - Dec. 3, 1909 M. J – CULPEPER – Mr. George G. Thompson, jr., formerly of Culpeper, now district freight agent of the Southern railroad, with headquarters at Greensboro, N.C., and Miss Lawrence E. Holly, were married in Washington on Wednesday.—Exponent, Nov. 26

**THOMPSON, Minnie B.** – Sept. 23, 1910 M. J. – FAIRFAX – Mr. S. S. Holbrook and Miss Minnie B. Thompson were married here Wednesday morning by Rev. E. L. Goodwin, and left on an early train for a bridal tour to points in Maryland and West Virginia.

**THOMPSON, Nannie Lucille** – Feb. 4, 1910 M. J. – Invitations have been received here to the marriage of Mr. William M. Bragg, son of Mr. H. T. Bragg, of this town, to Miss Nannie Lucille Thompson, of Roanoke, Va. The ceremony is to take place at Trinity Methodist Church, Roanoke, on the fifteenth of this month. Mr. Bragg has the congratulations of this Haymarket friends.

**THOMPSON, Sallie** – Sept. 23, 1910 M. J. – FAUQUIER – Marriage licenses were issued in Washington on Thursday to the following Fauquier couples: Joseph B. Pulliam and Carolyn Spicer, both of Remington; Benjamin Gordon, of Markham, and India

Chadwell, of Hume; Joseph A. Jeffries, of Warrenton, and Sallie Thompson, of Washington.

**THORPE, Harvey** – Jul. 29, 1910 M. J. – The officiating minister, Rev. J. K. Efird, advises us that Mr. Harvey Thorpe and Miss Maggie Reid were not married until July 26, four days after our announcement of the marriage. Just a little mistake in the date that was all. Shall we announce two others ahead of time?

**TIFFANY, Curell Elgin** – Jul. 2, 1909 M. J. – FAUQUIER- Miss Mauzy Fletcher and Curell Elgin Tiffany were married at the home of the bride Tuesday, June 28$^{th}$, at high noon, in the presence of the immediate family. Miss Fletcher is the second daughter of T. N. Fletcher. She is also well known in the society of Baltimore and Washington, where she had visited. Mr. Tiffany is the cashier of Fauquier National Bank. Mr. and Mrs. Tiffany left on the noonday train for Baltimore, after which they will go North on a short trip.—Times Dispatch.

**TIFFANY, Luck Adair** – Apr. 15, 1910 M. J. – FAUQUIER – Miss Annie Isabelle Rogers, daughter of Mr. Jessie Rogers, and Mr. Luck Adair Tiffany, son of Mr. and Mrs. W. S. Tiffany, were quietly married at the parsonage at Upperville, Va., by Dr. I. B. Lake, Wednesday, March 30, at 3 p.m. They returned to the home of the groom, where a reception was given them.—Loudoun Mirror.

**TILDEN, Myron** – Apr. 12, 1907 M. J. – The marriage of Miss Grace Edna Senior of Washington, a frequent visitor here, and Mr. Myron Tilden, has been announced.

**TIMBERLAKE, Lillian Somer** – Jun. 11, 1909 M. J. – LOUDOUN – Mr. J. Mack Clagett, a well known stockman and farmer, of Clarke county, and Mrs. Lillian Timberlake were married in New York on Tuesday. Mrs. Clagett was formerly Miss Lillian Somer, of New York, and her first husband was Shelby Timberlake of Clarke.- Enterprise.

**TODD, Gordon Livingston** – Oct. 22, 1909 M. J. - CULPEPER – An approaching marriage that will prove very interesting to Culpeper is that of Miss Adalena Bettus Rixey to Mr. Gordon Livingston Todd. The cards are out and the marriage will take place in the chapel of the university at 6 o'clock on Tuesday, Oct. 26. Miss Rixey is well known in Culpeper as Miss Lena Rixey, eldest daughter of Mr. and Mrs. Rixey, formerly of Culpeper.

**TOLSON, Herbert** – Oct. 17, 1885 M. G. - At the brides residence of Bellifair Mills on Thursday 3 P.M. Miss Jennie Page Johnson to Mr. Herbert Tolson, of Stafford County, Va.

**TRIBBY, H. Gordon** – Dec. 31, 1909 M. J. – LOUDOUN – A very pleasant marriage occurred at the parsonage, Saturday, Dec. 18, 1909, when Miss Eliza F. Payne became the bride of Mr. H. Gordon Tribby, Rev. D. L. Blakemore pronouncing the solemn words that made them man and wife. After the bridal trip to Washington and other points, the young couple will make their home in Hillsboro, this county.

**TRIPLETT, Cleighton Addison** – Sept. 23, 1910 M. J. – FAUQUIER – A quiet, but pretty wedding took place Wednesday evening, September $7^{th}$, at the home of Mr. Le Blond Burdett, in Tacoma Park, D.C., when Miss Nellie Gerrald McClaren and Mr. Cleighton Addison Triplett, of Rectortown, Va., were married.

**TRIPLETT, Elsie Annette** – Jun. 10, 1910 M. J. – Miss Elsie Annette Triplett, daughter of Mr. and Mrs. H. F. Triplett, and Mr. James Albert Weaver, a prominent young merchant of Bristow, Va., were married at the home of the bride's parents at Gainesville, Va., on Wednesday, June 8, the Rev. Mr. Welch, pastor of Sudley church, officiating.

The bride was becomingly attired in a suit of alice blue pongee and wore a large picture hat to match, trimmed with maline.

The wedding march was rendered by Mrs. Welch, wife of the pastor.

Among those present at the ceremony were: the Misses Galleher, of Gainesville; Miss Virginia Richardson, of Fairfax; Mr. P. J. Triplett, of Wilmington, N.C.; Mr. and Mrs. R. Triplett, of Portsmouth, Va., and Mr. and Mrs. T. Marstellar, of Greenwich.

**TROW, Walter Gordon** – Nov. 25, 1910 M. J. – LOUDOUN – The marriage of Miss Elizabeth Edmonds Harper, daughter of the late Robert Harper, of Leesburg and Washington, and Dr. Walter Gordon Trow, of Southern Virginia, took place Wednesday evening at 8 o'clock, at Metropolitan church, Washington. Rev. Paul Hickok performed the ceremony and the bride was escorted and given in marriage by her brother, Mr. Bernard F. Harper. Her sister, Miss

Roberta Wallace Harper, was her only attendant. Dr. Earl Clark, brother-in-law of the bridegroom, was best man. Messrs. Harry F. Harper, J. William Harper and Leslie Holt were the ushers. Following the ceremony a reception was held in the home of the bride's mother, Mrs. R. W. Harper, in Park road, for the bridal party and out-of town guest. The young couple will make their future home at Hallwood, Va.

**TRUITT, Roy C.** – May 3, 1907 M. J. – Miss Mary Elizabeth Kibler, daughter of Mr. James Kibler, who formerly lived here, was married to Roy C. Truitt of Lincoln City, Del., on April 23. Mr. Truitt is a well to do young business man of that place. Mr. Kibler moved to Lincoln City from Manassas about two years ago.

**TUCKER, Phoebe E.** – Oct. 21, 1910 M. J. – FAIRFAX – A marriage license was issued in Washington, Wednesday, to Geo. E. Lambert and Phoebe E. Tucker, both of this town. –Herald.

**TULLOSS, Lena Francis** – Apr. 8, 1910 M. J. – At the home of the bride Wednesday morning at 9 o'clock Miss Lena Francis Tulloss, daughter of Dr. W. R. Tulloss, of Haymarket, was quietly married to Mr. Owington Gordon Delk, of Smithfield, Va., in the presence of the immediate family and a few friends. The ceremony was performed by Rev. R. Gamble See, pastor of the Presbyterian church, of Marshall, Va.

The bride was attired in a handsome traveling costume of champagne cloth with hat and gloves to match. Mr and Mrs. Frank B. Simpson, of Smithfield, were among those present from a distance. The groom is a brother of Mrs. Simpson.

The bridal party took the morning train for a wedding tour which will include New York, Niagara and other points North. They will reside in Smithfield.

**TULLOSS, Mary E.** – Apr. 29, 1910 M. J. – A marriage license was issued in the clerk's office yesterday to Mr. Wadsworth T. Powers, of Bellfair Mills, Va., and Miss Mary E. Tulloss, daughter of Dr. W. R. Tulloss, of Haymarket. The marriage will take place on Saturday, May $7^{th}$.

**TULLOSS, Mary E.** – May 13, 1910 M. J. – A beautiful wedding was solemnized Saturday at noon at the home of Mrs. Annie Tulloss, in Fauquier county, when her granddaughter, Miss Mary E. Tulloss, daughter of Dr. W. R. Tulloss, of Haymarket, became the bride of Mr. Wadsworth T. Powers, of Stafford county.

The ceremony was performed by Rev. Dr. Shopoff in the presence of a number of friends and relatives. The parlor was beautifully decorated with cut flowers and potted plants. The bride entered on the arm of Mrs. R. W. Powers, as matron of honor, and was met at the altar by the groom and his best man, Mr. Ellis Perry, of Stafford county. The bride, who is one of Fauquier's most charming women, was becomingly attired in gray silk and carried brides-roses. Her matron of honor wore blue silk and carried pink roses.

After the ceremony a wedding dinner was enjoyed by the guests. The happy couple left immediately for Stafford where an elegant supper was given at the home of Mrs. Mary Powers, after which they left for their new home, carrying the best of wishes with them.

**TULLOSS, W. R.** – Feb. 1, 1907 M. J. – Dr. W. R. Tulloss and Miss Fannie Clark of The Plains were married in Washington last Tuesday evening. After a short tour they will return to his home in Haymarket.

**TURNER, Joseph** – Nov. 18, 1910 M. J. – Mr. Joseph Turner, of Culpeper, and Miss Annie Gibson, daughter of Mrs. Fannie Gibson, of Hickory Grove, were married yesterday at Aldie, Loudoun county. The bride is a niece of former Mayor T. O. Taylor, of this place.

**TYREE, J. A.** – Oct. 21, 1910 M. J.- FAUQUIER – At 9 o'clock Wednesday morning, the 12$^{th}$ inst., in the home of the father, Mr. A. D. Kelly, the marriage of Miss Nanny G. Kelly to Dr. J. A. Tyree, of Blackstone, Va., was impressively solemnized by Rev. Fleet James, the uncle of the bride.

**UTTERBACK, Edward Clinton** – Jan. 7, 1910 M. J. – FAIRFAX – Miss Eva May Harrison and Edward Clinton Utterback, of Clifton station, were married at Rockville, Md., Monday afternoon by the Rev. W. D. Keene, pastor of the Southern Methodist church, at the home of the minister.—Herald, Dec. 31.

**UTTERBACK, Lillie L.** – Jun. 22, 1906 M. J. - A marriage license was issued in Washington Saturday to Silas D. Glascock of Marshall, and Lillie L. Utterback of Haymarket.

**VANBERG, Mr.** – Aug. 17, 1906 M. J. - Miss Lizzie Horton, daughter of Mrs. Dora Horton of Potomac and Mr. Vanberg of Clifton were married in Washington last Tuesday.

**VETTER, Stella** – Dec. 30 , 1910 M. J. – Mr. Quilla Robertson and Miss Stella Vetter, daughter of Mr. Jacob Vetter, of Wellington, were married at the Lutheran church, in this place, on Wednesday morning, Rev. J. K. Efird, pastor of the church, officiating.

The bride, who is a pretty brunette, was gowned in a princess white silk, trimmed in white satin, and carried a bouquette of flowers.

Mr. Frank Bell was best man and Miss Nina Vetter, sister of the bride, was maid of honor.

The bride's travelling suit was of Navy blue cloth with hat and gloves to match.

After a sumptuous luncheon the happy pair left on the midday train for a trip to Baltimore and Philadelphia.

**VOGEL, Carrie** - Sept. 21, 1906 M. J. – Mr. Jos. Rollins and Miss Carrie Vogel, daughter of Mr. Phillip Vogel – all of this county – were married on Tuesday afternoon at St. Joseph Church at the Catholic Institute. The happy couple left on the evening train for Latrobe, Penn., where they will make their future.

**VOGLE, Jacob C.** – Oct. 1, 1909 M. J. – Marriage licenses were issued at the Clerk's office this week to Henry B. Wingfield, of Hanover county, and Miss Eunice L. Lynn, of Prince William county, and to Jacob C. Vogle, of Pennsylvania, and Miss Mary E. Rollins, of Prince William county.

**WAGENER, Sadie Vass Van** –Dec. 31, 1909 M. J. – CULPEPER – A marriage of interest to the people of Culpeper is that of Mrs. Sadie Vass Van Wagener to Mr. R. A. Schoolfield, of Danville. The marriage took place on Tuesday evening, the twenty-first of this month, in New York, at the Waldolf-Astoria. Mr. Schoolfield first married Miss Belle Vass, who died several years ago. Miss Sadie Vass, is a daughter of Mr. James Vass, formerly of Culpeper, and is well remembered by many of her schoolmates as a sweet and lovely girl in every way.

**WAGER, Charles Crawford** – Sept. 24, 1909 M. J. – CULPEPER –Mr. Charles Crawford Wager, formerly of Culpeper, now a prominent real estate man in Pittsburg, and Miss Marie Kolback were married at Eric, Pa., on Saturday last, September 11th. Mr. Wager's many Culpeper friends extend their congratulations.—Exponent, Sept. 17

**WAITE, Robert** – Jul. 8, 1910 M. J. – A marriage license was granted in Washington on Tuesday to Mr. Robert Waite and Miss Lizzie Davis, both of this county.

**WALKER, Ewell** – Nov. 25, 1910 M. J. – Miss Maude Eleanor Allensworth, daughter of Captain and Mrs. Walter S. Allensworth, was married Wednesday night to Mr. Ewell Walker, of Washington. Mr. Walker is a government employee of that city.

**WARING, William** – Jan. 18, 1907 M. J. – Mr. William Warning and Miss Maggie Scott were married yesterday at the residence of the officiating minister, Rev. Robert Smith.

**WARREN, Frederick Albert Ernest** – Nov. 4, 1910 M. J. – FAIRFAX – Miss Lelia Reynolds, daughter of Mr. and Mrs. Francis H. Reynolds, of Fairfax county, and the Rev. Frederick Albert Ernest Warren, of Chase City, Va., were married in Christ Protestant Episcopal church, Alexandria, Wednesday afternoon, the rector, Rev. W. J. Morton, officiating. Rev. Mr. Warren is a native of England, and was ordained at the Episcopal Theological Seminary last June.

**WARRING, William** - Apr. 5, 1907 M. J. – Married at the residence of the officiating minister, Rev. Robert Smith, on Friday last, Miss Sadie Redmon to Mr. William Warring—both of Prince William.

**WATSON, Carolyn Bell** – Jun. 25, 1909 M.J. – FAUQUIER – Dr. Alexandria B. Moore, of The Plains, Fauquier county, Va., a recent graduate of the University of Virginia, and Miss Carolyn Bell Watson, of Falls Church, Va., who graduated last year from the University Training School for Nurses, were quietly married at Christ Episcopal Church, Charlottesville, Sunday afternoon, June 20th, Rev. Harry B. Lee officiating. Only a few intimate friends were present.

**WEAVER, James Albert** – Jun. 10, 1910 M. J. – Miss Elsie Annette Triplett, daughter of Mr. and Mrs. H. F. Triplett, and Mr. James Albert Weaver, a prominent young merchant of Bristow, Va., were married at the home of the bride's parents at Gainesville, Va., on Wednesday, June 8, the Rev. Mr. Welch, pastor of Sudley church, officiating.

The bride was becomingly attired in a suit of alice blue pongee and wore a large picture hat to match, trimmed with maline.

The wedding march was rendered by Mrs. Welch, wife of the pastor.

Among those present at the ceremony were: the Misses Galleher, of Gainesville; Miss Virginia Richardson, of Fairfax; Mr. P. J. Triplett, of Wilmington, N.C.; Mr. and Mrs. R. Triplett, of Portsmouth, Va., and Mr. and Mrs. T. Marstellar, of Greenwich.

**WEBER, Philip P.** – Nov. 11, 1910 M. J. –Mr. Philip P. Weber and Miss Gertrude Garrison, of Independent Hill, were married at the Lutheran parsonage by Rev. J. K. Efird, November 9, 1910.

**WEBSTER, Eva** - May 27, 1910 M. J. – Cards are out announcing the approaching marriage of Mr. C. Maurice Hopkins of this place, and Miss Eva Webster. Miss Webster is a native of Boston but has been residing with her mother, Mrs. Julius Daniel Webster, at their new Washington home. The happy nuptial event is to take place at Epiphany Episcopal church Wednesday afternoon, June the first.

**WEEDON, Charles James** – Jun. 11, 1909 M. J. – Mr. and Mrs. Andrew M. Wright announce the marriage of their daughter, Katherine Florence To Mr. Charles James Weedon, of Washington, D.C., June 5th, 1909.

**WEEDON, P. T.** – Oct. 12, 1906 M. J. – Mr. P. T. Weedon of Washington, formerly of this county, and Miss Martha W. Perry of Philadelphia were married on Tuesday last.

**WELLS, Frank** - Jan. 25, 1907 M. J. – Miss Judie Breen and Mr. Frank Wells were married Jan. 9, 1907, at St. Joseph's Church and will make their future home at Bull Run.

**WENRICH, Wilson N.** – May 3, 1907 M. J. – Mr. Wilson N. Wenrich of this place and Miss Bessie V. Gold, daughter of Mr. and Mrs. William H. Gold of Hagerstown, Md., were married at high noon on Tuesday last at the home of the bride, Rev. J. Spangler Keiffer of Zion Reformed church, conducting the ceremony. The bride was attired in a beautiful blue silk costume.

Miss May Wenrich and Mr. Charles C. Wenrich, sister and brother of the groom, and a large number of the relatives and friends of the bride were present.

After the ceremony a dinner was served, and on reaching here that evening, the groom's parents gave a reception.

The bride, who is one of the most popular young ladies of Hagerstown, was the recipient of many beautiful presents and the groom was the recipient of a handsome token of esteem from the dramatic club of Bull Run Council.

**WENZER, Mamie** – Oct. 29, 1909 M. J.- Mr. Wm. J. Randall, of Wellington, and Miss Mamie Wenzer, of Fairfax county, were married last week in Washington.

**WHALEY, Grace** – Nov. 5, 1909 M. J. – LOUDOUN – Miss Grace Whaley, daughter of W. F. Whaley, of Loudoun, and Gray H. Easter, of Washington, were married Tuesday by Rev. George Cummings, of the Presbyterian church. The bride was attended by her sister, Miss Orra Whaley, and the groom by Richard Swindell, of Washington.

**WHEATON, George** – May 3, 1907 M. J. – Mr. George Wheaton and Miss Mildred Woodyard were married on Sunday last at the residence of the officiating minister, Rev. T. D. D. Clark.

**WHIP, M. E.** – Apr. 15, 1910 M. J. – Mr. M. E. Whip, who formerly lived in Manassas, and Miss Belle German, of Marshall, Va., were married in Marshall Sunday afternoon. Mr. Whip is a tie and lumber inspector for the Baltimore & Ohio Railway Co., with headquarters at Mt. Vernon, Indiana.

**WHITE, D. S.** – Sept. 17, 1909 M. J. – Mr. D. S. White and Mrs. Letitia Marshall Marston, both of Washington, were quietly married last Saturday evening at the home of Mrs. Marston's mother, Mrs. Marshall, on West street. Rev. W. T. Gover performed the ceremony. Only a few friends of the family were present.

**WHITE, Flossie Elizabeth** – Jan. 14, 1910 M. J. – CULPEPER – The home of Mr. and Mrs. Somerville J. White was the scene of a very quiet home wedding last Wednesday at 1 p.m. when the oldest daughter, Flossie Elizabeth, was given in marriage to Mr. Frank A. Cammack, of Washington, D. C., Rev. Thomas F. Grimsley, officiating. None witnessed the ceremony save the immediate relatives of the bride and groom. Immediately after the ceremony the couple left via C. & O. for Richmond, from where they will extend their tour to Florida, returning about Feb. 1, to make their home in Washington, D. C.

**WHITE, James R.** – Mar. 18, 1910 M. J. – Miss Katherine Cushing, daughter of Mr. and Mrs. Robert B. Cushing, of near Wellington, became the bride of Mr. James R. White, a prominent druggist of Dublin, Montgomery county, Va., on Monday morning, Rev. Dr. Hammer performing the ceremony. The young couple left for Washington on the Branch train. They will be at home in Dublin, Va., after March 24th.

**WHITE, John Goldsborough** – Oct. 1, 1909 M. J.- The marriage of Mr. John Goldsborough White, formerly of Haymarket, now of El Paso, Texas, to Miss Mary Sydnie Matthews, of Van Buren, Arkansas, is announced to take place at the home of the bride, on the sixth of October. Mr. White has the sincere congratulations of many friends here.

**WHITE, Mary W.** – May 6, 1910 M. J. – FAIRFAX – Mr. Clarence M. Leith, son of Dr. R. D. Leith, of Vienna, and Miss Mary W. White, daughter of Mr. Wm. G. White, of Baltimore, were married at the New Jerusalem Swedenborgain church in the latter city on the 19th inst., Rev. Arthur Mercer, of Brooklyn, N. Y., officiating. After an extensive wedding tour, they will reside in Detroit, Mich., where Mr. Leith holds a responsible position with the U. S. Fidelity and Guarantee Company.—Herald, April 29.

**WHITMER, Roxie** – Dec. 20, 1907 M. J. – Mr. W. H. Evans and Miss Roxie Whitmer were married yesterday at the Lutheran parsonage, Rev. J. K. Efird, officiating.

**WHITMER, Virgie R.** – Jan. 21, 1910 M. J. – Mr. Robt. A. Payne and Miss Virgie R. Whitmer were married yesterday afternoon at the home of Mr. Arthur Raymond, at Buckhall. Rev. H. S. Willey performing the ceremony.

**WIGFIELD, Bertie** – May 20, 1910 M. J. – FAUQUIER – Mr. Gilbert Fletcher and Miss Bertie Wigfield, both of Bethel, were married in Washington, D. C., on Tuesday last, by the Rev. J. B. McLaughlin, Mr. and Mrs. Fletcher are both well known in Warrenton, and the Democrat extends to the young couple congratulations, and wishes for them years and years of happiness.

**WILLIAMS, Anna Maline** – Feb. 28, 1896 M. G. - Mr. Thomas P Smith jr., of this county, was married at Campbells, N. Y., to Miss Anna Maline Williams, of that place on the 18th instant.

**WILLIAMS, Bertha F.** – Dec. 30, 1910 M. J.- Among the marriage licenses issued in Washington, on Saturday was one to Mr. Hilton Jones and Miss Bertha F. Williams, both of Prince William county.

**WILLIAMS, Charles Ashby** – Jan. 14, 1910 M. J. – LOUDOUN – Charles Ashby Williams, farmer and business man, of Middleburg, Loudoun county, and Miss Augusta M. Ewing were married Tuesday afternoon at the home of the bride's brother-in-law, Silas Cather, in Winchester, by Rev. H. M. Richardson, of the United Brethren church.

**WILLIAMS, Eppa H.** – Jan. 21, 1910 M. J. – A marriage license was issued in Washington Wednesday to Mr. Eppa H. Williams and Miss Evelyn T. Tapscott, both of Prince William county.

**WILLIAMS, James N.** – Mar. 18, 1910 M. J. - Rev. T. D. D. Clarke performed the ceremony which united in marriage Mr. James N. Williams, of Washington, and Miss Ella M. Carrico, of Prince William county, on Wednesday, at the Baptist Parsonage.

**WILLIAMS, Janie A.** – Apr. 12, 1907 M. J. – Miss Janie A. Williams of Mississippi, who, with her parents, visited Mr. J. B. T. Thornton in 1905, and a niece of Congressman John Sharp Williams, was married Wednesday, April 3, to Lieut. Butler.

**WILLIAMS, Ruth** – Dec. 30, 1910 M. J. – Mr. Henry Nicholas King, son of Mr. and Mrs. A. N. King, of Nokesville, and Miss Ruth Williams, of near Luray, Page county, were married at the home of the bride's parents, Mr. and Mrs. R. L. Williams, on Wednesday, Dec. 12, Elder Pitman of the Baptist church, officiating.

The bride was attired in a becoming gown of white messalline and carried a bouquet of bride's roses. The bride is a most attractive young lady and her departure from the home of her childhood is the source of much regret to her numerous friends and relatives.

Mr. King, the groom, who holds the position of lumber inspector for the Pennsylvania Railway Company has his head quarters in Florida.

On Monday a reception was tendered the wedding couple at the home of the groom's parents, in their new home near Nokesville.

A sumptuous dinner was served and congratulations extended to the happy pair. Mr. and Mrs. King will leave for Florida, their future home, within a few days with the good wishes of all.

Among those present at the reception, from a distance, were; Mr. H. W. Herring and family; Mr. A. J. Bradley; Mr. and Mrs. E. T. Garber; Mr. and Mrs. Jno. Hedrick; Mr. and Mrs. Benjamin King, of Washington; Mr. and Mrs. Thos. F. King, of Manassas; Mr. Samuel Flickinger, of Nokesville; Mr. M. T. King; Miss S. Yates; Mr. and Mrs. W. T. Allen and Mr. Clay Wood.

**WILLINGHAM, Minnie** –Apr. 22, 1910 M. J. – LOUDOUN – Theo. M. Bascue and Minnie Willingham were married at the Methodist Parsonage, this place Wednesday, the 13$^{th}$ inst., Rev. D. L. Blakemore officiating. The bridal couple will make their home at Round Hill.

**WILSON, George** – Sept. 2, 1910 M. J. – The engagement of Miss Nannie Rosenberger, daughter of Mr. G. R. Rosenberger, of this place, to Mr. George Wilson, of Alexandria, is reported.

**WILSON, George William** – Sept. 23, 1910 M. J. – Mr. and Mrs. Geo. M. Rosenberger announce the marriage of their daughter Nancy Elizabeth to Mr. George William Wilson on Wednesday, September 21, 1910, at Bristow, Va. At home after October 1$^{st}$, The Nansemond, 22 and N street, N. W. Washington, D. C.

**WILSON, Robert Scott** – Oct. 8, 1909 M. J. – FAUQUIER – The wedding of Miss Emma L. Pearson to Mr. Robert Scott Wilson, both of this county, is announced to take place in the Baptist church at Marshall, Va., October 9$^{th}$ at 6:15 p. m. No cards will be issued.—Democrat. Oct. 2.

**WILT, Ella** – May 6, 1910 M. J. – CLIFTON – Mr. Rush Buckely, our popular young mail-carrier, and Miss Ella Wilt, were married Saturday returning Monday night to be welcomed by a merry crowd from Clifton, who serenaded them.

**WINE, C. H.** – Oct. 29, 1909 M. J. – FAIRFAX - Mr. C. H. Wine, of this place (Clifton), and Miss Mabel Florence, of Manassas, were married last week at Manassas. We wish them a long, happy prosperous life. Mr. Wine's new and commodious dwelling is being erected by Mr. Evans, of Manassas, and will soon be ready for occupancy.

**WINES, Benjamin F.** – Apr. 22, 1910 M. J. – Mr. Benjamin F. Wines and Miss Sadie Bell, both of Prince William county, were married Wednesday by Rev. J. N. Badger at his residence on Centre street.

**WINES, Maggie Cordelia** – Feb. 4, 1910 M. J. – FAUQUIER – James N. Reno and Miss Maggie Cordelia Wines were married at the home of the bride's sister near Auburn on Thursday, Jan. 20$^{th}$, 1910. Rev. David Campbell Mayers officiated. About twenty guests were present and an elaborate supper was served after the ceremony.

**WINGFIELD, H. B.** – Oct. 8, 1909 M. J. –Mr. W. S. Lynn's home was the scene of a very pretty wedding on Wednesday of last week when his daughter, Miss Eunice Lucille and Mr. H. B. Wingfield, of Richmond, were united in marriage by Rev. Mr. Leighton, pastor of Broad Street church, Richmond, of which the groom was a member.

The bride was becomingly attired in cream Lansdowne, made princess. She carried a shower bouquet of bride's roses and lilies of the valley and was attended by her sister, Miss Lois Lynn, who acted as flower girl during the ring ceremony. Among the out of town guests were Mrs. L. A. Clarke, Mrs. Aubrey Clarke, Mr. J. W. Gregg and wife, Mr. Wallace Gregg and wife, of Washington; Mrs. H. Clay Lynn and Mr. James Wingfield and mother, of Richmond.

Mr. and Mrs. Wingfield have gone on an extended bridal trip to New York, Niagara Falls and Canada, and will be at home to their friends after November 1, at their future residence on Broad street, Richmond. The presents were handsome and numerous.

**WINGFIELD, Henry B.** – Oct. 1, 1909 M. J. – Marriage licenses were issued at the Clerk's office this week to Henry B. Wingfield, of Hanover county, and Miss Eunice L. Lynn, of Prince William county, and to Jacob C. Vogle, of Pennsylvania, and Miss Mary E. Rollins, of Prince William county.

**WINTER, George S.** – Aug. 19, 1910 M. J– FAUQUIER – Mr. and Mrs. Geo. B. Stone, of Warrenton, have announced the engagement of their daughter, Belle, to George S. Winter. The wedding will take place on August 17$^{th}$. Miss Stone is one of the most attractive and popular girls of the younger set and has spent several winters in Washington. Mr. Winter is a native of Washington. For the past year he has been in the employ of the canal commission in Panama, where the young couple will reside.—Democrat.

**WISE, Alice Nutt** – Oct. 12, 1906 M. J. – Cards are out announcing the marriage of Mr. W. Preston Gibson, brother to Mrs. R. S. Hynson of this place, to Miss Alice Nutt Wise of Leesburg.

**WISE, Katharine Garrett** – Dec. 31, 1909 M. J. – LOUDOUN – Rev. J. Alfred Garrett, son of Capt. W. E. Garrett, of Leesburg, and Miss Katharine Custis Wise, of Norfolk were married at the home of the bride in Norfolk, on Wednesday afternoon, Rev. Dr. A. J. Fristoe officiating. We extend your best wishes to the young couple.

**WOLFE, Allen S.** – Jul. 27, 1906 M. J. – Mr. Allen S. Wolfe and Miss Bessie L. Dulley both of Washington, D.C., were united in marriage by Rev. J. K. Efird at the Lutheran parsonage, Manassas, Va., July 21, 1906.

**WOLFE, May** – Jun. 11, 1909 M. J.– Mr. Lemuel J. Davis and Miss May Wolfe, of upper Prince William, were married last Wednesday.

**WOLFE, Virgie** – Dec. 24, 1909 M. J. – Mr. Chas. N. Davis and Miss Virgie Wolfe, of near Hoadley, were married Wednesday at the home of Rev. W. M. Smoot, of near Occoquan, who performed the ceremony.

**WOLFE, Virgie** – Dec. 24, 1909 M. J. – The following marriage licenses were issued this week at the clerk's office: Monday, Lewis M. Swartz, Culpeper county, and Miss Pearl L. Kelley, Fauquier county, Chas. N. Davis and Miss Virgie Wolfe, both of Prince William; Tuesday, John F. Donovan, Rockingham county and Miss Florida V. Allison, Loudoun county; Wednesday, Aubrey Flynn, Fauquier county, and Miss Annie L. Thomas, Prince William county; Thursday, Wm. E. Beahm, Rappahannock county, and Miss Edith G. Priest, Fauquier county; Geo. Spinks, Fauquier county, and Miss Bessie Baggott, Prince William county.

**WOOD, Daisie** – Dec. 3, 1909 M. J. – FAIRFAX – Miss Daisie Wood, daughter of Mrs. H. V. Wood, of Fort Myer Heights, and Mr. C.

R. Mateer, of Colvin Run, were married in Brown's Chapel Wednesday, Nov. 17, by The Rev. C. H. Wagner, of Herndon.

**WOOD, Edith** - Feb. 1, 1907 M. J. – Mr. Frank Smith and Miss Edith Wood, sister of Mrs. Jos. Herring of this place, were quietly married Tuesday morning at the residence of the officiating minister, Rev. S. H. Flory. Frank, in entering the matrimonial state, has sprung a surprise upon his many friends of the community. Being an old sailor he will doubtless know how to steer his matrimonial craft free of the reefs of domestic disaster.

**WOOD, George Augustus** – Dec. 24, 1909 M. J. – Mr. George Augustus Wood and Miss Ali Elizabeth Ross were married on Wednesday, Dec. 15, at the home of Mrs. Jessie Griffith, the Rev. W. S. Jackson, officiating.

**WOODHULL, Rogers** – Apr. 29, 1910 M. J. –Miss Anne Patterson, one of the most popular young ladies to visit this vicinity, is now the guest of Miss Jane DePauw. Her engagement to Mr. Rogers Woodhull, of Dayton, Ohio, is announced, the marriage to take place in the early autumn.

**WOODY, Oscar S.** – Oct. 7, 1910 M. J. – Marriage license was issued Wednesday in Washington to Mr. Oscar S. Woody and Miss Lelia Bullard. Miss Bullard is one of the most popular young ladies of Clifton. Mr. Woody, who has made Clifton his home for a number of years, is connected with the mail service between New York and London. They will make Clifton their home.

**WOODYARD, Mildred** – May 3, 1907 M. J. – Mr. George Wheaton and Miss Mildred Woodyard were married on Sunday last at the residence of the officiating minister, Rev. T. D. D. Clark.

**WOOLFE, Robert Raymond** – Nov. 4, 1910 M. J.- The approaching marriage of Mr. Robert Raymond Woolfe, formerly of this place, to Miss Elinor Sohnson Riffe, of Hinton, W. Va., has been announced. The ceremony will take place November sixteenth. Mr. Woolfe's friends here wish him much happiness.

**WORKMAN, Charles E.** – Nov. 5, 1909 M. J. – A marriage license was issued at the clerk's office on Thursday, October 28, to Mr. Chas. E. Workman, of Rockingham county, and Miss Nettie E. Ritenour, of Fauquier county.

**WORTHINGTON, Elizabeth Lewis** – Jun. 18, 1909 M. J.- ALEXANDRIA – Mr. Angus MacDonald Crawford, of San Antonio, Tex., son of Dr. Angus Crawford of the Theological Seminary, near Alexandria, and Miss Elizabeth Lewis Worthington, daughter of Mr. and Mrs. George V. Worthington, formerly of this city, but now of Washington, were married Saturday night at Christ church, Georgetown.

**WRIGHT, Katherine Florence** – Jun. 11, 1909 M. J. – Mr. and Mrs. Andrew M. Wright announce the marriage of their daughter, Katherine Florence To Mr. Charles James Weedon, of Washington, D.C., June 5$^{th}$, 1909.

**WRIGHT, Orin** – Apr. 22, 1910 M. J. – FAUQUIER – Mr. Orin Wright, of Fairfax and Mrs. Nannie Follen, of this place were quietly married in Washington on Monday last. They returned to Warrenton on Tuesday and spent several days here after which they left for their future home in Fairfax.—Democrat, April 16$^{th}$.

**WRIGHT, Orin A.** – Apr. 29, 1910 M. J. – A marriage license was issued in Washington last week to Orin A. Wright, of Oakton, Prince William county, and Mrs. Anna D. Follen, of Warrenton.

**WYNKOOP, Bessie** – Jan. 21, 1910 M. J. – LOUDOUN – Miss Bessie Wynkoop, of Woodgrove, and Mr. Zimmerman, of Washington, were quietly married at the home of the bride's father, Mr. Thos. J. Wynkoop, of Woodgrove, Wednesday afternoon. After a brief wedding tour they will reside in Washington.

**WYNKOOP, Bessie Dear** – Feb. 4, 1910 M. J. – LOUDOUN – Cards are out announcing the engagement of Miss Bessie Dear Wynkoop, daughter of Mr. and Mrs. J. T. Wynkoop, of Woodgrove, Loudoun county, to Mr. Harvey J. Zimmerman, of Washington and also formerly of Pittsburg, Pa. The ceremony will be performed by Rev. I. B. Lake, pastor of the Baptist Church, Upperville, Va.—Warrenton Democrat.

**WYNKOOP, Lulu A.** – Dec. 31, 1909 M. J. – LOUDOUN – The announcement is made of the marriage of Mr. Ernest L. Munday, of Waxpool, and Miss Lulu A. Wynkoop, of Round Hill, Va., which took place at the residence of Mr. and Mrs. Lucius H. Thadew, 2213 M. St., N. W. Washington, D.C., at noon on Saturday. The ceremony was performed by the Rev. G. W. Popkins, of Waxpool, Va., in the presence of a few intimate friends of the contracting parties, after which the happy couple left for their future home, Ashburn, Loudoun county, where they will be pleased to receive their many friends.—Mirror, Dec. 17.

**ZIMMERMAN, Mr.** – Jan. 21, 1910 M. J. – LOUDOUN – Miss Bessie Wynkoop, of Woodgrove, and Mr. Zimmerman, of Washington, were quietly married at the home of the bride's father, Mr. Thos. J. Wynkoop, of Woodgrove, Wednesday afternoon. After a brief wedding tour they will reside in Washington.

**ZIMMERMAN, Harvey J.** – Feb. 4, 1910 M. J. – LOUDOUN – Cards are out announcing the engagement of Miss Bessie Dear Wynkoop, daughter of Mr. and Mrs. J. T. Wynkoop, of Woodgrove, Loudoun county, to Mr. Harvey J. Zimmerman, of Washington and also formerly of Pittsburg, Pa. The ceremony will be performed by Rev. I. B. Lake, pastor of the Baptist Church, Upperville, Va.—Warrenton Democrat.

## A

Abbott
  Grace · 42, 135
Abel
  Mattie Lee · 1, 105
Acheson
  H. W. · 1, 124
Adams
  Jessie · 7, 84
  Marjorie Owen · 1, 49
  R. C. L. · 139, 143
Adrian
  Edith · 1, 52
Alexander
  J. R. H. · 1, 34, 53, 101
Allen
  Guy · 2, 44
  W. T. · 92, 166
  William Lewis · 2, 74
Allensworth
  Maude Eleanor · 2, 161
  Walter S. · 2, 161
Allison
  Florida V. · 2, 5, 8, 43, 48, 58, 89, 122, 146, 150, 154, 168
Amidon
  Clymedia · 2, 84
Anderson
  Ford G. · 2, 141
  Geneva T. · 2, 18
  Irva · 3, 106
  Lloyd · 3, 36
Andes
  Miss · 3, 73
Andrews
  Alexander B. · 28, 129
Ankers
  Lelia V. · 3, 17, 35, 97
  William · 3, 97
Anthony
  Mattie · 30, 51
Antonsanti
  Louis · 3, 85
Armstrong
  William · 3, 109

Arnold
  Alverta · 4, 77
  Claude E. · 4, 77
  Maurice H. · 4, 77
  Sallie · 4, 5
  Thomas · 4, 77
Arrington
  James Irving · 4, 5
Ashton
  Horace · 5, 121
  John Thornton · 5, 121
  Ruth · 5, 121
Austin
  Bertha · 42, 135
  Bertha S. · 31, 32, 151
  Wm. Edward · 32, 151

## B

Badger
  J. N. · 9, 56, 79, 104, 105, 106, 120, 154, 167
Baggott
  Bessie · 2, 5, 8, 43, 48, 58, 89, 122, 146, 151, 154, 168
Bailey
  Robert M. · 5, 103
  Robt. M. · 6
  William E. · 6, 143
Baker
  C. W. · 6, 110
  D. D. · 6, 110
Ball
  Bessie Robena · 6, 138
  Murray L. · 6, 16
  Samuel H. · 6, 138
Ballard
  Robt. T. · 6, 143
  Sargent I. · 7, 84
Bancroft
  Owen M. · 7, 148
Bascue
  Theo. M. · 7, 166
Bateman
  Amelia · 7, 37
Bayliss
  Elizabeth Virginia · 7, 106

Beach
   Mary L. · 7, 45, 67, 85
Beahm
   Wm. E. · 2, 8, 58, 89, 122, 146
Beales
   Elmer L. · 8, 113
Bell
   Chas. W. · 8, 15
   Edward · 8, 106
   Essie · 8, 123
   Frank · 128, 160
   G. W. · 8, 123
   Geo. W. · 8, 15
   Sadie · 9, 167
Bennett
   Harrison M. · 42, 135
   Mabel · 41, 134
   Maitland C. · 42, 135
Berkley
   F. P. · 9, 99
   Mary Pattison · 9, 99
Berry
   Dalias · 9, 152
   Dallas · 9, 152
   Owens · 9, 152
Beverley
   Harry · 9, 87
   R. H. C. · 9, 87
Beverly
   May · 28, 129
Biebetheiser
   Beatrice · 39, 137
Birdsall
   Eli · 9, 119
   Millard · 9, 119
Black
   Sam · 109, 145
Blackwell
   Eva Ashton · 10, 64, 152
   Grayson McLean · 10, 64, 152
   Moore Carter · 10, 64, 152
Blair
   William Richards · 10, 144
Blakemore
   D. L. · 7, 54, 91, 99, 118, 155, 157, 166
Blakesmore
   D. L. · 2, 45

Blood
   Colonel Richard · 42, 134
Bodine
   Lera · 10, 110
Boehin
   J. J. · 20, 47
Boley
   Cassie · 11, 91, 92
   William · 11, 92
Bolling
   Mary · 11, 140
   Mary Field · 11, 140
   Sallie Stuart · 11, 140
Bondurant
   Elmo · 11, 79
Booker
   Samuel Edward · 11, 145
Boorman
   Alice · 42, 135
   Catharine · 42, 135
Borden
   Emma C. · 12, 19
Boston
   F. R. · 53, 63
Boulware
   Ballard Preston · 12, 102
Bowen
   Inez · 30, 51
   M. H. · 13, 76
   P. B. · 13, 76
   Walter · 12, 75
   Walter F. · 12, 75
   Walter Fullerton · 12, 76
Bowman
   D. F. · 13, 57
Bradford
   Mary E. · 13, 119
Bradley
   A. J. · 92, 166
   Myrtle · 13, 36
Brady
   Grace · 13, 44
   Norman · 14, 114
   Samuel · 14, 38
Bragg
   H. R. · 14, 155
   H. T. · 14, 155
   W. Magnese · 14, 154

William M. · 14, 155
Brandt
   Martha · 14, 120
Brawner
   Charles E. · 14, 99
   Charley Waugh · 14, 99
   Harvey · 15, 52
   P. D. · 15, 52
   Susie · 15, 52
   Virginia Harvey · 52
Brazewell
   Lena Belle · 8, 15
Breckenridge
   Aleck N. · 63, 136
Bredrup
   C. P. · 15, 66
   Robena Olive · 15, 66
Breeden
   Annie L. · 15, 79
   John S. · 15, 79
Breen
   Judie · 16, 162
   Lillian E. · 6, 16
Brenneman
   J. Irwin · 16, 22
Brenton
   George C. · 16
Bridges
   Benjamin · 16, 114
   Bertha Alice · 16, 114
Bridwell
   Albert L. · 16, 80
   Daisy M. · 16
   Wm. C. · 16, 81
Brill
   Harry · 16, 56
Britton
   J. F. · 54, 119
   John · 17, 114
Brooks
   C. W. · 39, 50
   Goldie Kalb · 3, 17, 35, 97
   Lawrence · 17, 43
   Mary E. · 17, 78
Brown
   Gedney · 30, 51
   Grace S. · 17, 137
   John · 56, 104

T. P. · 34, 121
W. V. · 17, 123
Browning
   Irma · 17, 50
Bryant
   Media F. · 17, 124
Bubb
   Abram M. C. · 18, 115
Buchanan
   A. C. · 18, 98
   Lephia · 18, 98
Buckely
   Rush · 19, 166
Buckley
   Jos. L. · 2, 18
Bullard
   Lelia · 19, 169
Burdett
   Le Blond · 107, 157
Burkhardt
   Rev. · 55, 132
   W. H. · 33, 53, 55, 59, 67, 132
   William H. · 35, 104
Bushong
   J. Frank · 12, 19, 20, 47
   J. Locke · 12, 19, 47
   Joseph Locke · 20, 46
   M. J. · 12, 19
   Mahlon · 20, 47
Butler
   Bertha E. · 20, 59
   Daniel · 20, 59

# C

Caldwell
   Virginia Prudence · 20, 93
Calhoun
   Joseph · 21, 83
Callaway
   Annie Belle · 21, 83
   Carrie · 21, 83
   Elizabeth · 21, 83
   Elizabeth Sue · 20, 21, 83
   J. L. · 21, 83
   J. S. · 21, 83
   James · 21, 83

Jos. · 21
Julia · 21, 83
Sue · 21, 83
Thos. · 21, 83
Callehder
  Edward · 142, 150
Calvert
  Alfonso · 22, 137
  D. J. · 22, 150
Cammack
  Frank A. · 22, 163
Cammann
  H. Schuyler · 22, 55
Campbell
  Thomas H. · 18, 98
Cannon
  Joseph T. · 28, 129
  Oswold · 22, 79
Canter
  Harry M. · 36, 82
Carlin
  Congressman · 24, 69
Carney
  Quenton A. · 22, 126
Carpenter
  Bertha · 16, 22
  Grace · 23, 95
  J. F. · 22, 95
  W. J. · 16, 22
Carr
  Caleb · 42, 134
  Nellie L. · 88, 93
Carrico
  Ella M. · 23, 165
Carrington
  A. B. · 8, 106
Carruthers
  Blanch · 79, 154
  Lutie · 57, 97
Carson
  J. B. · 21, 83
  James B. · 21, 83
  Mr. · 23, 88
  Thos. C. · 21, 83
Carter
  Ada · 78, 117
  Dulany F. · 23, 98
  George Calvert · 1, 124

Harry · 23, 141
Harry C. · 23, 140
Henley · 108, 133
Henry C. · 23, 140
J. A. · 78, 117
Samuel Henley · 23, 57
Carver
  Eizabeth McDonald · 24, 69
  Elizabeth · 24, 69
Cassell
  Lloyd T. · 24, 36
Cather
  Cordelia L. · 24, 150
  Silas · 54, 165
  W. H. · 24, 150
Catlett
  Pauline · 24, 148
Chadwell
  India · 25, 65, 85, 122, 146, 156
Chamberlain
  Edward Matthews · 25, 113
Chamberlin
  Charles B. · 42, 135
Chapman
  William G. · 5, 121
Charlton
  Edith · 25, 137
Chase
  John A. · 30, 51
  Robbie · 30, 51
  Sandborn · 30, 51
Chesher
  Jas. R. · 25, 117
Chisolm
  George · 25, 101
Church
  Capt. Benjamin · 42, 134
Clagett
  Gertrude Dulaney · 25, 70
  J. Mack · 25, 156
  Wm. B. · 25, 70
Claggett
  Samuel · 29, 130
Clark
  Bessie · 25, 80
  Earl · 70, 158
  Fannie · 25, 159

T. D. D. · 3, 36, 38, 49, 56, 58,
   71, 79, 80, 82, 96, 100, 106,
   127, 135, 149, 163, 169
W. H. · 13, 36
Clark.
   T. D. D. · 16
Clarke
   Aubrey · 102, 167
   L. A. · 102, 167
   May · 26, 154
   Sallie · 26, 154
   Sarah Gertrude · 26, 153
   T. D. D. · 23, 165
   Thomas · 32, 151
   W. D. · 26, 153
Clarkson
   H. M. · 26, 27, 28, 29, 86, 87,
      124, 128, 129
   Henry Mazyck · 27, 128
   Hugh · 28, 129
   Hugh T. · 26, 63, 87, 136
   Hugh Thompson · 26, 86
   Jean · 27, 28, 128, 129
   Lee M. · 28, 129
   Thomas · 27, 86
   Thomas B. · 28, 129
   Walter · 27, 86
   Walter B. · 63, 136
   Walter Beaumont · 29, 124
Clayton
   J. B. · 30, 51
   Julia Florence · 30, 51
   Katie · 30, 51
   Louise Adelaide · 29, 30, 50, 51
   Marion · 30, 51
   W. F. · 30, 51
   Wm. F. · 29, 50
Clement
   Small A. · 31, 153
Cleming
   Rev. · 108, 118
Clifton
   Zoa Langdon · 31, 151
Cline
   Annie L. · 32, 69
   Harry · 32, 69
   Lena · 8, 15, 17, 32, 69, 123,
      126, 157, 158

W. H. · 32
Walter A. · 32, 68
Cloud
   Lillie · 32, 145
Cocke
   William R. C. · 33, 48
Cockerille
   Coleman · 33, 104
Cockrell
   Edwin · 44, 139
   S. K. · 9, 123
   Selwyn K. · 81, 120
Colbert
   Frank · 33, 130
Cole
   Howard Elton · 33, 34, 53
   Stockton W. · 34, 121
Coleman
   T. F. · 79, 117
Colvin
   Thos. L. · 34, 44
Commander
   Charles · 30, 51
Compton
   Earl · 34, 147
   Robert F. · 34, 35, 126
   Robert French · 35, 126
Concklin
   E. F. · 34, 53
Conklin
   Edward Franklin · 35, 104
Conner
   A. · 3, 73, 114, 120
   Abraham · 35, 81
   Abram · 76, 99
   Elizabeth K. · 35, 81
   William · 35, 81
Connon
   Robert Elmer · 3, 17, 35, 97
Coons
   J. A. · 3, 35
   Menora · 3, 35
Cornell
   Wm. · 36, 124
Corner
   Thomas · 4, 77
Cornwell
   B. C. · 36, 135

Daisy M. · 36, 135
Willie · 36, 126
Council
  Rev. · 66, 137
  V. H. · 13, 119, 139, 150
Cowne
  Amanda B. · 24, 36
Coxen
  Harry · 13, 36
Cragg
  Thomas Mark · 36, 82
Crawford
  Angus · 36, 170
  Angus MacDonald · 36, 170
  Dellie W. · 37, 72
Creamer
  Margaret Ada · 37, 146
Crenshaw
  Elizabeth · 26, 87
  Katherine · 27, 86
  Nathaniel Bacon · 26, 86
Crittenden
  William J. · 37, 105
Crosby
  Luna E. · 37, 107
Cross
  Jas. H. · 7, 37
  Pemmie Tim · 37, 103
  Wilmer · 38
  Wilmer B. · 38, 82
Crouch
  Albert · 14, 38
  Elias · 39, 73, 127, 138
  Frank · 38, 138
  Hattie V. · 14, 38
  Inez · 38, 39, 72
  Leonora · 39, 73, 127, 138
  Mary Anna · 39, 132
Cullen
  Harry A. · 39, 137
  N. J. · 39, 137
  Wm. W. · 39, 137
Cummings
  George · 49, 163
Curtis
  Miss · 39, 50
Cushing
  Katherine · 39, 164

Robert B. · 39, 164

# D

Daley
  Edward A. · 40, 146
Dandridge
  Edmund Pendleton · 40, 99
Daniel
  Julius · 80, 162
Darlington
  Elizabeth · 40, 142
  J. J. · 40, 142
Darr
  Ruth · 30, 51
Davidson
  Anna Bell · 88, 93
Davies
  H. Thornton · 41, 134
  Harriet I. · 42, 135
  Hawes Thornton · 40, 78
  J. Jenkyn · 40
  John J. · 41, 134
  Madie W. · 40, 77
  W. Willis · 32, 151
  Will W. · 40
  William Willis · 41, 133
Davis
  A. · 50, 86
  A. P. · 2, 34, 44
  Ada · 13, 44
  Alton A. · 43, 120
  Captain Lucian A. · 44
  Chas. N. · 2, 5, 7, 43, 48, 58, 89, 122, 146, 150, 154, 168
  Edna · 49
  Eppa · 43, 45
  Fannie · 43, 111
  Helen · 17, 43
  Hunter · 43, 139
  Irva H. · 34, 44
  Lemuel J. · 44, 168
  Lizzie · 44, 161
  Lucian A. · 13, 44
  Lucien · 44, 55, 111
  Nadine · 2, 44
  Richard · 43, 111

Sarah E. · 43, 45
Day
  Frederick M. · 7, 45, 67, 85
Daymude
  Alice J. · 45, 94
Deane
  Chas. Russe · 45, 149
Dearmont
  William A. · 45, 127
Decatur
  Annie E. · 46, 110
  Wilson · 45, 110
Delk
  Owington Gordon · 46, 158
Demory
  Oscar · 46, 139
DePauw
  Jane · 117, 169
  Miss · 26, 87
Devers
  Alfred · 46, 82
Dickerson
  Ora · 46, 116
Dinges
  Edna · 19, 47
  M. Gladys · 19, 46
  Mary Gladys · 20, 46
  Nellie · 19, 47
  Vista · 19, 47
  Wm. H. · 19, 47
Dodd
  George Y. · 47, 143
  Thomas Franklin · 47, 143
Dodge
  Howard P. · 47, 70
  Sarah Katrina · 47, 70
Donovan
  John F. · 2, 5, 8, 43, 48, 58, 89, 122, 146, 150, 154, 168
Dorsey
  W. B. · 9, 119
Downs
  Minnie C. · 48, 77
Du Bose
  Alice Watts · 33, 48
  George · 33, 48
Dulaney
  Colonel · 97, 133

Dulany
  Eva Randolph · 48, 123
  Richard Hunter · 48, 123
Dulley
  Bessie L. · 49, 168
Duncan
  Etta · 49, 144
Dunn
  Frank L. · 1, 49
Duval
  V. W. · 13, 76
Dyer
  Edith · 49

# E

Early
  M. G. · 32, 68
Easter
  Gray H. · 49, 163
Eastham
  Blanche Byrd · 50, 65
Eckhart
  Clara · 50, 86
  Lillian · 50, 153
Eddington
  C. M. · 13, 76
Eddins
  Hunter · 89, 94
Edmonds
  Will · 39, 50
Edwards
  W. M. · 17, 50
Efird
  Charles E. · 30, 51
  J. K. · 6, 13, 16, 17, 29, 36, 37, 43, 45, 49, 50, 54, 55, 57, 61, 72, 75, 78, 96, 107, 115, 117, 124, 126, 127, 146, 156, 160, 162, 164, 168
  M. Otho · 29, 50
  Milton Otho · 30, 51
Elliott
  Frank · 1, 52
Ellis
  Grace · 52, 107
  James V. · 52, 107

Jas. B. · 52, 107
Mandy · 52, 107
Maude D. · 52, 107
Embrey
   C. W. · 14, 52
   Charles William · 15, 52
   Murry A. · 53, 70
Embry
   Lilly · 53, 63
English
   Alvin · 53, 100
   C. Albert · 34, 53
   Charles A. · 33, 53
   Charles Albert · 33, 53
   Chas. A. · 34, 53
   Myra Gardner · 33, 53
Ennis
   Ada V. · 54, 66
   Claude · 54, 119
   Maud · 54, 120
   Nelson L. · 54, 125
   Thos. E. · 54, 119
Evans
   E. D. · 54, 98
   E. K. · 54, 91
   W. H. · 54, 164
Ewing
   Augusta M. · 54, 165

# F

Fair
   Charles · 54, 115
   Charles A. · 61, 116
   Delia F. · 54, 55, 115
Fairfax
   Hamilton · 22, 55
   Henry · 22, 55
   Jno. W. · 22, 55
   Katharine Van Ransslear · 22, 55
   Lucien · 44, 55, 111
   Rosier · 49
   Willie · 55, 70
Faithfull
   C. M. · 13, 76
   Clarence · 13, 76

Fately
   Carrie · 56
Ferguson
   Anna Louise · 55, 131, 132
   Bettie · 56, 104
Ferneyhough
   Robert E. · 56, 84
Fetzer
   Minnie M. · 16, 56
Fewell
   E. N. · 56, 71
   Emma · 56, 71
   William F. · 57, 69
Fleming
   Frances · 139, 143
   Francis · 108, 133
   Virginia · 57, 97
Flemming
   Francis Lee · 23, 57
   Mary · 23, 57
   Richard Bland Lee · 23, 57
Fletcher
   Gilbert · 57, 164
   Mabel · 139, 143
   Mauzy · 57, 156
   T. N. · 57, 156
Flickinger
   Samuel · 92, 166
Florance
   Georgia · 13, 57
   J. A. · 58, 80
   Robert H. · 58, 79
Florence
   Mabel · 58, 166
Flory
   S. H. · 144, 169
Flynn
   Aubrey · 2, 5, 8, 43, 48, 58, 89, 122, 146, 150, 154, 168
Follen
   Anna D. · 58, 170
   Nannie · 58, 170
Ford
   Ethel · 30, 51
Forsyth
   Josephine · 58, 130
Foster
   J. W. · 59, 67

Margaret Mitchell · 59, 67
Fox
  Irvin · 20, 59
Free
  Mabel · 59, 75
  Mabel Gertrude · 59, 71
  W. R. · 59, 60, 71, 75
French
  Sandford William · 61
  Sandford Williams · 116
  Sanford William · 61, 116
Fristoe
  A. J. · 61, 168

# G

Galt
  Alexander · 4, 77
Gamble
  Cary · 28, 63, 66, 74, 94, 108, 129, 136
  Rev. · 95
Garber
  E. T. · 92, 166
Garner
  Newton · 61, 84
  Pearl · 61, 84
Garrett
  J. Alfred · 61, 168
  W. E. · 61, 168
Garrison
  Gertrude · 61, 162
German
  Belle · 61, 163
Gheen
  Jos. E. · 62, 123
Gibbons
  Cardinal · 87, 141
Gibson
  Annie · 62, 159
  Fannie · 62, 159
  Jno. A. · 34, 53
  Robert A. · 59, 67, 74, 95
  Stuart A. · 82, 106
  W. Preston · 62, 168
Giddings
  E. B. · 40, 78

Gilkeson
  Bettie · 62, 144
  Carlisle H. · 62, 143
  Sam F. · 62, 144
  Samuel F. · 62, 144
Gilless
  Mr. · 27
Gillis
  Commodore · 63, 136
  Florence S. · 63, 136
  Helen · 63, 136
  Julia · 63
  W. W. · 63, 136
Gilliss
  Charles James · 63, 136
  Chas. James · 62, 136
  Florence · 28, 129
  James · 63, 136
  Jas. · 63, 136
  Walter · 63, 136
Ginon
  Rev. · 14, 99
Glascock
  Mason · 53, 63
  Silas D. · 64, 159
Glass
  Chester · 64, 90
  Dorothy Beatrice · 64, 90
Glenn
  Governor · 28, 129
Gold
  Bessie V. · 64, 162
  William H. · 64, 162
Goldrose
  Mrs. Max · 8, 15
Goode
  Mr. · 64, 118
Goodman
  Warren W. · 10, 64, 152
Goodwin
  E. L. · 80, 155
Gordon
  Benjamin · 24, 65, 85, 122, 146, 155
Gough
  Joseph · 65, 124
Grafton
  W. · 65, 120

Grasty
  Eilbeck · 50, 65
Gray
  Edgar · 65, 73
  George D. · 65, 73
  Hazel · 65, 116
  Maud B. · 66, 68
  Melvin C. · 54, 66
  Minerva · 66, 109
  Rosie · 65, 73
  Tom · 65, 116
  Turner · 66, 109
Grayson
  Geo. B. · 15, 66
  T. Keller · 66, 137
Green
  Carrie B. · 7, 45, 67, 85
  Lelia · 42, 135
  Thomas Francis · 59, 67
  Willard · 67, 91
Gregg
  J. W. · 102, 167
  Wallace · 102, 167
Griffin
  William · 68, 81
Griffith
  Benjamin · 68, 69
  Daniel H. · 66, 68
  Jessie · 133, 169
  Pearl · 68, 69
Grimsley
  Thomas F. · 22, 163
Groff
  R. L. · 68, 110
Guthree
  D. · 68, 91
Guthrie
  H. E. · 62, 143

# H

Hable
  Estelle · 139, 143
Hale
  Fleeta Anna · 32, 68
  Fleta A. · 32, 68
  John T. · 69, 117
  W. F. · 32, 68
  William F. · 32, 68
Haley
  J. J. · 68, 69
  Josephine · 57, 69
Hall
  Florence · 41, 42, 134, 135
  J. E. · 60, 71
  M. D. · 24, 69
  Martha P. · 32, 42, 135, 151
  Richard Dulany · 25, 70
Halley
  Ospah · 55, 70
Halpenny
  Bertha A. · 53, 70
  J. · 53, 70
Hamilton
  Hugh · 70, 78
  Susan · 70, 78
  Susan Fitzhugh · 70, 78
Hammer
  Rev. Dr. · 39, 164
Hammill
  Perry · 44
  R. C. · 44, 139
Hammond
  H. C. · 13, 76
  Mrs. Dr. · 6, 103
  W. G. · 54, 125
Hamner
  Rev. Dr. · 5, 8, 14, 38, 120, 122, 138
Hanneman
  Clara F. · 42, 135
Hanson
  Laura · 4, 77
Hardy
  Charles Willoughby · 48, 70
Harper
  Bernard F. · 70, 157
  Elizabeth Edmonds · 70, 157
  Harry F. · 71, 158
  J. William · 71, 158
  L. F. · 62, 144
  R. W. · 71, 158
  Robert · 70, 157
  Roberta Wallace · 70, 158
Harrell

A. H. · 56, 71
J. Claude · 59, 71
Jannette Lambert · 88, 93
Harris
  Edith M. · 37, 72
  Williams · 39, 72
  Wm. · 38, 72
Harrison
  Burnley · 73, 152
  Ernest P. · 72, 152
  Eva May · 72, 159
  Mary Belle · 21, 83
  W. S. · 21, 83
Hay
  Robena · 38, 82
Haymarker
  Dell M. · 65, 73
Hayth
  Geo. E. · 39, 73, 127, 138
Heath
  Miss · 108, 133
Heddings
  Roy · 3, 73
Hedrick
  Jno. · 92, 166
  John · 73, 90
  Ray · 76, 99
  Sallie · 76, 99
  W. P. · 73, 90
Heflin
  Eva · 73, 127
  Laura C. · 2, 74
Heineken
  Averick Parker · 74, 94
  C. A. · 74, 94
  Christian A. · 74, 88
  Emma · 74, 95
  Herman · 74, 95
Heistand
  Florance G. · 74, 125
Henry
  Arthur Lee · 13, 76
  William Alexander · 75, 96
Hensel
  Chas. A. · 26, 86
Herndon
  Alidion · 75, 117
  Hattie M. · 75, 127

Herrell
  Elizabeth · 12, 76
  J. Claude · 59, 75
  James Edward · 12, 76
  Janie · 12
  Jas. E. · 12, 75
  Jeanie S. · 12, 75
  Jeanie Shields · 12, 75
  Robert · 13, 76
Herring
  Edward · 76, 99
  H. W. · 92, 166
  Hastings W. · 76, 100
  Jos. · 144, 169
Heyl
  Wm. McLean · 48, 77
Heymond
  Arthur P. · 4, 77
  Ella M. · 4, 77
  Jane · 4, 77
Hibbs
  E. Humphrey · 40, 77
Hickok
  Paul · 70, 157
Hicks
  N. W. · 30, 50
Higgins
  Ambrose F. · 17, 78
Hildebrand
  S. V. · 8, 11, 15, 52, 92, 113
Hilderbrand
  S. V. · 11, 92
Hill
  A. M. · 21, 83
  Orrin K. · 78, 117
Hilleary
  Richard · 70, 78
  Richard Washington · 70, 78
Hines
  Paul · 4, 77
Hinks
  Edwin S. · 10, 65, 70, 78, 152
Hitt
  Rosa · 22, 79
Hixson
  Byron F. · 19, 47
  Caludius · 79, 154
  Lydia · 11, 79

Nelson · 11, 79
Walter S. · 107, 113
Hobart
  Harrison C. · 15, 79
Hodges
  Nannie · 30, 51
Hoffman
  Lettie May · 79, 117
  Lillian C. · 58, 79
  Wm. H. · 58, 80
Holbrook
  S. S. · 80, 155
Holden
  B. J. · 56, 105
  Estelle · 12, 76
  Isabella · 20, 84
Holland
  Walter · 25, 80
Hollis
  C. W. S. · 63, 136
  Rev. · 46, 140
Holly
  Lawrence E. · 80, 155
Holmes
  Bessie E. · 16, 80
Holt
  Leslie · 71, 158
Holtzclaw
  C. B. · 64, 118
Hooker
  Walter · 32, 69
Hopewell
  Harry W. · 80, 104
Hopkins
  C. Maurice · 80, 162
  Stephen · 42, 134
Hore
  W. W. · 13, 76
  Walter · 13, 76
Hornbaker
  Frank · 32, 42, 135, 152
Horton
  Clarence · 80, 97
  Dora · 81, 160
  J. M. · 81, 97
  Lizzie · 81, 160
Hottell
  Restry · 81, 120

Hottle
  Cora · 68, 81
  J. S. · 68, 81
  Milton · 35, 81
House
  I. A. · 38, 82
  John Nathaniel · 81, 110
Howard
  Harry H. · 139, 143
Hower
  Fannie · 16, 81
Hume
  Mamie Lee · 81, 125
Hundley
  May W. · 13, 76
Hunt
  Eppa · 38, 82
  Eva · 38, 82
  S. W. · 38, 82
  Silas · 38, 82
Hunter
  John C. · 36, 82
  Mabel Isabelle · 36, 82
Hutchinson
  Ruth · 20
  Warren · 61, 84
Hutchison
  Annie M. · 46, 82
  Benjamin B. · 82, 106
  C. S. · 38, 82
  G. A. · 21, 83
  Gustavus A. · 20, 83
  H. G. · 21, 83
  Isabelle · 21
  Quinton · 2, 84
  R. A. · 21, 83
  Robert A. · 20, 84
  Susan · 20, 21, 83, 84
  Westwood · 21, 32, 69, 83
Hutton
  Henry I. · 56, 84
  Margaret · 56, 84
Hynson
  A. A. · 32, 151
  R. S. · 39, 62, 132, 168
  Reid · 32, 151

## I

Iden
  B. F. · 6, 84
  Pauline Elizabeth · 7, 84
Irving
  Virginia · 84, 109
Ish
  Lavinia · 21, 83
  M. A. · 85
  Mabel R. · 85, 149
  Mollie · 85, 97
  Sallie E. Atkinson · 85, 149

## J

Jackson
  Paul · 85, 95
  W. S. · 133, 169
Jacobs
  Jos. M. · 7, 45, 67, 85
James
  Fleet · 89, 159
Janney
  Chas. H. · 85, 92
  Cornelia Hamilton · 85, 92
Jefferies
  J. P. · 3, 85
  M. H. · 3
Jeffries
  Joseph A. · 25, 65, 85, 122, 146, 156
  Nannie · 3, 85
Jenkyn
  J. · 78
Johnson
  Jennie Page · 86, 157
  Wm. G. · 50, 86
Johnston
  Miss · 63, 136
Joliffe
  Mary C. · 26, 86
  William H. · 26, 86
Jolley
  Ada Berry · 87, 154
  J. D. · 87, 154

Jolliffe
  Blanche · 87, 115
  Mary C. · 26, 87
Jonas
  Harvey · 60, 71
  Lila · 60, 71
Jones
  Bessie · 9, 87
  Elizabeth · 63, 136
  Elizabeth Winter · 9, 87
  Hilton · 87, 165
  John Marshall · 87, 141
  T. Marshall · 9, 87, 88, 141
Jordan
  C. E. · 13, 23, 76, 88
  Charles E. · 88, 93
  Charlotte J. · 74, 88
  Lucile · 23, 88
  Viola Lucile · 88, 93

## K

Keagy
  Fannie · 32, 68
Keene
  W. D. · 72, 102, 155, 159
Keiffer
  J. Spangler · 64, 162
Keller
  Carl Baxter · 88, 93
  Chas. · 88, 93
  Wm. P. · 89, 94
Kelley
  Pearl L. · 2, 5, 7, 43, 48, 58, 89, 122, 146, 150, 154, 168
Kelly
  A. D. · 89, 159
  Nanny G. · 89, 159
Kent
  Clara Bell · 4, 77
Kerr
  Harry Hyland · 64, 90
  James · 64, 90
Key
  John Baltzell · 90, 145
Keys
  E. G. W. · 90, 91

Grover C. · 90, 113
John W. · 90, 100
Owen · 90, 91
Keyser
  Charles · 27, 86
Kibbler
  Gertrude · 141, 149
  J. L. · 2, 74
Kibler
  Gertrude · 142, 149
  J. L. · 65, 116, 141, 149
  James · 90, 158
  M. · 142, 149
  Mary Elizabeth · 90, 158
Kilmer
  Rebekah S. · 20, 47
Kincheloe
  Andrew · 90, 91
  D. E. · 54, 91
  Lillie · 73, 90
  Mable M. · 67, 91
  Pearl · 54, 91
  Sallie · 90, 91
  W. W. · 67, 73, 90, 91
King
  A. N. · 92, 165
  Benjamin · 92, 166
  Gardner · 11, 91
  Henry Nicholas · 92, 165
  M. T. · 92, 166
  Thos. F. · 92, 166
Knot
  Philip M. · 85, 92
  Robert F. · 85, 92
Kolback
  Marie · 93, 160
Korson
  Albert · 88, 93

# L

La Monta
  Owen · 18, 98
La Motthe
  J. D. · 89, 94
Laird
  W. H. · 2, 141

Lake
  I. B. · 20, 57, 93, 97, 131, 156, 170, 171
  James Ludwell · 20, 93
Lambert
  Colin H. · 88, 93
  Geo. E. · 93, 158
  George Hunter · 88, 93
  Hattie · 88, 93
  L. G. · 88, 93
  Virgie Eudora · 88, 93
Lane
  Jas. M. · 45, 94
Lann
  Walter · 74, 94
Larkin
  C. M. · 95
  Lizzie J. · 95
Lawrason
  Eliza · 45, 149
Laws
  Edith · 85, 95
  H. Kinzel · 13, 19, 47, 76, 85, 95
  Lillie · 73, 90
  Sallie · 95, 135
Layman
  John E. · 23, 95
Leach
  Mrs. · 63, 136
Leadbeater
  William G. · 5, 121
Leahy
  Catherine T. · 96, 146
Leavell
  Byrd · 50, 65
Ledman
  Birdie May · 89, 94
  Eva · 96, 114
Lee
  Fannie Stuart · 75, 96
  Harry · 11, 140
  Harry B. · 112, 161
  Nannie M. · 96, 111
  Sadie · 96, 100
  William F. · 75, 96
  William T. · 57, 96
Lefever

William · 3, 97
Lefevre
   John · 38, 82
   William · 3, 17, 35, 97
LeHew
   Miss · 63, 136
Leighton
   Rev. · 101, 167
Leith
   Clarence M. · 97, 164
   R. D. · 97, 164
Lemmon
   J. Southgate · 97, 133
   Janet Southgate · 97, 133
Leonard
   Earnest · 85, 97
Lesier
   Katie · 80, 97
Lewis
   J. Marye · 32, 152
   Julia · 12, 76
   Marion · 4, 77
   Sallie · 79, 154
Lickey
   Clara · 23, 98
Linaweaver
   J. L. · 18, 98
   Otto · 18, 98
Lindamood
   Bertie F. · 54, 98
Link
   A. C. · 45, 127
   A. G. · 19, 47
Lipscomb
   William Harold · 41, 134
Litellier
   A. · 108, 110
Littlejohn
   Horace T. · 98, 155
Littleton
   Edgar · 34, 53
   Richard Conway · 9, 99
Lloyd
   A. S. · 40, 99
   Lee Cockrell · 14, 99
   Mary Robertson · 40, 99
   Rev. · 33, 48
Locke

   W. F. · 44, 139
   William French · 75, 96
Long
   Mattie · 76, 99
   Simeon · 76, 99
   W. C. · 32, 68
Loose
   Althea E. · 41, 134
Loud
   Dolly · 63, 136
Love
   Geo. · 100, 112
Loveless
   Blanche · 100, 118
   Emma A. · 90, 100
Lowe
   Archie L. · 96, 100
   Lillie · 53, 100
   M. C. · 53, 100
Lowndes
   Ada Linton · 100, 154
Lucas
   Mr. Lucas · 37, 105
Lunsford
   Annie M. · 100, 112
Lupton
   Nellie B. · 20, 47
Luttrell
   David Harris · 101, 111
Lutz
   Cora · 1, 101
   S. S. · 1, 101
Lynch
   G. W. · 109, 145
   Leo A. · 25, 101
   Margaret Ellen · 101, 115
   Martin · 101, 115
   W. E. · 101, 116
Lynn
   B. W. · 12, 102
   Eunice L. · 101, 132, 160, 167
   Eunice Lucille · 101, 167
   H. Clay · 102, 167
   Lois · 101, 167
   Mary Elizabeth · 12, 102
   Pearl · 102, 155
   Sallie · 102, 150
   W. S. · 101, 167

# M

MacMillan
  Jeannette · 4, 77
Macon
  Francis A. · 29, 130
  J. Conway · 102, 153
Maconnaughey
  Samuel S. · 102, 143
Maddox
  Charles H. · 102, 112
  Julia M. D. · 37, 103
  Nellie Rae · 5, 6, 103
  Webb · 139, 143
Magill
  John Randolph · 103, 133
Maitland
  Sir Richard · 42, 134
Makely
  Carrie · 12, 76
Malone
  Horner · 13, 76
Maphis
  Fred D. · 19, 47
Marcher
  John E. · 103, 137
Marlow
  Edward Grandison · 35, 104
  Frances Edwards · 35, 104
Marshall
  Lou · 63, 136
Marstellar
  T. · 157, 162
Marsteller
  Monnie Elizabeth · 33, 104
  S. A. · 33, 104
Marston
  Letitia Marshall · 104, 163
Martin
  Gertrude · 80, 104
  William M. · 56, 104
Martins
  C. J. · 1, 105
Mason
  Mary · 37, 105
  Miss · 95
  Rich · 139, 143
  Richard · 108, 133
Mateer
  C. R. · 105, 169
Matthew
  Laura · 105, 112
Matthews
  Arabella D. · 106, 120
  Benjamin F. · 3, 106
  Charles B. · 106, 120
  Eva May · 82, 106
  Mary Sydnie · 106, 164
Maxwell
  P. J. · 30, 51
Mayers
  David Campbell · 125, 167
Mayhugh
  Garnett T. · 7, 106
  Mamie · 8, 106
  Noah · 52, 107
McClaren
  Nellie Gerrald · 107, 157
McClosky
  William C. · 107, 113
McCoy
  W. E. · 37, 107
McDaniel
  Laura · 108, 124
McDonald
  Bessie · 108, 118
  Roderick · 139
  William · 108, 141
McElroy
  Elizabeth Joliffe · 26, 86
McFarland
  Vera · 113
McGill
  John · 12, 60, 71, 76, 108, 133
McGlone
  Elizabeth · 108, 111
  George A. · 108, 110
  I. V. · 108, 110
  John J. · 108, 110
  Rose · 108, 110
McIntosh
  Chas. Brower · 66, 109
  Frank W. · 84, 109
McIntyre
  Louisa M. · 3, 109

Major · 4, 109
McKay
   Kathryn · 63, 136
   Thomas · 63, 136
   Virginia · 63, 136
McLaughlin
   J. B. · 3, 57, 102, 109, 112, 164
McLean
   J. W. · 109, 145
   Louise · 109, 145
   Wilmer · 109, 145
McLearen
   Owen · 10, 110
McLeod
   D. C. · 24, 148
   William Scott · 139, 143
McLinn
   Ina · 6, 110
McMichael
   Mae · 81, 110
McQuinn
   Geo. · 46, 110
Meade
   Elizabeth · 110, 152
   Hallie · 28, 63, 129, 136
Meeks
   Helen · 25, 113
Meetze
   Manton · 110, 153
Mercer
   Arthur · 97, 164
Merchant
   Lula McLain · 68, 110
Meredith
   J. C. · 108, 111
   Thos. S. · 108, 110
Mertz
   Amelia · 111, 112
   J. A. · 111, 112
Metz
   Thomas A. · 96, 111
Miller
   Edna D. · 32, 68
   H. R. · 6, 103
Mills
   Monk · 43, 111
   Myrtle · 44, 55, 111
   Richard · 44, 55, 111
Milton
   Katharine Braden · 101, 111
Moffett
   Irma M. · 111, 141
Moller
   J. F. · 32, 69
Moncrief
   L. J. · 105, 112
Money
   Guilford · 100, 112
Monroe
   John Matthew · 49, 144
Montague
   Frederick · 111, 112
Moore
   Alexandria B. · 112, 161
   Benjamin T. · 26, 86
   Helen · 42, 135
Morgan
   Edna M. · 102, 112
   W. J. · 85, 149
Morris
   F. E. · 14, 155
   Maggie A. · 100, 112
Morrison
   Annie · 113, 119
Morton
   W. J. · 125, 161
   William J. · 5, 121
Moses
   James · 25, 113
   Vera McFarland · 25
Moss
   Ada · 4, 77
Muddiman
   Dave · 107, 113
   Geo. · 107, 113
   Henry · 107, 113
   Lucy Margaret · 107, 113
Muldrow
   Alma · 30, 51
Munday
   Ernest L. · 113, 170
Murphy
   Miss · 90, 113
Myer
   Elizabeth · 32, 151
Myers

Genevieve · 8, 113
Howard · 114

# N

Nalls
   Maud · 14, 114
Nash
   Emily · 114, 115
   Mattie · 60, 71
   Thelma · 60, 71
Neely
   David T. · 109, 145
Neff
   I. M. · 113, 114
   Mary Elizabeth · 114
Neil
   Walter · 96, 114
Nelms
   Rev. · 61, 116
Nelson
   Birdie M. · 114, 120
   Caroline Peyton · 17, 114
   Charles Emory · 16, 114
   Geo. W. · 17, 114
   Joseph · 54, 55, 115
   Silas · 115, 118, 119, 123
Nesbit
   Edith · 115, 116
   Scott · 115, 116
Neufer
   Anna J. · 18, 115
Neville
   Nellie · 18, 98
   Robert · 48, 123
Newman
   Daniel · 114, 115
   Margaret E. · 32, 151
   W. A. · 95
   W. W. · 87, 115
Neylon
   Peyton · 101, 115
Nicol
   Pauline · 7, 84
Noble
   Laz · 115, 116
Nolan

Nicholas · 65, 116
Noonan
   Mary Gertrude · 101, 116
   May · 101, 116
Norwood
   John H. · 23, 57

# O

O'Neil
   Dennis · 46, 116
   John K. · 46, 116
Oertley
   David · 13, 76
Oliver
   Sarah · 30, 51
   Will · 30, 51
Orrison
   Agnes Elizabeth · 61, 116
   Foster · 61, 116
   Ruby · 61, 116
   W. W. · 61, 116
Owen
   Carrie · 78, 117
   Janie · 78, 117
Oyster
   Geo. M. · 32, 69

# P

Packard
   Rev. · 33, 104
Painter
   Luther Lee · 79, 117
Pancoast
   Joseph H. · 117, 153
   Lousie E. · 117, 153
Parker
   Joseph · 32, 151
Partlow
   Wallace E. · 75, 117
Patrick
   Father · 25, 101
Patterson
   Anna · 69, 117

   Anne · 117, 169
   Bettie · 25, 117
   Grace · 115, 118, 119, 123
   William · 100, 118
Pattie
   L. Frank · 41, 134
   Luther J. · 118, 120
Payne
   Eliza F. · 118, 157
   James · 118, 142
   Lavigious · 108, 118
   Miss · 64, 118
   Robt. A. · 118, 164
   Roxie · 119, 123
   Sanford J. · 13, 119
   W. W. · 119, 122
   William Gaston · 87, 141
Peabody
   Harvey J. · 113, 119
Peacock
   Florence · 9, 119
   H. B. · 9, 119
Pearson
   Bertie I. · 115, 118, 119, 123
   Emma L. · 119, 166
   James H. · 54, 119
   Lelia · 120, 126
Pendleton
   W. H. K. · 40, 78
Perry
   Ellis · 121, 159
   Elsie L. · 43, 120
   Martha W. · 120, 162
Peterkin
   Bishop · 40, 99
Peyton
   Catherine · 139, 143
   Nanette · 65, 120
   Robt. · 65, 120
Phelps
   Charles · 29, 130
Piggott
   Fenton L. · 106, 120
Pine
   L. Adelia · 42, 135
Pitkins
   Janette · 81, 120
Pitman
   Elder · 92, 165
Plaster
   Hubert T. · 34, 53
Pleasants
   C. E. · 108, 141
Polen
   Bertha J. · 118, 120
   Peter · 66, 109
Polley
   Jas. P. R. · 14, 120
Popkins
   G. W. · 3, 97, 113, 171
Pote
   Roy R. · 114, 120
Powell
   Llewellyn · 5, 121
Powers
   Mary · 121, 159
   R. W. · 121, 159
   Wadsworth T. · 121, 158, 159
Price
   Belle · 28, 129
   Fannie · 34, 121
   J. M. · 34, 121
   Mary · 28, 129
   Mrs. · 119, 122
Priest
   Edith G. · 2, 5, 8, 43, 48, 58, 89, 122, 146, 151, 154, 168
Proskey
   Alex. · 4, 77
Pulliam
   Joseph B. · 24, 65, 85, 122, 146, 155
Purcell
   George · 13, 76
   J. R. · 122, 149
   Mamie · 122, 149
Putnam
   Ida B. · 62, 123

---

# R

Ragsdale
   J. W. · 30, 50, 51
Rainer
   Lena · 17, 123

Randall
  J. I. · 8, 9, 15, 123
  Lucien · 119, 123
  William · 123
  Willie C. · 115, 118, 119, 123
  Wm. J. · 123, 163
Randolph
  Archibald Cary · 11, 48, 123, 140
Ratcliffe
  G. Raymond · 31, 32, 151
Ratrie
  Alice Sophenia · 123, 147
  H. H. · 124, 147
Raymond
  Arthur · 118, 164
  Frank Kellog · 108, 124
Reading
  Robert Lee · 29, 130
Redmon
  Sadie · 124, 161
Redmond
  Virginia · 36, 124
Reeves
  Correne J. · 1, 124
  Courtney · 1, 124
  Eliza · 65, 124
  Henry W. · 1, 124
Reichley
  J. C. · 32, 152
  Jac · 42, 135
Reid
  Anna Elise · 29, 124
  Hezekiah · 17, 124
  Maggie · 125, 156
Reldrow
  Albert · 30, 51
Remington
  Ralph Elwood · 81, 125
Renner
  Mollie · 54, 125
Reno
  James N. · 125, 167
Reynolds
  Francis H. · 125, 161
  Lelia · 125, 161
Rhodes
  Clinton C. · 19, 47

Rice
  Robert H. · 74, 125
Richardson
  H. M. · 54, 165
  Virginia · 157, 162
Rickert
  Edith · 42, 135
Ridout
  Corner · 4, 77
Riffe
  Elinor Sohnson · 125, 169
Riley
  John · 120, 126
  Laura · 36, 126
Rison
  Frances S. · 22, 126
Ritenour
  Nettie E. · 126, 169
Ritterbusch
  Daniel W. · 44, 139
Rixey
  Adalena Bettus · 126, 156
  Congressman · 35, 126
  John F. · 34, 35, 45, 126, 127
  Mary Barbour · 34, 35, 126
  Rear Admiral · 35, 126
  Sallie · 45, 127
  Thomas P. · 45, 127
Roberts
  A. M. · 73, 127
Robertson
  Elizabeth M. · 127, 149
  Everett P. · 75, 127
  Quilla · 127, 160
  T. R. · 63, 136
  Thomas Ross · 27, 28, 128, 129
  Westcott · 28, 129
  Wm. R. · 28, 129
  Wm. V. · 58, 130
Robinson
  F. L. · 31, 41, 133, 151
  Leslie F. · 7, 84
  Robert · 130, 148
  Robt. · 130, 148
  Rosa · 33, 130
  W. · 27, 39, 73, 86, 127, 138
  Walter · 131, 147
  Walter H. · 131, 147

Rogers
  Annie Isabelle · 131, 156
  Jessie · 131, 156
  W. B. · 14, 155
  W. T. C. · 55, 132
  Wade Hampton · 39, 132
  William Thomas Clagget · 55, 131
Rollins
  Jos. · 132, 160
  Mary E. · 101, 132, 160, 167
Roop
  Hervin U. · 37, 105
Rosenberger
  G. R. · 132, 166
  Geo. M. · 132, 166
  Nancy Elizabeth · 132
  Nannie · 132, 166
Rosensteel
  Father · 37, 103
  Rev. Father · 37
Ross
  Ali Elizabeth · 133, 169
Roszel
  Richard Julian · 97, 133
  Rosa · 103, 133
  Rosalie · 108, 133
Round
  Emily Maitland · 41, 134
  Geo. C. · 41, 133
  George C. · 41, 134
  George Carr · 41, 134
  Nora Vera · 41, 133
  Norma V. · 32, 151
  Norma Vera · 41, 133
  Ruth Althea · 41, 134
Ruffner
  John · 95, 135
Russell
  Jas. · 36, 135
Rust
  Ashby · 63, 136
  Elizabeth · 63, 136
  Esther May · 62, 63, 135, 136
  Jno. D. · 63, 136
  John R. · 62, 63, 136
  Nannie A. · 63, 136
  Robert A. · 63, 136

Rutherford
  Beatrice · 21, 83
Ryan
  Thomas F. · 108, 110
Ryer
  Henry C. · 17, 137

# S

Sabine
  Annie Leona · 22, 137
Saffer
  F. E. · 39, 137
  M. Lillian · 39, 137
Salisburg
  George A. · 25, 137
Sampson
  Miss · 62, 144
Sanbourn
  Grace F. · 103, 137
Sanders
  Angie · 66, 137
  W. W. · 66, 137
Sanford
  Harry Rider · 61, 116
Saunders
  Edna · 139, 143
Sayers
  Maria A. · 39, 73, 127, 138
Sayres
  Rebecca · 38, 138
Schaffer
  Phoebe · 138, 152
Schoolfield
  R. A. · 138, 160
Schue
  Joseph Milton · 6, 138
Schwab
  Lucile R. · 138, 150
  Lucille Rosamond · 138, 150
  William W. · 138, 150
Scott
  E. W. · 139, 143
  Maggie · 139, 161
See
  R. Gamble · 46, 158
Selby

Dr. · 108, 133, 139, 143
John Hunter · 139, 143
Selecman
  Marguerite · 43, 139
  Rowena · 44, 139
  W. R. · 43, 139
  Senior
    Grace Edna · 139, 156
Sewell
  Frank · 10, 144
Shackelford
  Hattie · 46, 139
  R. B. S. · 11, 140
  R. S. B. · 11, 140
Shannon
  Emma · 62, 144
  Rev. · 15, 66
  Walter · 58, 80
Shell
  Octavia J. · 24, 69
Shelton
  William · 140, 145
  Wm. F. · 140, 145
Shepherd
  Harriet V. · 23, 140
  Ida · 108, 141
Shepperd
  Hattie · 23, 141
Shirley
  Ethel · 2, 141
  Sergeant J. W. · 2, 141
Shopoff
  Rev. · 121, 159
Shriver
  M. Jeannette · 87, 141
Shryock
  George H. · 111, 141
Shumate
  S. Sidney · 141, 149
  Sydney · 142, 149
  W. G. B. · 142, 149
Simpson
  Charles Augustus · 40, 142
  Edith · 118, 142
  Frank B. · 46, 158
  Lella Cannor · 142
  Thomas P. · 142
Sinclair
  Bruce · 52, 107
  C. A. S. · 142, 150
  Talbott · 142, 150
Sisson
  Blanche · 6, 143
  E. B. · 6, 143
Skinner
  Susan E. · 102, 143
Slaughter
  Delia · 108, 133
  Delia Towles · 139, 143
  J. W. · 108, 133
  John Philip · 139, 143
Smith
  A. J. · 62, 143
  Ad. E. · 109, 145
  Catherine Louise · 47, 143
  Charles Edward · 11, 145
  Charles G. · 10, 144
  Charlotte · 41, 134
  Cora E. · 6, 143
  Eleanor G. · 62, 144
  Elizabeth · 62, 143
  Florence Lyon · 10, 144
  Frank · 144, 169
  Jno. W. · 23, 140
  John Ambler · 49, 144
  Lillian · 140, 145
  Lillie Erva · 140, 145
  Margaret · 62, 144
  Marian · 62, 144
  Mildred Earle · 11, 145
  Philip · 62, 144
  Robert · 14, 38, 90, 100, 102, 124, 139, 140, 143, 145, 161
  Robert L. · 140, 145
  Robt. · 6, 143
  Simon Asburn · 109, 145
  Thomas P. · 145, 165
  Walter · 62, 144
Smitten
  Ina Mary · 90, 145
  W. B. · 90, 145
Smoot
  Elder · 44, 55, 111
  W. M. · 43, 168
Snowden
  D. Edgar · 5, 121

Somer
  Lillian · 25, 156
Sours
  Henry · 32, 145
Spaight
  Thos. L. · 96, 146
Speeden
  Marion · 139, 143
Spicer
  Carolyn · 24, 65, 85, 122, 146, 155
Spies
  Anna E. · 37, 146
  Edward Emerentia · 37, 146
Spindle
  Lillian W. · 40, 146
Spinks
  Charles · 131, 147
  Charles H. · 131, 147
  Geo. · 2, 5, 8, 43, 48, 58, 89, 122, 146, 151, 154, 168
  George · 5, 146
  Nellie · 131, 147
  Roy · 131, 147
Stark
  Robert Caleb · 124, 147
Starkweather
  C. Lee · 44, 139
  Mrs. · 110, 152
Stellwagen
  Edward · 63, 136
  Miss · 63, 136
Stephan
  M. · 13, 76
  Michael · 13, 76
Stephens
  Lillie M. · 34, 147
Stevens
  Bertha · 130, 148
  P. J. · 130, 148
Stone
  Belle · 148, 167
  Geo. B. · 148, 167
Stoneburner
  Bessie E. · 7, 148
Stonnell
  S. B. · 24, 148
Stradley

Wilmer · 122, 149
Strother
  A. W. · 141, 142, 149
  F. A. · 2, 7, 9, 18, 54, 98, 148, 152
  John S. · 127, 149
  Lewis E. · 85, 149
  Stuart · 141, 142, 149
Sublett
  G. H. · 45, 149
Sullivan
  Harry Brown · 138, 139, 150
Suthard
  Landy · 102, 150
Sutherland
  Nora · 22, 150
Swann
  C. Orrick · 142, 150
  Louise J. · 142, 150
Swart
  Hamilton · 24, 150
Swartz
  Lewis M. · 2, 5, 7, 43, 48, 58, 89, 122, 146, 150, 154, 168
Sweeney
  J. N. · 30, 51
Sweet
  Wm. Elisha · 31, 151
Swetnam
  E. R. · 9, 152
  Roberta R. · 9, 152
  Roberta Randolph · 9
Swetnan
  Bettie K. · 72, 152
  Jennie · 73, 152
  Roberta Randolph · 152
Swindell
  Richard · 49, 163
Switzer
  Jack L. · 138, 152
Sydenstricker
  C. L. · 96, 114
Sydnor
  Chas. W. · 110, 152
Sylvester
  Maj. · 67, 91
Syme
  William · 5, 121

# T

T. D. D. Clark
  T. D. D. · 16, 49
Talbot.
  Robert · 29, 124
Talbott
  Francis Boswell · 10, 65, 152
Taliaferro
  Agnes Marshall · 31, 153
  C. C. · 102, 153
  Francis Armistead · 102, 153
  Win. · 31, 153
Tapscott
  Evelyn T. · 153, 165
Tate
  Allen Ernest · 50, 153
Tayloe
  Wesley · 89, 94
Taylor
  Anna · 12, 76
  Anna Louise Forbes · 13, 76
  Fannie · 110, 153
  Henry B. · 117, 153
  Oliver C. · 26, 153
  Selina · 12, 76
  T. O. · 62, 159
Templeman
  H. W. · 87, 154
Thadew
  Lucius H. · 113, 170
Thomas
  Annie L. · 2, 5, 8, 43, 48, 58, 89, 122, 146, 150, 154, 168
  Charles H. H. · 100, 154
  Elizabeth · 79, 154
  Pickton · 55, 104
  W. S. O. · 17, 137
Thomasson
  Nannie · *See* Thompson
Thompson
  A. H. · 96, 111
  Ernest A. · 102, 155
  Ethel · 99, 155
  George G. · 80, 155
  H. A. · 99, 155
  Hugh · 26, 29, 86, 130
  Minnie B. · 80, 155
  Nannie Lucille · 14, 155
  Sallie · 25, 65, 85, 122, 146, 156
Thornton
  J. B. T. · 20, 40, 41, 78, 134, 165
  R. Ewell · 41, 42, 134, 135
  W. W. · 42, 135
Thorpe
  Harvey · 124, 156
Tiffany
  Curell Elgin · 57, 156
  Luck Adair · 131, 156
  W. S. · 131, 156
Tilden
  Myron · 139, 156
Timberlake
  Lillian · 25, 156
  Shelby · 25, 156
Timmons
  Jessie · 30, 51
Timons
  Annie Joe · 30, 51
Todd
  Gordon Livingston · 126, 156
Tolson
  Herbert · 86, 157
Tomlinson
  Robt. · 30, 51
Tompkins
  H. F. · 42, 135
Townsend
  George B. · 1, 49
Tribby
  H. Gordon · 118, 157
Triplett
  Cleighton Addison · 107, 157
  Elsie Annette · 157, 161
  H. F. · 157, 161
  Orion · 47, 143
  P. J. · 157, 162
  R. · 157, 162
Trow
  Walter Gordon · 70, 157
Truitt
  Roy C. · 90, 158
Tucker

Clinton R. · 75, 96
Phoebe E. · 93, 158
Tulloss
  Annie · 121, 158
  Lena Francis · 46
  Mary E. · 121, 158
  W. R. · 25, 46, 121, 158, 159
Turner
  Bessie · 4, 77
  Joseph · 62, 159
  Nancy Byrd · 4, 77
  Thornton · 4, 77
Tyler
  Norton · 28, 129
Tyree
  J. A. · 89, 159

# U

Unddlekauf
  Walter · 89, 94
Utterback
  Edward Clinton · 72, 159
  Lillie L. · 64, 159

# V

Van Nest
  S. B. · 32, 69
Vanberg
  Mr. · 81, 160
Vass
  Belle · 138, 160
  James · 138, 160
  Sadie · 138, 160
Vetter
  Jacob · 127, 160
  Nina · 128, 160
  Stella · 127, 160
Vogel
  Carrie · 132, 160
  Phillip · 132, 160
Vogle
  Jacob C. · 101, 132, 160, 167

# W

W. T. Gover
  W. T. · 5, 16, 33, 39, 56, 68, 69, 79, 104, 117, 130, 137, 146, 163
Wagener
  Sadie Vass Van · 138, 160
Wager
  Charles Crawford · 92, 160
Wagner
  C. H. · 105, 169
Waite
  Robert · 44, 161
Walker
  Ewell · 2, 161
  Katherine M. · 84, 109
Wallace
  Mayor · 1, 105
Warning
  William · 139, 161
Warren
  Frederick Albert Ernest · 125, 161
Warring
  William · 124, 161
Washington
  Pattie · 142, 150
Waters
  Mirand · 30, 51
Watson
  Carolyn Bell · 112, 161
  W. F. · 81, 125
Weaver
  James Albert · 157, 161
Weber
  Philip P. · 61, 162
Webster
  Eva · 80, 162
  John · 30, 51
Weedon
  Charles James · 162, 170
  P. T. · 120, 162
Welch
  Rev. · 157, 161
Wells
  Frank · 16, 162

Welsh
  Homer · 52, 59, 107, 130
Wenrich
  C. C. · 14, 155
  Charles C. · 64, 162
  May · 64, 162
  Wilson N. · 64, 162
Wenzer
  Mamie · 123, 163
Whaley
  Grace · 49, 163
  Orra · 49, 163
  W. F. · 49, 163
Wheaton
  George · 163, 169
Whip
  M. E. · 61, 163
White
  D. S. · 104, 163
  Fanny · 28, 129
  Flossie Elizabeth · 22, 163
  James R. · 39, 164
  John Goldsborough · 106, 164
  Mary W. · 97, 164
  S. R. · 1, 52, 131, 147
  Somerville J. · 22, 163
  Wm. G. · 97, 164
Whitmer
  Roxie · 54, 164
  Virgie R. · 118, 164
Whitmore
  C. W. · 43, 120
Wigfield
  Bertie · 57, 164
Wilkinson
  Alce · 42, 134
  Lawrence · 42, 135
Will
  Wm. R. · 39, 132
Willey
  H. S. · 118, 164
  W. S. · 130, 148
Williams
  Anna Maline · 145, 165
  Arthur · 89, 94
  Bertha F. · 87, 165
  Charles Ashby · 54, 165
  Eppa H. · 153, 165
  Frances Swann · 142, 150
  Harvey · 60, 72
  James N. · 23, 165
  Janie A. · 20, 165
  John Sharp · 20, 165
  R. L. · 92, 165
  Richard P. · 3, 86
  Ruth · 92, 165
Willingham
  Minnie · 7, 166
Wilson
  Alice · 139, 143
  George · 132, 166
  George William · 132, 166
  Robert Scott · 119, 166
Wilt
  Ella · 19, 166
Wiltshire
  J. H. · 36, 45, 94, 124
Wine
  C. H. · 58, 166
  W. T. · 120, 126
Wines
  Benjamin F. · 9, 167
  Maggie Cordelia · 125, 167
Winfrey
  E. W. · 17, 50, 87, 115
Wingfield
  H. B. · 101, 167
  Henry B. · 101, 132, 160, 167
  James · 102, 167
Winter
  George S. · 148, 167
Wise
  Alice Nutt · 62, 168
  Katharine Custis · 61, 168
Wisnant
  M. A. · 30, 51
  W. A. · 30, 51
Wisner
  Dr. · 42, 135
Wolfe
  Allen S. · 49, 168
  George L. · 18, 115
  May · 44, 168
  Virgie · 2, 5, 7, 43, 48, 58, 89, 122, 146, 150, 154, 168
Wood

Clay · 92, 166
Daisie · 105, 168
Edith · 144, 169
George Augustus · 133, 169
H. V. · 105, 168
Woodhull
   Rogers · 117, 169
Woodruff
   William A. · 61, 116
Woody
   Oscar S. · 19, 169
Woodyard
   Mildred · 163, 169
Woolfe
   Robert Raymond · 125, 169
Workman
   Chas. E. · 126, 169
Worthington
   Elizabeth Lewis · 36, 170
   George V. · 36, 170
Wright
   Andrew M. · 162, 170
   Katherine Florence · 162, 170
   Orin · 58, 170
   Orin A. · 58, 170
Wyatt
   Marion B. · 26, 86
Wynkoop
   Bessie · 170, 171
   Bessie Dear · 170, 171
   J. T. · 170, 171
   Lulu A. · 113, 170
   Thos. J. · 170, 171

# Y

Yates
   S. · 92, 166

# Z

Zimmerman
   Harvey J. · 170, 171

www.ingramcontent.com/pod-product-compliance
Lightning Source LLC
Chambersburg PA
CBHW071418160426
43195CB00013B/1736